The Politics

of Selfhood

D1611799

PUBLIC WORLDS

Series Editors Dilip Gaonkar and Benjamin Lee

RICHARD HARVEY BROWN, EDITOR

The Politics

of Selfhood

Bodies and Identities

in Global Capitalism

PUBLIC WORLDS, VOLUME 13

UNIVERSITY OF MINNESOTA PRESS

MINNEAPOLIS LONDON

Copyright 2003 by the Regents of the University of Minnesota

All rights reserved. No part of this publication may be reproduced, stored in a retrieval system, or transmitted, in any form or by any means, electronic, mechanical, photo-copying, recording, or otherwise, without the prior written permission of the publisher.

Published by the University of Minnesota Press
111 Third Avenue South, Suite 290
Minneapolis, MN 55401-2520
http://www.upress.umn.edu

Library of Congress Cataloging-in-Publication Data

    The politics of selfhood : bodies and identities in global capitalism / Richard Harvey Brown, editor.
        p.   cm. — (Public worlds ; v. 13)
    Includes bibliographical references and index.
    ISBN 0-8166-3754-7 (HC : alk. paper) — ISBN 0-8166-3755-5 (PB : alk. paper)
    1. Capitalism—Social aspects.   2. Feminist theory.   I. Brown, Richard Harvey.
II. Series.
    HB501 .P6359 2003
    330.12'2—dc21

                                                                                        2003005844

Printed in the United States of America on acid-free paper

The University of Minnesota is an equal-opportunity educator and employer.

12 11 10 09 08 07 06 05 04 03   10 9 8 7 6 5 4 3 2 1

Contents

Richard Harvey Brown

Introduction: Theorizing the Body/Self

in Global Capitalism

Character and identity have been topics of concern since Homer, but such interest has accelerated and become more intense since the nineteenth century when Baudelaire, Nietzsche, Dostoyevsky, and others challenged the primacy of reason in man, nature, and history and instead advanced personal psychological experience as the ultimate arbiter of meaning. Social scientists have moved in the opposite direction, from a focus on individual and essential identities toward an emphasis on collective, socially constructed selves, even investigating cultural identities as a basis for political mobilization (Cerulo 1997; Calhoun 1987). For example, social movements usually involve a struggle for recognition by marginalized groups, often against even larger categories of identity, such as the nation, which is invoked by elites.

Efforts to theorize the body/self as a social artifact also have come from social history, clinical practice in psychiatry and psychoanalysis, feminist scholarship, anthropology, cognitive science, and philosophy. Here I merely mention a few approaches that seem promising for a developing sociology of the body in relation to selfhood in global capitalism. These include ideas of Karl Marx and Norbert Elias; thoughts of Émile Durkheim and Marcel Mauss and their later elaboration in poststructural writers such as Pierre Bourdieu and Michel Foucault; certain anthropological works in the structuralist tradition such as those by Mary Douglas; and some insights of symbolic interaction and neo-Weberian sociology. Two other rich and relevant approaches, feminist theory and critical theory, are treated and deployed respectively by Philip Jenks in chapter 2 and Lauren Langman in chapter 8 of this volume.

Cast in this theoretical matrix, certain common threads run through the substantive topics of the essays gathered here. One such theme is how the body is constructed in various ways—ways that emphasize or give form and significance to the body's different aspects, in different contexts, for different purposes. Another theme is the political and psychological influences of electronic media in the shaping of selves and sensualities and, reciprocally, how social actors can use these media for self definition or civic discourse. The essays also address global capitalism, not only as a context for constructing bodies and selves, but also as a direct force in these processes, as, for example, in the international trade in sex, labor processes, and televisual personae. Moreover, by taking a distinctly cross-cultural and comparative approach, we avoid essentialist definitions of bodies or identities and instead are obliged to explore the political, economic, institutional, and cultural settings of corporeality, identity, and representation.

These studies also seek to overcome rigid distinctions between "interpersonal" and "mass" as ideal types of social relations. This distinction is valuable for seeing trade-offs and relations between emotionally rich but often exclusive and arbitrary "life-worlds" of personal solidarity and the prospects for democracy and efficiency of "systems," however alienated and alienating they may be (Habermas 1987, 1989). The distinction between interpersonal and mass relations also points to a key fact of human life—its corporeality and finitude. The fact that we live in and through bodies, that we both have and are bodies, imposes limits on the possible experience that we can have as starting points for understanding and for building social theory. Although there are only so many people we can know really well, mass communication both radically extends the scope of our indirect knowledge and has become indispensable to the operations of advanced societies. "A head of state, however deep his or her feelings of generalized care for the people of the nation, could never answer all mail personally. The spirit may be willing, but the flesh is weak. At some point on the ascending scale of numbers, stories give way to statistics, personalized appeals to typifications" (Peters 1991, 26). Thus we have sought to show how embodied selves and the politics of identities operate within "systems" and how systems of capital and mass communication have deeply entered the life-worlds and the phenomenological experience of the body/self.

Richard Harvey Brown

≈ viii ≈

From such a perspective, bodies and identities are simultaneously re-sources and constraints, objects of domination and agents of resistance. Bodies/selves are principal fields of political, economic, and cultural activity, dominant tropes through which the tensions and crises of society are represented, usually in media of mass communication. The women's movement, lobbies for the elderly, pro-choice and pro-life movements, moral parries over pedophilia or repressed memories, AIDS research and education, abortion clinics and propaganda for family planning, global sports spectacles, organ donor networks, campaigns for safe sex, chastity, or preventive medicine—all are major aspects of the politics of bodies and identities in contemporary capitalist societies.

The essays in this volume are grouped into three broad topics. Margaret Tally and Philip Jenks respectively treat the female working/welfare body in the neoliberal corporate state. Antonella Fabri and Lauren Langman explore how male and female bodies are culturally and politically constructed in the Americas. The essays by Timothy Luke, Eva Illouz, Timothy McGettigan, Lauren Langman, and Richard Harvey Brown unfold relations between the body/self, media, and consumption in postmodern capitalist societies.

One of the less explored aspects of transformations in global capitalism is their embodied psychosocial impact on its workers, especially women. Transnational companies have experienced and imposed numerous shocks in the past decade, including divestitures, affirmative action, downsizing, and mergers. For women as well as men, the impacts have included heavier workloads, speedups, and fear of losing one's job. In chapter 1, "The Illness of Global Capitalism: Female Employees on 'Sick Leave' and the Social Meaning of Pain," Margaret Talley examines the increase in the number of women in particular who have taken leaves of absence owing to stress and sickness. She first explores the circumstances under which such women felt ill, describing their symptoms and the meaning that illness played in their work and family lives. She also explores the practical impact of taking a sick leave in terms of women's overall conditions of employment. Talley then focuses on two broader themes: first, the culture of illness for women, that is, how illness often is a response to social conditions that women feel powerless to overcome; second, the more general point of how global capitalism, in all its transformations and radical shifts, has caused reciprocal transformations in the lives of its workers, even when they are not fired. In this context, illness becomes a generalized response to too much work, too little positive meaning, and a sense that there is no end in sight. Talley concludes by speculating on how these women, and workers in general, might be able to respond through more direct forms of democratic action that encourage greater health rather than those passive methods of resistance that many women now employ.

The state, as well as private firms, seeks to surveil and govern the body. Thus, Philip Jenks explores how the body/self is disciplined by the liberal state through the constitution and corporalization of the categories of public and private. In chapter 2, "The Problematics of Democratic Action within Disciplinary Liberalism: The Norplant Case and the Postmodern Body," Jenks examines the specific mechanisms by which these categories are applied to bodies within the frameworks of postmodern fragmentations of identity and the capitalist political economy. Recently, Norplant has been "prescribed" by judges and political representatives as a condition for parole, or the receipt of welfare, in milieus that display little concern for the right to privacy. The growing debate over the medical safety of Norplant and its role in the American welfare state also delineates an increasing tension over the relationship between public and private bodies. By examining the case of Norplant, Jenks illuminates not only the value and limits of previous theorization of these issues, but also the possibilities for democratic political actions. Within the context of a postindustrial, "flexible" political economy and emergent postmodern cultural trends, the possibility of a durable democratic politics is constrained not only by a decentering of the subject, but also by a decentering of the corporeal basis for subjectivities. While postmodern developments have opened a myriad of challenges to more traditional pluralist and Marxist inquiries into power, they often have stopped short of theorizing their own contributions to democratic political action. Yet no political theory is adequate if it is not grounded in corporeal human relations, for these relations are necessary conditions for what is called the political.

Jenks's study of reproductive technologies provides this embodiment for political theory by showing the gendered character of American social, political, and private relations. To do this, he works through some of the more complex contributions of Michel Foucault and Hannah Arendt. In a very general sense, Foucault's analytics open up a consideration of broader nongovernmental forms of political and social power, providing a more capacious genealogy of domination. Because Foucault sees power "everywhere," some have wrongly accused him of nihilism. This charge may be an overstatement, especially insofar as Foucault sees power as creative or enabling and not just repressive. Nonetheless, Foucault's works offer little in the way of meaningful political reconstruction (except the vibrant yet limited notion of resistance).

Jenks places the discourse of Norplant within a Foucauldian framework of power. This provides for a critique of liberalism and the hegemonic components of new reproductive technologies, but it offers little to help us comprehend or formulate democratic action, although the body is integral to human action. Jenks asserts that Foucault only describes the body as acted upon, never acting. By contrast, argues Jenks, the spontaneity of natality and its capacity to unite humans through difference carries with it an emancipatory potential that is realized in Hannah Arendt's conceptualizations of natality, potentia, action, and power. These concepts offer a framework for maintaining the benefits of Foucault's critique while providing the means for reconstituting public spaces in which sustained democratic action is possible.

Jenks then elucidates the limits, benefits, and difficulties of Arendt's post-Enlightenment framework in the context of feminist discourse. Feminist landscapes must be "embodied" in a manner that extends beyond both Foucauldian and Arendtian analyses; that is, the construction of gender roles is vital to any inquiry into the production of the subject. Feminist readings of new reproductive technologies within the framework of a Foucauldian–Arendtian critique enable a more succinct analysis of the corporeal. Jenks elaborates this analysis through a consideration of trends toward disembodied discourse in positivism and postmodernism. Thus he aims not merely to show that this or that technology is "bad" or "good" but, more importantly, to illuminate the social contexts within which operate both new reproductive technologies (such as Norplant) and the political (including technical) discourses about them.

Males were the target of the 1980s massacres sponsored by the Guatemalan state (and the United States), which almost swept away the indigenous Maya-speaking population. This created one of the conditions for a politics directed toward the bodies of indigenous women. Women, after all, are understood by both ladino and indigenous people to be the primary bearers and reproducers of Maya culture. Thus, one of the legacies of decades of violence in Guatemala has been the creation of a body of women that has become the object of control through "normalization" at both the local and national levels. In chapter 3, "Genocide or Assimilation: Discourses of Women, Bodies, Health, and Nation in Guatemala," Antonella Fabri examines a post–civil-war program of national health development in that country. She explores how such programs operate as a form of cultural repression (or even genocide) or, alternately, how they can serve as vehicles of assimilation of the Maya body/self into a national identity and body politic.

Maya feminism in Guatemala has close affinities with discourses of the colonial constitution of the Other and of the difficulty of self-representation by the subaltern, in this case the Maya people and, in particular, Maya women. Within Guatemalan organizations that focus on Indian women's issues, women are allowed to express themselves only through a dependence on the authorized male or ladino voices, which restrict voices of Indian women to their bodies and to reproductive and nurturing functions. Thus women are the subalterns within an already subordinated social group (the Maya people), and their position as such is continuously re-created. Yet these discourses of the female body—much like women's veils in eighteenth-century Europe—can also be used as a facade to escape closer surveillance, or even as a means of resistance. Indeed, the formation of organizations for women might be interpreted as a space of resistance appropriated *by* women or, conversely, as the designation *of* woman as the body upon which practices of domination are inscribed.

Fabri interprets the subordinate condition of women within the nation-state as a heritage of Spanish colonization. She sees the national policy of assimilation to ladino culture and the present subordination of Indian women (and indigenous culture generally) as an extension of this legacy of the Conquest. Whereas the Maya are attempting to dis-internalize the heritage of invasion and domination, so the medical system is using the invasion produced by the recent violence to create a healthy, ladino, social body. Health care, maternity, food preparation, and hygiene are the programs targeted at indigenous women. These programs constitute rules to be followed in order to insert the social body of Indian women into a modern Guatemalan nation and also, in effect, to insert modern ladino culture into Indian women's bodies, often literally. As this postcolonial discourse is embodied in Maya women, they become the new subjects who will make Indians law-abiding, docile bodies. From the silence imposed through violence, the body becomes a new terrain for struggles for power. A new speaking subject is socially engineered by health development programs as a gendered, ethnic, and subordinated body that can function as a civilian of the new society. Nonetheless, within these new discourses, silences of the body are again imposed on the subaltern.

One can also view consumption as a means through which one creates one's body/self as an aesthetic production, as in Nietzsche, or as a means by which selfhood actively produces its own subjugation to capital and class domination, as in Marcuse; that is, at the same time that consumption subjugates, it also provides various joys of group membership, recognition of solidarity, and realms of empowerment. Most considerations of consumer-based subjectivities have been located in nations in which large sectors of the population have discretionary incomes that permit consumer choices and consumer-based expressions of selfhood. In poorer countries, people participate in global consumerism more through the imagination. But here, too, the dialectic of domination/empowerment is evident. It is thus interesting to compare the meanings and expressions of consumer-based subjectivities in a major Latin American society, such as Brazil, with those of the United States. In North America, with its Puritan legacies of work and self-control, consumer-based hedonistic identities can be seen as part of the postindustrial political economy. In Brazil, by contrast, with its legacies of Catholicism and aristocratic rule, consumer-based hedonistic identities are more continuous with premodern legacies.

These differences can be seen in a comparative semiotics of shopping malls, beaches, and, particularly, festivals. Thus, in chapter 4, Lauren Langman examines the American Super Bowl and the Carnival of Rio. Much as Carnival is central to Brazilian culture and identity, the Super Bowl stands as a central trope of the American body/self. A comparison of these two spectacles shows how certain men and women in each culture construct and articulate their identities, but under sociocultural conditions that are neither similar nor of their own choosing. Legacies of past generations, mediated through power-laden social-symbolic interactions, weigh down upon present forms of selfhood. With globalized techno-capital now apparently triumphant, mass-mediated consumerism has become the leitmotif of the present age. For the wealthy nations and privileged sectors of developing societies, articulations of lifestyles and identities based on consumption have become ubiquitous. Notwithstanding universalizing aspects of globalization, the specific social meanings and expressions of identities based on spectacles and consumption always are embedded and embodied within local social formations with their own unique histories. Langman shows how this occurs, and what it might mean for social theory, through close comparative analyses of Carnival in Brazil and the Super Bowl in the United States.

Bodies and identities, time and space, sex and power, work and knowledge, even the market and the state are not natural givens. Instead, they are names of historical constructs that authority must hold in constant check within the bodybuilding regimes of global capitalism. Such psychosocial-physical nexes, where body shops overlap with bodies politic, is the topic of Timothy Luke's inquiry in chapter 5, "From Body Politics to Body Shops: Power, Subjectivity, and the Body in an Era of Global Capitalism." Luke explores the terms and conditions under which bodies are always being built by the body politics and body shops of contemporary capitalist society. Human bodies cannot be separated from the natural and artificial environments within which they are positioned. Likewise, the coevolution of bodies with tools and machines greatly affects how the body mediates processes of construction within any environmental setting. By reexamining the relations of time and space, work and knowledge, and market and state in processes of building bodies, Luke discloses some of the deep technology at work within the body politic and body shop. His investigation of the dynamics of bodies and bodybuilding reveals assumptions, both corporal and ontological, that underpin modern nation-states and markets.

In "advanced" societies such as the United States, but elsewhere as well, the more relationships are consciously constructed, that is, entered and exited in a purposive fashion by individuals, the less stable and secure will be their normative basis; that is, with more scope and freedom to shape selves and relations, norms are more likely to be up for grabs and actors are more likely to wage microscopic wars in the zone of everyday life. Because individuals—pinioned beneath the state and the market—have to turn themselves into the center of their own lives, and because readymade recipes no longer can guide action, actors are left to haggle and bargain over the norms that should underpin their relations. Paradoxically, at the same time that "intimate relations" and "feelings" become paramount to one's identity, actors entering relations for a variety of purposes, interests, needs, and values are likely to argue vehemently about these relationships. As love, family, and parenthood are undermined by the state and assaulted by the market, people increasingly are faced with contradictory demands. On the one hand, we are expected to make ourselves the center of our own life plan, even at the cost of estrangement from our intimates; on the other hand, because of the "homelessness" entailed by fading communities and traditions, we are in an ever more urgent need of intimacy and personal relations to alleviate these losses in social solidarity. Thus, the same forces that drive us to seek intimate personal relations are also those that undermine those very relations, and drive us to talk about them incessantly, all with an ever-growing frenzy.

In chapter 6, "Reinventing the Liberal Self: Talk Shows as Moral Discourse," Eva Illouz argues that these conditions are found in microcosm on talk TV. Indeed, Illouz challenges highbrow views of American talk shows and argues that these shows are in fact a kind of deliberative moral discourse about identity in late-liberal societies. Critics of "trash talk shows" have decried their alleged thirst for sensationalism and shock, much as nineteenth-century reformers campaigned against popular recreations. But the public outrage that is ritually poured over talk shows obscures a few simple questions: What are talk shows about? What makes them such a popular culture form? What segment of the contemporary imagination do they capture? Moreover, what makes talk shows the target of the elite outcry that they cheapen sensibility and threaten cultural values?

Illouz answers that the appeal of talk shows can be explained by their cultural meanings. In particular, talk shows conflate aspects of the private sphere with the claims and modes of argumentation of the public sphere. But why is the private realm of such interest to talk shows and why is it telescoped with the codes and modes of argumentation of the public sphere? Illouz argues that talk shows mimic the de-privatization and embattled character of the life-world and simulate an "ideal speech situation" to cope with the increasing contentiousness of everyday life; that is, to retrieve the meanings of talk shows, Illouz addresses their codes and conventions against the backdrop of contradictions in contemporary political ideas, recent transformations of the family, changes in the psychology and roles of everyday life, and the impact of media on the formation of identity. Indeed, it is precisely these forces that account for the intense dramatic staging of emotions in certain talk shows. These shows perform the ritual claim not only that personal and intimate relations are of paramount importance to daily life, but also that they are difficult because there are no preestablished normative guideposts on which individuals can lean to resolve their disputes. Intimate relations have become central to the constitution of late modernity, yet the impossibility of knowing and deciding in advance how such intimate relations should be conducted leaves actors peculiarly vulnerable to others, as well as to the nay-saying voices within themselves.

Hence, talk shows deal symbolically with a basic question of late or postmodernity: How should we talk—and argue—about ourselves and others, when no moral foundation can preside over our discussions? And, paradoxically, the answer that talk shows give to this question is generally the same one that is offered by Jürgen Habermas, Richard Rorty, and Jean-François Lyotard: speak sincerely and honestly, listen, be open and fair about the rules, do not silence the other, keep the conversation going. Thus the linguistic format of the talk show itself provides a response to our cultural conundrum. The world of talk shows is underlain by the assumption that language is the paramount reality of personal relationships and that these can and, in fact, *ought* to be argued over, and that they exist, or can be made to work or continue, only through conversation. Moreover, even if the principal parties cannot agree, there usually still is a decision—by the audience. Thus the staging of talk shows as confrontations and disputations is also a staging of the populist democratic assumption that social bonds can be discussed, negotiated, and repaired through arguments and communications in which the *public* is the ultimate judge.

We often speak and write about the impact of media that we view, but much less is understood of how being the objects/subjects of media surveillance affects our comportment and sense of self. In chapter 7, "Reflections in an Unblinking Eye: Negotiating the Representation of Identities in the Production of a Documentary," Timothy McGettigan describes a research project conducted during a cross-country trip on the Green Tortoise, an adventure travel bus company. In the context of this adventure trip, McGettigan was able to observe and participate in the shooting of a documentary film titled *Songs of the Open Road*. This journey across the United States provided an opportunity to investigate the nature and power of "simulations" in a manner that is much richer than Baudrillard's (1988) impressionistic passage through the American landscape.

The presence of a motion-picture documentary team during this Green Tortoise journey created a variety of unique opportunities to evaluate the construction of self in a postmodern "cinematic society" (Denzin 1995). The gaze of the cameras often influenced the flow, transitions, and character of both mundane and spectacular events. At the same time, the film crew made significant efforts to minimize the "contaminating" effects of their documentation process. Thus, the process of recording footage for a motion picture became an integral component of the deconstructive social critique and redefinition of self that often evolves during the course of Green Tortoise adventure trips. Consequently, rather than compromising the reality that they sought to capture, the influences of the documentary team had the result of enhancing the reflexive exploration of identity that is a feature of the "normal" environment on the Green Tortoise. In addition, observing the documentary team at work created an opportunity to reflect upon and reevaluate the justifications for the author's own self-serving and somewhat voyeuristic project. From this fieldwork, McGettigan is able to speculate on the reflexive "mediated" nature of American identity and society in general.

Lauren Langman explores how hegemony operates in, on, and through the body in different social-historical formations in chapter 8, "From Subject to Citizen to Consumer: Embodiment and the Mediation of Hegemony." In all complex societies there have been great inequalities of prestige, wealth, and power, as well as different ideological legitimations for these inequalities. Langman argues that the effectiveness of various legitimations—their character and their capacity to elicit willing compliance to domination and hegemony—have depended on their being embodied by the persons whom they shaped as subjects; that is, legitimations "work" only if they are literally incorporated into the body/self of the persons in, through, and over whom they operate.

The key to understanding the processes by which hegemony and its legitimation are mediated through embodiment is the mode of communication that is characteristic of each social formation—oral, scribal, reading or print capitalism, and electronic. This is because each mode of communication privileges certain of the senses and particular bodily dispositions and disciplines (or lack of them). Some of these processes of domination are captured theoretically by the cultural Marxism of the Frankfurt School in Germany and by Antonio Gramsci in Italy, who argued that culture played an autonomous role and was not simply a reflection of the forces of production. For Gramsci (1975), the willing assent of peoples was based on "hegemony," that is, elite control of culture and consciousness. Ruling-class intellectuals articulated and disseminated worldviews in which elite interests were mystified as the "general good." This ideological leadership defined reality, meanings, and morality to sustain power and privilege by colonizing the everyday life experiences of the masses. Hegemony thereby shaped ordinary people's perceptions, values, judgments, and conduct so that elite claims to authority became "common sense," oppressive social arrangements were taken for granted, and alternatives and critiques were marginalized or demonized as bizarre, pathological, or heretical. For Gramsci, then, ideas have political consequences in that intellectuals, who are part of or allied to elites, construct worldviews with value orientations, and these come to naturalize what is historically arbitrary, and thereby to mystify elite interests as the "general good."

But Gramsci's formulation begs the question why people would so willingly renounce their class interests. At this point, Langman turns to considerations of the body and notes that the same media that sustain the larger systems of domination and administration also create social organizations and values that construct the body, colonize desire, and foster particular forms of consciousness that reproduce each person's subjugation; that is, the dominant mode of communication preconditions the body and disposes desire to embrace certain modes of thought and feeling that typically serve hegemonic interests. Here Langman argues that a shift of psychoanalytic thinking—from its theory of biologistic drives to a sociological theory of bodily desire colonized by media—helps us to understand the motivational impetus (the willingness) of "willing assent."

Socialization into modes of communication ranges from the hand signals of hunting with a father, to singing while weaving with a mother, to learning to read and write in school. For example, the bodily discipline of *reading*—sitting still by oneself and paying close attention—helped to create disciplined individuals who embodied virtues necessary for modern states and markets and who needed and were receptive to the collectivist ideology of nationalism, which, in turn, was spread largely through print. Likewise, as Richard Harvey Brown notes in the following essay, the contemporary socialization into communication of children in late-capitalist societies begins with exposure to television, film, and computer games and the Internet, as well as interaction in peer groups in which bodily appearance and fashion become important aspects of social evaluation and individual subjectivity. Such an audiovisual, electronic, sensate schooling of the body is an important moment in the acquisition of willing bodily assent into the hegemonic culture of spectacle and consumption.

Modern social theory continues to vacillate between two radically opposite visions of the person. Behaviorists and rational choice theorists posit a wholly atomized individual who is an automaton responding to psychological stimuli or interests. And structuralists describe a wholly socialized individual—a marionette dancing by the strings of norms and institutions. Both of these visions neglect the subjective realities of selves who interpret, react to, and reproduce themselves and their worlds. In chapter 9, "Narration and Postmodern Mediations of Western Selfhood," Brown moves beyond this behaviorist/structuralist duality by exploring how bodies are shaped socially and historically through narratives of self-creation and self-realization. Reflexive individuals, on this account, are best thought of as moral agents who construct and reconstruct social realities through the creation of narratives of selves in society. Such narratives cluster in communities of discourse that develop their own standardized genres, a process that employs the agreed-upon world of the social. Although shaped by preexisting genres and archetypal plots, individual and collective efforts to locate selves in a social narrative are nonetheless spaces for moral discourse on identity and forms of life in the struggle to master social, psychological, and historical contingencies. These narrative discourses regularly leave traces on the body, whether through fashion, fitness, or self-denial. Indeed, corporeality is a key site for narrative mastery of social circumstances with various disciplines of the body marking cultural identities, age cohorts, and individual merit.

According to Brown, the most recent turn in the long history of modern narration of the self through discipline of the body has come in response to the intense barrage of media and the sensory assaults of consumer culture that are the condition of postmodern capitalism. The ensuing media-created narrations have redefined the relation between body and self. Whereas earlier narrations of selfhood were typically religiously or heroically motivated to reflect inner grace, moral strength, or earned achievement, today rock stars, supermodels, and other celebrities provide the most influential paradigms of self-narration.

Like identities, bodies have become infinitely more malleable. Experimenting with appearance, sexuality, and body image has become the rule. For example, the earlier question "What do you want to be when you grow up?" has come to include one's gender. Although some of this experimentation takes place in the "high culture" of performance art, it is more often the case that advertisements, films, and celebrity culture take the lead in defining new roles for selves, and new ways to tell and become them. Because these images are typically commodified, and represented through mass media, surface tends to triumph over depth.

As sentiment and senses become more private and subjective (that is, less grounded in copresentness and, hence, less intersubjectively validated), they become more free, but also more unstable and malleable, more easily manipulated by influence at a distance through advertising, emulation of celebrities, and the pursuit of televisual dreams. Prepackaged self-images are available through mass-produced simulations that transform desires and are marketed to the audiences for whom subjectivity is realized as consumption.

If narratives take their cues from a barrage of pop cultural images, is there any sense in speaking of an "authentic" or "autonomous" autocreated self? Are not poststructuralist or postmodern perspectives that reveal the fiction of the individual, as she is dissolved into a pastiche of texts, more in tune with the contemporary scene? In response, Brown argues that poststructuralist and postmodern thinkers—like the structuralists before them—accord too much attention to the many obstacles faced in the achievement of viable selfhood. Indeed, the very practices of critique and deconstruction of narratives presume that there is a story to be told. What remains, then, is the political and moral challenge of self-narration in a reified and commodified culture.

References

Armstrong, Tim. 1996. "Introduction" to Tim Armstrong, ed. *American Bodies: Cultural Histories of the Physique*. New York: New York University Press.
Bataille, Georges. 1987. *Erotism*. London: Marion Boyars.

Baudrillard, Jean. 1988. *America*. Trans. Chris Turner. New York: Verso.

———. 1994. *Simulacra and Simulation*. Ann Arbor: University of Michigan Press.

Brown, Richard Harvey. 1989. *Social Science as Civic Discourse*. Chicago: University of Chicago Press.

Calhoun, Craig. 1987. "Populist Politics, Communications Media and Large Scale Social Integration." Working Paper 16, Center for Psychosocial Studies, Chicago.

Cerulo, Karen A. 1997. *Identity Designs: The Sights and Sounds of a Nation*. New Brunswick, N.J.: Rutgers University Press.

Denzin, Norman. 1995. *The Cinematic Society: The Voyeur's Gaze*. London: Sage.

Diggins, John Patrick. 1998. *Max Weber: Politics and the Spirit of Tragedy*. New York: Basic Books.

Douglas, Mary. 1970. *Purity and Danger: An Analysis of Concepts of Pollution and Taboo*. Harmondsworth, England: Penguin.

Durkheim, Émile. 1960 [1893]. *La Division du travail social*. 7th ed. Paris: Presses Universitaires de France.

———. 1965. *The Elementary Forms of Religious Life*. New York: Free Press.

Durkheim, Émile, and Marcel Mauss. 1963. *Primitive Classification*. Chicago: University of Chicago Press.

Elias, Norbert. 1982. *The Civilizing Process*. Trans. Edmund Jephcott. New York: Pantheon Books.

———. 1987. *Involvement and Detachment: Contributions to the Sociology of Knowledge*. Cambridge: Blackwell.

———. 1991. *The Society of Individuals*. Malden, Mass.: Blackwell.

Falk, Pasi. 1994. *The Consuming Body*. London: Sage.

Featherstone, Mike, Mike Hepworth, and Brian S. Turner, eds. 1991. *The Body: Social Process and Cultural Theory*. London: Sage.

Foucault, Michel. 1979. *Discipline and Punish: The Birth of the Prison*. Trans. Alan Sheridan. New York: Random House.

———. 1980. *The History of Sexuality*, vol. 1, *An Introduction*. Trans. Robert Hurley. Harmondsworth, England: Penguin.

———. 1988. *Madness and Civilization: A History of Insanity in the Age of Reason*. Trans. Richard Howard. New York: Random House.

Friedman, Jonathan. 1994. *Cultural Identity and Global Processes*. Thousand Oaks, Calif.: Sage.

Giddens, Anthony. 1991. *Modernity and Self-Identity: Self and Society in the Late Modern Age*. Stanford, Calif.: Stanford University Press.

Goffman, Erving. 1959. *The Presentation of Self in Everyday Life*. New York: Doubleday.

———. 1961. *Asylums: Essays on the Social Situation of Mental Patients and Other Inmates*. New York: Doubleday.

Gramsci, Antonio. 1975. *Philosophy and Culture in the Young Gramsci*. St. Louis: Telos.

Habermas, Jürgen. 1987. *The Theory of Communicative Action*, vol. 2, *Lifeworld and System*. Trans. Thomas McCarthy. Boston: Beacon Press.

———. 1989. *The Structural Transformation of the Public Sphere*. Trans. Thomas Burger. Cambridge: MIT Press.

Joseph, May. 1999. *Nomadic Identities: The Performance of Citizenship*. Minneapolis: University of Minnesota Press.

King, Anthony, ed. 1997. *Culture, Globalization, and the World System: Contemporary Questions for the Representation of Identity*. Minneapolis: University of Minnesota Press.

Lacqueur, Thomas. 1990. *Making Sex: Body and Gender from the Greeks to Freud.* Cambridge: Harvard University Press.

Langman, Lauren. 2001. Cyber-Feudalism: From Medieval Selfdom to Post-industrial Servdom. Manuscript. Department of Sociology, Loyola University, Chicago.

Lash, Scott, and Jonathan Friedman, eds. 1992. *Modernity and Identity.* Oxford: Basil Blackwell.

Luhman, Niklas. 1986. *Love as Passion: The Codification of Intimacy.* Cambridge: Polity Press.

Marcuse, Herbert. 1969. *Eros and Civilization.* Boston: Beacon Press.

Mauss, Marcel. 1979 [1936]. "Body Techniques." In *Sociology and Psychology: Essays.* London: Routledge and Kegan Paul.

Mead, George Herbert. 1970 [1934]. *Mind, Self, and Society.* Chicago: University of Chicago Press.

Mellor, Philip A., and Chris Shilling. 1997. "Introduction" to *Re-forming the Body: Religion, Community, and Modernity.* London: Sage.

O'Neill, John. 1985. *Five Bodies: The Human Shape of Modern Societies.* Ithaca, N.Y.: Cornell University Press.

———. 1989. *The Communicative Body: Studies in Communicative Philosophy, Politics, and Sociology.* Evanston, Ill.: Northwestern University Press.

Preston, P. W. 1997. *Political/Cultural Identity: Citizens and Nations in a Global Era.* London: Sage.

Scott, Sue, and David Morgan, eds. *Body Matters: Essays on the Sociology of the Body.* London: Falmer/Taylor and Francis.

Simmel, Georg. 1978. *The Philosophy of Money.* Trans. Tom Bottomore and David Frisby. London: Routledge and Kegan Paul.

Synnott, Anthony. 1992. "Tomb, Temple, Machine and Self: The Social Construction of the Body." *British Journal of Sociology* 41.1 (March): 79–110.

Turner, Brian S. 1992. *Regulating Bodies: Essays in Medical Sociology.* London: Routledge.

———. 1994. *The Body and Society: Explorations in Social Theory.* London: Sage.

Weber, Max. 1991 [1904–5]. *The Protestant Ethic and the Spirit of Capitalism.* New York: HarperCollins.

Margaret J. Tally

1

The Illness of Global Capitalism:

Female Employees on "Sick Leave"

and the Social Meaning of Pain

The shift in modern society from an industrially based to a postindustrial economy has generated profound changes in the ways our lives are organized. The shift has entailed the increasing advent of technology in all spheres of our work lives (Rifkin 1995; Reich 1991) and the downsizing and restructuring of formerly large hierarchical businesses and organizations. In addition, there are larger trends toward the globalization of the economy, and the withdrawal of loyalty of workers from companies and even nations as they attempt to cope with uncertainties of employment. Further, the jobs that remain in advanced economies are different from traditional forms of labor. Service work and "knowledge work," to use a term employed by Robert Reich (1991), are two growing areas of employment that differ sharply from more traditional industrial or agricultural labor. Both offer new expectations and different forms of status, authority, and control.

Scholars seeking to assess these changes have theorized that they result in shifting identities among workers (Kunda 1992). These questions are part of a broader inquiry into the postmodern self as a social construction that is subject to radical transformations (Giddens 1991; Kunda 1992; Hirschhorn 1988). Gideon Kunda (1992), for example, has explored how organizational cultures in high-tech industries influence the ways individual knowledge workers must adapt their social identities to their work environments. Charles Heckscher (1996) also has studied how organizations that are in the throes of downsizing alter employees' overall sense of identification with and to their organizations.

These explorations are critical forays into the broader discussion of how changes in the organizations of work are transforming the ways we relate to our jobs and to each other as workers. What new images of work and of workers are emerging in Western, postindustrial societies? How are these new images connected to particular kinds of labor, such as service work and knowledge work? How are these kinds of workplaces organized, and how do workers adapt to these new organizational cultures? How, finally, do those workers respond when they are unhappy with the changes in their work life? Do they continue to identify with their jobs in the same way, or do they offer resistance to the imposed values and norms of the workplace? As one window into these processes, Kunda (1992) explores high-tech engineers and their inculcation into a high-intensity work culture. The term *culture* has been applied in organizational theory to the study of management to mean "the shared rules governing the cognitive and affective aspects of membership in an organization, and the means whereby they are shaped and expressed" (Kunda 1992, 8). A "strong culture" in this framework refers to an intense identification with the goals and values that the upper management of a company might espouse. The "hearts and minds" of employees have been won over or, as Kunda points out,

> Under normative control, membership is founded not only on the behavioral or economic transaction traditionally associated with work organizations, but, more crucially, on an experiential transaction, one in which symbolic rewards are exchanged for a moral orientation to the organization. In this transaction a member role is fashioned and imposed that includes not only behavioral rules but also articulated guidelines for experience. In short, under normative control it is the employee's self—that ineffable source of subjective experience—that is claimed in the name of the corporate interest. (Ibid., 11)

Kunda finds that there is an orchestrated effort on the part of management to create a "strong culture" by which engineers will identify with the goals of the organization so fully that they do not balk at the intensive workloads increasingly required of them.

Other research, conducted by scholars such as Arlie Hochschild and Robin Leidner, focuses on how another group of workers, service personnel, are inculcated into the strong cultures of their organization (Hochschild 1989; Leidner 1993). Hochschild finds, for example, that women who are employed as airline stewardesses are not only required to perform physical labor as part of their job, but in fact are required to perform a kind of "emotional labor" of service for customers. "Emotional labor" refers to the "emotional style of offering the service [as] part of the service itself" (Hochschild 1983, 5).

Leidner, too, looks at service workers, such as those in the insurance industry as well as food-service workers at McDonald's. She also finds that intensive efforts are made on the part of the companies to inculcate in workers an identification with the company's goals. In addition, in interactions with customers, service workers are also required to display a distinct set of emotional attributes, including various performances of gender.

The conflicts that arise between the stated norms of the organization, the tacit ways that things get done, and the personalities of the workers can create tensions in the very identity of the service worker who is asked to alter a formerly personal attitude in the professional performance of his or her job. As Leidner writes:

> The routines of interactive service workers, in short, are structured to make them be certain kinds of people. Some of the qualities built into their routines are ones that workers might well judge positively—cheerfulness or aggressiveness, helpfulness or control. Similarly, routines may match workers' ideas of appropriate manliness or womanliness. Other aspects of the routines, such as those demanding subordination, passivity, or insincerity, may be harder for workers to incorporate into their self-images. Interactive service workers have to determine whether they want to be the kinds of people their routines demand, and whether it is possible for them, while at work, to be the kinds of people they want to be. (Leidner 1993, 188–89)

In the work of Kunda, Hochschild, and Leidner, there is the sense that the needs of the organization require the workers to adapt aspects of their personality to fulfill the needs of the job. These organizations exert a kind of normative control that has been described by Kunda as "the attempt to elicit and direct the required efforts of members by controlling the underlying experiences, thoughts, and feelings that guide their actions" (1992, 11). The work of a strong culture is to inculcate employees so that they will so strongly identify with the goals of the organization that they will alter their own identities to meet the needs of the organization. The metaphor of "family" has sometimes been used to describe how these members of an organization feel. At the same time, a "strong culture" impels individuals to comply with a work environment that may have strong forms of control within the labor process itself. The work of the strong culture, then, is to inculcate the worker not only to identify with the goals of the company, but also to accept the structure of the job itself, which could be highly rationalized or Taylorized, and alienating.

One of the less explored aspects of these studies is the ways in which workers could be said to resist the kinds of normative controls that exist in organizations that have strong cultures. Indeed, even in work organizations with strong cultures that encourage individuals to work harder and to offer emotional labor, workers do not always passively accept these constraints. In order to begin to outline some of the forms of worker resistance, it might be helpful to explore work cultures where service workers conduct their jobs, and further, how these workers respond to these conditions. Can we identify forms of resistance to these "strong cultures" that ask workers to adopt specific identities in the performance of their jobs?

To examine this question in more detail, I offer a descriptive account of one particular group of workers—female customer service representatives—and one innovative means they adopted for responding to the conditions of their workplace. As part of a larger ethnographic project exploring the impact of downsizing on white-collar workers, I was engaged in field research in a telephone company (hereafter, "the company") in the mid- to late 1990s. I was able there both to observe interactive service workers at their jobs and to interview them and their managers and executives in mid-level management. These interviews were conducted both on and off of their job sites, and were followed up with additional interviews in response to emerging research questions.

In trying to understand the meanings embedded in these women's responses to questions about their work life, serious questions emerged about how they experienced the changing conditions of their jobs. For example, the majority of those interviewed spoke about how too much work was expected of them for them to do a good job. In addition, they described how they were experiencing stress in response to the way their work life was organized. In trying to understand their occupational lifeworld, it was critical to apprehend the meanings they attached to being "stressed" or "burned out," and to understand how they responded to these conditions. I discovered that many of these women had been either absent from their jobs on disability or on "stress leave" during the period in which I was observing the company. In interviews with benefits administrators and managers, there was a clear sense that there had indeed been an increase in absenteeism during the period in which I was at the company. I would argue that, both metaphorically and literally, illness, whether real, imagined, or invented, became one of the means of using the system to their advantage, as well as a real response to the increasingly unacceptable conditions of their job. In this way, it could be said that these women literally used their bodies to respond to and resist work conditions they found to be intolerable.

As Pei-Chia Lan argues in her study of cosmetic retailers in department stores and direct selling, workers' bodies are not a topic that has been actively theorized in studies of labor (Lan 1998). Writers such as Foucault (1977) have explored how the body is inscribed with relations of power and knowledge; similarly, social theorists such as Bourdieu have shown how the body becomes a site for the expression of class tastes and interests (Bourdieu 1985). As Lan points out, however, social theory has not taken the next step of assessing how the labor process itself inscribes particular power relations through the manipulation of the body. In addition, in terms of the question of resistance, theories of labor have not dealt with how workers might use their bodies as a means either to resist or to negotiate some autonomy within conditions of work that they find intolerable. As Lan observes:

> The labor process should be seen as a battleground that involves contested power practices as well as workers' agency and resistance. It is a process of negotiation among various and unsettled power dynamics, and incessant bargaining between workers and employers/managers in their everyday work. This situation becomes more significant in the labor process of service workers, who have overtaken manufacturing workers in most industrialized societies. (Lan 1998, 231)

How these female customer service representatives or "reps" used sick leave also provides an interesting example of how the macro changes in the economy impacted on these women's sense of identification with their company. Indeed, many of these women went from accepting the metaphorical identification of their company as a "family" to employing sick leave to extract the maximum benefits from an organization with which they no longer identified. And, in fact, there also was an increase in the amount of actual sickness and pain that these women experienced as a result of these macro changes. The sheer volume of work they had to contend with increased exponentially, which created often intolerable levels of stress. Depression and "burnout" arose in the wake of simply too much work, in addition to the emotional labor they were already expected to perform on their job.

In this essay, I will touch on two aspects of the meaning of pain for these women: the instrumental use of pain, whether real or invented, as a lever to extract benefits from a company with which they no longer identified; and physical pain as a response to increasingly higher levels of work. I begin by exploring some of the structural features of the job. Then I look at how these female reps responded to these structural conditions, in terms of both real and imagined illnesses, as well as using sick leave as a strategy of negotiation and resistance. Finally, I will broaden the discussion by exploring more generally how recent changes in the nature of work have influenced the changing identity and sense of loyalty among service workers.

Structural Features of the Job

The job of customer service representative had a long history in the company I studied. The essential aspects of the job remained consistent, even while it was transformed historically as machines changed the way in which the job was done. The job of the customer service representative was to ensure that phone customers received good service on their account. The reps were responsible for billing, orders, selling, and collections of customers' accounts. They did this through direct phone contact with customers, who would call in to receive assistance. Initially staffed by men, the job of phone operator and then customer service representative became "gendered" as a female occupation in the early part of the last century. As Stephen Vallas notes, the fact that women came to occupy this job effectively meant that the job became a "ghetto" for women and deprived them of opportunities for mobility in the company:

> The Company's conception of women as inherently different from men set in motion structural processes that would endure for over a century. The feminization of the switchboard . . . began a pervasive system of sex segregation that reserved virtually all rewarding, skilled jobs for men. It also reached into efforts to challenge the Company's authority, introducing divisions into the workers' movement to establish trade unions. . . . Furthermore, the influx of vast numbers of women into the . . . system affected the Company's relationship with its workers, inviting managers to adopt a protective and eventually paternalist stance toward its largely female work force. (Vallas 1993, 42–43)

In addition to the work environment being largely gendered and paternalist, the job itself was highly structured and monitored. Fixed hierarchies were in place, and the workers were closely monitored, with supervisors being able to plug into a worker's switchboard to ensure that she was in compliance with the company's rules regarding proper behavior toward customers.

The strong culture of the company was dedicated to ensuring that elaborate codes of conduct were strictly adhered to. The rules were to be precisely followed, and no deviations were allowed in the performance of one's job. As part of this effort, and early on in the history of the company, an intensive effort was directed at controlling the worker's bodily and emotive behavior. As Vallas writes, "by 1915 one operator told an inspector for the federal government that she and her fellow switchboard workers were not allowed to turn their heads—not even allowed to smile, to fold hands or to cross their feet, nor even to lean back in their chairs" (ibid., 48). The Taylorization of this pink-collar position meant that increasing efforts would be made to rationalize every aspect of the job, to minimize the worker's autonomy in performing the job and maximize the scripted and rote nature of the work.

In order to ensure loyalty in this structured work environment, the company worked hard to maintain a "family" atmosphere, both through paternalistic management practices and through literally hiring several members of an extended family for different jobs in the company. In addition, the majority of the workers hired, particularly in the earlier parts of the century, were largely white and not first-generation immigrants. This too ensured a kind of homogeneity and "family" atmosphere in the company. Finally, company buildings were usually located in the neighborhoods in which workers lived, so that not only relatives, but friends from the neighborhood also worked in the same building, which also lent itself to a communal and familial atmosphere. Representatives often spoke of how their supervisors used to be like family members, for example, giving them clothes that their own children had outgrown and, more important, finding jobs for their relatives and neighbors.

In addition to the strong culture of believing that one was part of a "family," a second aspect of the normative culture focused on the issue of service. The women were inculcated to serve the customer, though this aspect of their job transformed during the course of the twentieth century. In fact, as the job became ever more mechanized and automated as the relevant technologies progressed, the women felt more estranged from their jobs, and less able to identify themselves as serving the public. As Vallas notes:

> Traditionally, even after management's application of Taylorism to their jobs, operators had found some compensation from the visible fact that it

was they who conveyed scarce information to subscribers, responded to emergencies, and metaphorically wove their local communities together. When machines began to perform this function, consigning operators to auxiliary roles in both the work process and local community, many felt a profound sense of personal loss. (Vallas 1993, 54)

In general, though, two aspects of the job contributed to a strong culture and sense of identification with the company: the notion that these women were somehow part of a family and that they were dedicated to service. These feelings were echoed by many of the older women who had been at the company in the "old days." As one man noted:

> You just knew when you saw someone that they worked for the company. They just had a certain look about them. I remember seeing people on the subway, and knowing they worked for the company just by the way they talked and dressed. We all looked alike and felt like we were part of a big family. (Male, 51, trainer, human resources, April 15, 1998)

In terms of the identification with service, one woman observed:

> I used to feel great about being able to help someone who was upset with his or her bill. It's such a great feeling when you know what to do. To get them an answer when they are upset. (Female, 41, former rep, May 16, 1998)

One of the most significant changes that the company had undergone occurred in the 1980s, when it became both divested and deregulated. From being one of the largest telephone companies in the country, it now became simply one more competitor in a vastly deregulated market, having to actively compete for customers.

In addition to deregulation and divestiture, the company had also undertaken a massive effort at downsizing in the late 1980s and early 1990s, and had significantly reduced the overall size of its workforce by the time I began my interviews. Although the bulk of the reduction in the workforce had been directed at management, incentives to retire early also were being offered craft workers, of whom the customer service representatives were part. Large numbers of representatives did in fact take these incentives, which meant that many of the representatives I spoke with were "new hires." Because they had only been there a short time, they were less familiar with others on the job, had less of a "family feeling," and were less experienced in performing the job effectively.

Another large-scale shift in the job, which occurred in the 1980s as a result of affirmative-action initiatives, was that there were now large numbers of African-American females occupying the rep job in the greater metropolitan area. Some critics have speculated that these hirings were a cynical move designed simply to increase the minority numbers for the Equal Employment Opportunity Commission while placing African-Americans in the most difficult job in the company with the fewest opportunities for mobility. However, for African-Americans, the rep job offered an opportunity that they would not have had previously when the company was essentially segregated and almost entirely white. For these women, the company offered a kind of stability and protection in an urban labor market that had historically provided few opportunities to African-American women.

Another large-scale change had to do with the vastly increased volume of business the company experienced by the early and mid-1990s and its efforts to maintain or increase profits in a newly competitive environment. The economy had strengthened and the bull market was ascendant, which meant that more and more businesses were being created and expanding, which in turn meant more business for the company. In addition, advances in telecommunications technology allowed the company to offer a wide array of new services, and thus there were many more kinds of products and services to offer an expanding customer base.

In addition to and as a consequence of the increasing volume of work, the job itself had been subjected to a speedup by management, so that reps were now responsible for working with customers at a much faster rate. In fact, the Public Service Commission had fined the company for not responding fast enough to customers. Rather than hiring and training additional reps, however, management responded by pressuring the reps on the job to respond at a much faster rate to avoid additional fines. Because of large-scale retirements and firings, a larger and more complex range of products, and the high turnover rate of this stressful job, there were now even fewer reps to handle a vast increase in volume.

Responses to New Conditions of the Job

The advent of deregulation, divestiture, increased volume, and subsequent speedup of the job held profound implications for the reps' sense of identification with the company. In addition, these changes had important ramifications for the ability of reps to play out the service role of their job. Moreover, many of the older workers now simply no longer felt that they were part of a family. As one of these older workers exclaimed, "The first time [with the company] I married for love; the second marriage is for money!" (female, 47, former rep, June 1997). Another older rep observed, "Now the company is so bottom-line driven, they don't care about us anymore, all they want is the profits" (female, 38, rep, December 1995).

Part of the reason for this loss of "family feeling" was that reps no longer felt that their company was protecting them. Earlier in this Taylorized environment, there had been too many rules, but at least there was a sense that the work itself was designed so that they could reasonably get it done. For example, earlier the job had been structured so that each rep had approximately one hour "on the line" answering customer calls, and one hour "off the line" to process the paperwork generated from working with customers. Now, the rep was expected to be "on line" for five and a half hours a day, with one hour for lunch, two fifteen-minute breaks, and one hour to process all the paperwork. Even though reps now do some of the "paperwork" on the screen itself as they are working with customers, there is still a good amount of "off-line" paperwork and follow-up details to be accomplished in any given transaction. The reps simply cannot process all the information they have generated with customers in one hour of their working day.

Far from feeling protected by supervisors, reps now felt increasingly vulnerable to a management structure that had accelerated the speed and volume of their work. When I spoke with managers about these changes, many of them too bemoaned the new work atmosphere that this speedup had created and blamed upper management for the changes, or even those outside management who were somehow orchestrating the new "bottom-line" ethos of the company:

> It's the folks out there, on Wall Street, who are driving the decisions we're making here . . . they want to see the numbers. (Male, 56, director, training)

In the new, bottom-line environment, the emphasis has steadily shifted from service to volume, which has meant in turn that it is harder to serve customers. Reps are routinely pressured to speed up their calls, and to sell more phone services than a customer might need or want or be able to afford. In earlier periods, the emotional labor that a rep performed coincided with a gendered sense of self as a nurturing, caring person who wanted to help people. Now that reps are no longer simply "helping," but trying to sell, there is a conflict with this earlier understanding of service. Put simply, many of the older reps felt somehow inauthentic, as one rep noted: "I hate having to try and push the new products on people, since I know most of them can't afford it anyway" (female, 43, rep, March 19, 1996).

Combined with this sense of inauthenticity was the fact that, because of a new, downsized work environment where their sense of job security was threatened, the older reps experienced a sea change in their sense of identification with the company, and in their identities as workers within it. In contrast, the younger workers had little knowledge of the "old days" and the sense of identification with the company as part of one big family. Hence, they experienced the company as simply a very intense and pressured work environment. The job was extremely Taylorized, offered little autonomy, and exacted stringent requirements in terms of the emotional labor that they had to perform. No matter how much work they were given, for example, they were still required to be polite, courteous, and helpful.

Thus, for both younger and older reps, there were ample reasons to feel disconnected from the company. The older reps went from feeling like loyal members of a big family to disgruntled and bitter workers who were going to use the company in the same way they felt it was using them. The younger reps simply viewed the company as a harsh and restrictive work environment, which meant that they too would look out for themselves and try to extract whatever benefits they could from the company. Both the younger and older reps, in sum, turned to the "sick leave" policy offered by the company as a vehicle to "get back" from the company some benefits to which they felt entitled.

During the time of my study, the company was changing its benefit plans for both "incidental absences" (first seven calendar days) and "short-term disability" (fifty-two weeks). Benefits administrators reported that various departments had identified an increase in their absences following the introduction in 1993 of the Family Medical Leave Act (FMLA). This act, inaugurated as part of the Clinton administration's effort to help working families, required that employers with more than fifty workers provide unpaid time off in the case of personal illness or to care for sick family members, with no disciplinary actions taken against them.

In addition to such cases as long-term absences for which workers applied as a result of the FMLA, they now also were routinely absent for short periods of time, with seven days or less being the norm. This was a result of the policy of the "step," which penalized workers for taking a day off from work by counting it against their attendance record as a week. Since they were being penalized for a week anyway, most reps simply decided to remain off the job for the period they were being "stepped" or penalized. Thus, the sick-leave policy of counting a day off as a week off in terms of a rep's attendance effectively meant that the reps would add informal vacation time, as they remained out of work for a week at any given time. As one rep explained:

Why should I rush back to work when they already stepped me for tak-
ing a day off? I might as well just take off and do what else I need to do.
I can call the insurance, whatever, which I can't get done during the week
anyway. . . . . They [the company] don't care and didn't believe me anyway.
I had a hard time getting them to accept my doctor's note. (Female, 24, rep,
March 1997)

Other companies might offer ten paid sick-leave days to employees, without a mark against their attendance record. Because this company had a
sick-leave policy that counted each sick day as up to five, it inadvertently
encouraged the reps to take the week off. As one woman explained, "You
know, I don't do this but a lot of people just plan their years using their
sick leave, so they can get more time. I wouldn't do that, but a lot of the
reps just think they're entitled to it" (female, 45, rep, April 1997).

It should be noted that the older reps were able to recount a time when
reps did not use the sick-leave policy in this way. They recounted taking off only as much time as they needed to get better. In part, this was
because they felt a loyalty to the company, and to their fellow reps, many
of whom would have to do more work to compensate for their absence.
Another reason was that, in previous times, their manager would not
count their absence as a "step" or mark against their attendance record.
The manager would tell reps to take as much time as they needed to get
better, and the reps in turn would take only as much time as they actually
needed. Now the managers routinely invoke the "step" process against
the reps, in many cases because they are new themselves to the job and
do not have the kind of relationship with their reps that managers once
held. Because the "step" process is activated now routinely, the older reps
respond by taking the entire week off.

The younger reps also took advantage of the "step" system, in part because of the social backgrounds that they came from. For example, many
of the younger workers were low-income, African-American women who
were used to surviving in tough, inner-city environments, and were less
schooled in the ways of the mainstream corporate world in which they
now found themselves. Upon entering the company, they quickly had
to develop a whole new set of skills for dealing with a white managerial
establishment and a widely diverse customer base. Many of these women
were faulted by their managers for such things as their use of "Black
English," their office attire, and their math and writing skills. Far from
identifying with the company, these younger reps instead perceived their
managers as hostile, unreasonable, and perhaps even racist.

In this environment, the younger reps viewed the "step" system as a means for extracting some "payback" for a job that was stressful and difficult. Many of these women had had to deal with public bureaucracies such as welfare, Medicare, and schools, and viewed the "step" system as one opportunity to use a policy to maximum advantage. Ironically, this seems to be an appropriate counterpart to the company's new attitude toward its workers, as resources to be used for maximum benefits.

It should also be noted that, for both younger and older reps, there were significant stresses from both within and without the company, which would lead them to needing time off from a difficult job. Many of these women were the mainstays in an extended family network where other relatives were significantly less well off, suffering problems of health, substance abuse, and, in some cases, incarceration. Many of the women were mothers, some single mothers, and had responsibilities for child care as well as for supporting their families financially. Many commuted long distances to their jobs, and were required to report to work regardless of weather conditions, because they were penalized if they took "snow days" (even if their children stayed home because school was canceled as a result of snow). Moreover, the conditions of the work itself were increasingly intolerable, not least because their supervisors were often new and poorly trained.

In this internal and external climate, many of the women started to develop health problems, some of which were quite significant and included such ailments as hypertension, high blood pressure, and adult-onset diabetes. Many also reported such work-related ailments as strained vocal cords, swelling in the ankles, sore wrists, and eyestrain. In sum, the use of sick leave represented a complex interplay of real health issues combined with a desire to extract as much time away from the company as was possible under the sick-leave policy.

The Changing Nature of Service Work

Customer service work has become a permanent feature of the employment landscape. As scholars in the field of service work such as Cameron Macdonald and Carmen Sirianni (1996, 1) point out, employment in this sector accounts for approximately 79 percent of nonagricultural jobs in the United States. Further, the majority of new jobs being created are, and likely will continue to be, in the service sector.

In the company I studied, the service work itself has shifted to include a strong sales component. This changes the kind of emotional labor that the rep now has to do. She is not only managing emotions with the goal of helping the customer, but must also include a selling component to the relationship. Customers, in turn, understand that the representative is not only in the "business" of helping them with their phone lines, but is also now a salesperson, and they are on their guard about being pressured into purchasing something they may not want or be able to afford. Added to this is a work environment where there is too much work to provide quality (or even adequate) service to customers. Customers respond by getting angry, or, as one rep offered, "they're always squawking at us."

In this environment, the rep job itself has become increasingly difficult to perform, and the emotional labor involved in dealing with irate customers and unreasonable managers is leading to increased amounts of emotional and physical fatigue. At the same time, the rep is now faced with a work climate that emphasizes competition over family and numbers over service. In this brave new world, the metaphor of "family" has been replaced by "the bottom line."

In this sense, "sick leave" and "disability leave" take on a new and important meaning. Other scholars (Taylor and Bain 1988) have noted the ways in which workers in telecommunications have begun to demonstrate both individual and collective forms of resistance to these new work conditions. However, in the case of the women I studied, the notion that there was somehow a collective form of resistance is hard to sustain. These responses were individual, fragmented, and ultimately mirrored the "every man for himself" ethos of the new corporate environment. In addition, I do not think the women were able to view their use of sick leave as a political response to an unreasonable work structure.

More important, the use of sick leave in and of itself cannot be understood as resistance. Rather, it is a kind of negotiation that the women engaged in to mediate between their physical distress and the company's policy to give them time off when they were sick. For many of these women, the sick-leave policy was understood as a kind of employee benefit, to be used to its maximum effect so long as it did not lead to even more punishment than a mark against their attendance—if they used too many of these "steps" they would be out of a job. Their tactic was to use as much sick time as possible to get their entitled time off, but not so much as to get them fired.

In the context of the overall history of the company, however, the use of sick leave by these women does represent an abandonment of the work ethic that had been instilled in them in earlier periods of the company's history. The strong culture of the company was such that workers considered it part of their duty to show up for work no matter what. If one was really sick, it was understood that the worker really did need the time off, and was not penalized for taking the time needed to get better. The strong culture, in other words, not only referred to the structure of the job, which was highly rationalized and Taylorized, but also to the ideological perception of the workplace as a family that one did not "abandon" by using sick leave excessively. In this new work environment, the strong culture had all but disappeared, and in its stead was a workplace inimical to the worker's needs. Illness became the primary response to this environment, to be employed on an "as needed" basis as a way to recover some autonomy and in many cases to try to regain one's physical well-being.

Although the use of sick leave can be understood to represent one form of resistance and negotiation, it remains the case that more collective forms of action are needed to fully address the changing work conditions of these women. If they have lost their sense of family, it may be that they can now more fully identify with collective forms of representation such as those suggested by the membership in their union. However, many of the women expressed concern that the union was not adequately addressing their situation. Because of their history with the union, the female reps had occupied a complicated but lesser status, and thus their concerns were not always put on the table in labor negotiations. Any kind of collective response, therefore, would have to address their status in the union itself.

In general, as the nature of service work shifts, in all likelihood an increase in absenteeism and the use of sick leave will continue. This is a result of the changing nature of a job that has increased the amount of stress experienced by service workers, as well as the loss of the work ethic that was based on identifying with the needs of the employer. In this sense, the social meaning of pain, as expressed through the use of sick leave, is a sign both of resistance and of frustration with the world of work.

References

Albrecht, Karl, and Ron Zemke. 1990. *Service America! Doing Business in the New Economy.* New York: Warner Books.

Bourdieu, Pierre. 1985. *Distinction: A Social Critique of the Judgment of Taste.* Cambridge: Harvard University Press.

Braverman, Harry. 1974. *Labor and Monopoly Capital: The Degradation of Work in the Twentieth Century.* New York: Monthly Review Press.

Foucault, Michel. 1977. *Discipline and Punish: The Birth of the Prison.* Trans. Alan Sheridan. New York: Pantheon Books.

Garson, Barbara. 1988. *The Electronic Sweatshop: How Computers Are Transforming the Office of the Future into the Factory of the Past.* New York: Simon and Schuster.

Giddens, Anthony. 1991. *Modernity and Self-Identity: Self and Society in the Late Modern Age.* Stanford, Calif.: Stanford University Press.

Heckscher, Charles. 1996. *White-Collar Blues: Management Loyalties in an Age of Corporate Restructuring.* New York: Basic Books.

Hirschorn, Larry. 1984. *Beyond Mechanization: Work and Technology in a Postindustrial Age.* Cambridge: MIT Press.

———. 1988. *The Workplace Within: Psychodynamics of Organizational Life.* Cambridge: MIT Press.

Hochschild, Arlie Russell. 1983. *The Managed Heart: Commercialization of Human Feeling.* Berkeley: University of California Press.

———. 1989. *The Second Shift: Working Parents and the Revolution at Home.* New York: Avon.

Kunda, Gideon. 1992. *Engineering Culture: Control and Commitment in a High-Tech Corporation.* Philadelphia: Temple University Press.

Lan, Pei-Chia. 1998. "'Bodily Labor' in Contemporary Service Jobs: Cosmetics Retailers in Department Stores and Direct Selling." In *Work, Difference and Social Change: Two Decades after Braverman's Labor and Monopoly Capital."* Binghamton, N.Y.: Binghamton University.

Leidner, Robin. 1993. *Fast Food, Fast Talk: Service Work and the Routinization of Everyday Life.* Berkeley: University of California Press.

———. 1996. "Rethinking Questions of Control: Lessons from McDonald's." In *Working in the Service Society,* ed. Cameron Lynne Macdonald and Carmen Sirianni. Philadelphia: Temple University Press.

Macdonald, Cameron Lynne, and Carmen Sirianni, eds. 1996. *Working in the Service Society.* Philadelphia: Temple University Press.

Reich, Robert. 1991. *The Work of Nations.* New York: Alfred A. Knopf.

Rifkin, Jeremy. 1995. *The End of Work: The Decline of the Global Labor Force and the Dawn of the Post-Market Era.* New York: Putnam.

Taylor, Phillip, and Peter Bain. 1998. "An Assembly Line in the Head: The Call Centre Labour Process." Paper presented at the 16th International Labour Process Conference UMIST, Manchester.

Vallas, Steven Peter. 1993. *Power in the Workplace: The Politics of Reproduction at AT&T.* New York: State University of New York Press.

2

The Problematics of Democratic Action within Disciplinary Liberalism: The Norplant Case and the Postmodern Body

The debate over the medical safety of Norplant and its role in the American welfare state delineates an increasing tension in relationships between public and private bodies. In the United States, Norplant has been "prescribed" by judges and political representatives as a condition for parole or the receipt of welfare in a milieu that displays considerable ambivalence over women's bodily autonomy. Indeed, more than a dozen attempts have been made to legalize a tie between Norplant and welfare. In many developing nations, where reproductive technologies are usually tested before they are released in Europe and the United States, Norplant marks the crucial transformation of birth control into population control.

In this essay, I examine the specific mechanisms by which the categories of public and private are constituted within the frameworks of postmodern fragmentation of human identity and the world political economy of disciplinary liberalism. By examining the case of Norplant, I hope not only to illuminate the value and limits of previous theorization of these issues, but also to develop an understanding of the possibility for democratic political actions. Indeed, that sustained egalitarian action is an actual possibility remains in question today. Within the context of a postindustrial, flexible political economy and emergent postmodern cultural trends, the possibility of durable democratic political action is constrained not only by a decentering of the subject, but by a decentering of the corporeal basis for subjectivities. Although postmodern developments in recent years have revealed the problematics of pluralist and Marxist inquiries into the nature of power, many of these developments have stopped short of theorizing their own contributions to democratic political action. I hope, in this study of reproductive technologies, to ground political theory in those corporeal human relations that are a necessary condition for what we call the political, and to highlight the gendered nature of American social, political, and private relations by working through some of the contributions of Michel Foucault and Hannah Arendt.

In a very general sense, Foucault's analytics of power opens up a consideration of broader nongovernmental forms of political and social power, providing a more capacious genealogy of power and domination. Because Foucault sees power "everywhere," some have wrongly accused him of nihilism (Dryzek 1994, 8). Although nihilism may be an overstatement, Foucault's works offer little (save the vibrant yet limited notion of resistance) in the way of meaningful political reconstruction. Foucault's broader concept of power allows for a threefold process of producing, analyzing, and manipulating the subject. Foucault places the subject within a field of "multiple force relations." The multiplicity of these relations allows for concepts such as "choice" and "resistance" to play an integral role in human power relations. Here I seek to place the discourse of Norplant into Foucault's framework of power. While this avenue provides a viable grounding for the critique of liberalism and the hegemonic components of new reproductive technologies, it offers less in the way of understanding action. The body is, in crucial ways, integrally related to human action. As I pursue the role of the body in power relations, I turn to the works of Elizabeth Grosz and Maxine Sheets-Johnstone, asserting that Foucault often describes the body as acted upon, but rarely acting.

Hannah Arendt's conceptualizations of power, potentia, action, and natality offer a framework for maintaining the benefits of Foucault's critique while providing the means for reconstituting ontological spaces where sustained democratic action is possible. The spontaneity of natality and its capacity to unite humans through difference carries with it an emancipatory potential that is never realized in Foucault's work because such a realization requires the constitution of viable public spaces. Arendt's framework thus complements Foucault's critique of modernity in that it offers not a "way out" of power, but a way through. Yet Arendt's post-Enlightenment philosophy also is plagued with racism and sexism.

Given these limits of her work, I have attempted to read Arendt "against the grain," throwing her more problematic assertions into question.

Feminist readings of new reproductive technologies within my synthesis of Foucault and Arendt produce a more succinct analysis of the body and a more detailed understanding of the construction of gender. This reading aims not to assign a particular irreversible ideology to all technology, but rather to gain a comprehensive understanding of the social context under which new reproductive technologies (such as Norplant) operate. Finally, it is important to recognize that Norplant is part of a larger process of disembodiment and incorporation in postmodern culture. I conclude with a consideration of this process and how it has worked its way through the discourses of both positivism and postmodernism. Fuller understanding of this process can inform an egalitarian politics of embodied subjectivities.

Here, I engage aspects of critical theory as being distinct from, but also continuous with, postmodern and poststructural accounts of power. Although contemporary theoretical accounts of power have often effectively uncovered sites and sources of resistance in response to more totalizing theories of domination in critical theory, such efforts run the risk of eliding relations of domination. There may be some merit in speaking of *totality* and *domination* in the context of global capital. Thus, contemporary attempts to construct political theories of power that cast off the contributions of Marxism and critical theory outright run the risk of presenting a less comprehensive theory of power. The parsimonious Gramscian equation for hegemony (hegemony = force + persuasion) may be helpful here (Gramsci 1971, 206–78). To some extent, postmodern and poststructural accounts of power can be read as attempts to focus with great clarity on the latter end of this equation. The ways in which power relations are *signified*, for example, play a fundamental role in formulating resistance and domination. Thinkers as diverse as James C. Scott, Donna Haraway, Judith Butler, Jacques Derrida, and Michel Foucault have all tapped into the role of signification in maintaining and reframing power relations. However, to approach power only on the levels of persuasion and signification involves the risk of ignoring the material and corporeal bases within which relations of signification are articulated. I believe that Derrida recognized this when he wrote *Specters of Marx* (1994). It is also worth noting that feminist critics of new reproductive technologies in the South, such as Sonia Corrêa, have presented articulate, viable critiques of power and new reproductive technologies from a feminist-Marxian perspective. By contrasting *and comparing* critical and poststructural theory as well as feminisms of the 1970s, 1980s, and 1990s, I seek to provide concepts of power and hegemony that elucidate relations of signification as well as relations of production and reproduction.

On the Disciplinary Discourse of Norplant

What sets the cultural logic of Norplant (and other new reproductive technologies) apart from other older techniques of contraception? Whereas older procreative and contraceptive methods divided women from men, thereby reinforcing cultural norms of women as vessels, new reproductive technologies divide women internally as well through cellular *micropractices*. A woman is separated from her womb, her fetus, and her choice to have a baby in very concrete ways. The growth of "fetal rights" through ultrasound, the separation of woman from womb ("surrogacy"), and the increase of diagnostic techniques to reveal a fetus's potential future health problems (genetic testing) all contribute to a more severe version of an old problem: in a literal sense, the woman's body has become a body divided against itself. Speaking formally, Anita Hardon describes Norplant as "a hormonal implant, consist[ing] of six silastic rods, each containing 36 milligrams of progestin levonorgestrel which can be effective for a period of five years" (Hardon 1994, 11). The slow release of the hormone progestin drastically reduces the possibility of successful ovulation. As a contraceptive, it is one of the most effective on the market with a pregnancy rate "lower than for IUD or pill users and comparable to surgical sterilization during the first three years of use" (National Women's Health Network 1991, 1). Norplant has the added feature of being *reversible* in that the effects of the steroid quickly dissipate upon removal.

The most commonly acknowledged side effects of Norplant include changes in menstrual bleeding patterns (irregularities, more frequent bleeding, amenorrhea). Pilot studies in Chile, Thailand, and Sri Lanka reported bleeding disturbances for 45 percent of Norplant users (WGNRR 1988). Masculinist and ethnocentric biases contribute to the misrepresentation of menstrual disturbance as an inconvenient side effect. But prolonged menstruation results in more clothing to wash, which is dangerous in communities where clean water is inaccessible. Observers in Haiti, for example, noted that the cost of clean water has led many Norplant recipients to use wastewater for cleansing (Jenks 2000, 31). Norplant researchers have not fully considered the medical, cultural, and emotional impact of prolonged and intermittent menstruation at a global level. In some cultures, women cannot worship or participate in other crucial social functions during their menstrual cycles. A ninety-day absence from places of worship, caused by irregular or prolonged menstruation, could easily contribute not only to personal religious alienation, but also to a decline of social status within the community (ibid., 32).

The Population Council has noted headaches, weight changes, depression, and acne as side effects. However, many health advocates have found that in addition to these problems, Norplant carries other risks. Norplant can adversely affect lipid metabolism, resulting in the development of cardiac problems. Another side effect that has been reported but was not included in the Population Council's releases is epilepsy. The Population Council's studies have also been criticized for not being representative: "Investigations were carried out with young, healthy, non-smokers. . . . 'Healthy' is understood [as]: without cardiovascular disease, without diabetes (preferably in the family), not overweight, without liver disease" (UBINIG 1988, 101). Moreover, Norplant is presented to many potential consumers (particularly in developing nations) as problem-free. The Bangladesh Fertility Research Program advertisement's entire text had six assertions: "a new birth control method, a wonderful innovation of modern science, this method is for women, this can be implanted under skin of arm, this will ensure sterility for 5 years, and when removed, can have child again" (ibid.). Such representations do not adequately integrate the physical and psychological pain that may result from the device. Whether a user develops migraines, depression, a seizure disorder, or cannot worship consistently as a result of menstrual irregularities, all of these "side effects" are potent forms of pain.

Yet, most forms of contraception have their own problems, so why target Norplant? Part of what sets these technologies apart is that they are provider-dependent for insertion and removal, thus opening up the opportunity for the intervention of others (the state, husbands, places of employment) into the reproductive aspects of a woman's life. Norplant (and Depo-Provera) is targeted as a form of patriarchal disciplinary control emanating from the certainty of what Arendt terms "the Archimedean point" (Arendt 1958). It is toward these forms of intervention that this analysis is directed.

Norplant cannot be considered "in itself." To *only* speak clinically about six silicone pins that can be implanted subdermally with a set of clearly delineated effects is to ignore the cultural, economic, and political contexts of the use of this technology. Norplant is an *effect* of the emergence of disciplinary liberalism—a political formation that mirrors the traditional liberal claims to autonomy while developing increasingly subtle modes of subject formation. These trends are not happenstance, but intimately related to the transition of Cold War industrial political economies into power relations of *improvement and flexibility*. As Ernest J. Yanarella and Herbert G. Reid note, postfordist political economies are directed toward producing an increasingly efficient production system involving workers termed "humanware" (Yanarella and Reid 1996, 200, citing "Hardware, Software, Humanware"). The term *humanware* points to the fusion between worker and technology. The introduction of Norplant into legal sentencing provides the "flexibility" for the worker to be an efficient, productive citizen. Moreover, these mechanisms of power are *gendered*, not only in the fact that to date all heavily marketed invasive contraceptive devices are "for" women, but also in that the structures of power relations within liberalism are masculinized. These structures are indebted to the masculinist concepts of sovereignty and "autonomy" that permeate the rhetoric of "choice" and "freedom" in the world political-economic landscape. In the following brief account of Norplant, I provide an examination of its application in the public sphere. Although it remains uncontested that thousands of women use this technology without any problems, the placement of Norplant within the economic-legal structure of the state nonetheless indicates a new problematic relation of power at the political, cultural, economic, and social levels. I will conclude by considering Foucault's and Arendt's contributions to the notions of power vis-à-vis postmodern identities and the emergence of a more subtly hegemonic postindustrial political-economic order.

In January of 1991, Tulare County Superior Court Judge Howard Broadman ordered Darlene Johnson (who was convicted of child abuse for flogging her children with a belt) to accept Norplant as a condition for her probation. Although no mention was made during the plea agreement of any forced contraception, Broadman stood firm, holding to his ruling after a second appeal. Arthur Caplan, who directs the University of Minnesota's Center for Biomedical Ethics, noted that this incident was part of a trend: "There is definitely a trend toward third-party involvement in reproductive decisions, including attempts to put women in jail for taking drugs that can affect the fetus" (Alexander 1991, A1). It is even more troublesome to consider that the sentence was not originally altered after it was disclosed that Johnson was a diabetic and had high blood pressure. Broadman indicated that if her physician refused to implant the device, the court would appoint one despite contraindications. At issue was the fact that Johnson originally consented. Considering how new the device was at the time, it is unsurprising that she did not then know what Norplant was. When she asked the court, Broadman responded, "well, it's like a birth control pill" and nothing more (*Appellant's Opening Brief* 1991, 45). The plaintiffs argued unsuccessfully that this was not a case of informed consent and therefore her agreement was nonbinding. Although other legal developments resulted in Johnson never using the device, Judge Broadman's "option" set a precedent in the United States. By 1993, Lynn Smith and Nina J. Easton were able to document similar cases in Florida, Illinois, California, Texas, and Nebraska (Smith and Easton 1993, 27).

Although this case was considered by many to be tragic and unjust, it might be argued that it is hardly representative of Norplant, of new reproductive technologies more generally, or of the broader issues of power and liberalism. Rather than being a deviation, however, this case indicates a larger public discourse over forced contraception, welfare mothers, and child abusers (Roberts 1997). On December 12, 1990, the *Philadelphia Inquirer* printed an editorial titled "Poverty and Norplant—Can Contraception Reduce the Underclass?" which argued that owing to increasing poverty among blacks, welfare mothers should be forced to use Norplant. Although the editorial met with considerable controversy, most criticisms were directed at the racism of the piece while ignoring its sexism and classism. Repeated attempts have been made throughout the United States to *encourage* Norplant as a condition for welfare. Kansas House Bill 2089 would have provided cash incentives of five hundred dollars initially and fifty dollars annually to each participant. Similar bills in thirteen other states were also proposed. In Baltimore's Laurence Paquin High School, a public school for pregnant teenagers, administrators introduced the drug. Many African-Americans in Baltimore are angered by the move. The school is predominantly black and some have condemned it as "social engineering" and "genocide." Sixty-one million dollars of Medicaid and health and welfare agencies' funding was spent on Norplant implantation, although very little has been allocated for removal. This is particularly worrisome, as it is costly to remove the device and those who do not remove it risk ectopic pregnancy. In the state of Oklahoma, the implant will not be removed unless medically necessary (Kaeser 1994, 11).

It is important here to realize how Norplant is located within the sociopolitical realm. The discourses of Norplant can discipline female criminals, "teach lessons," prevent "damage" to future children, reduce the number of blacks born, reduce the underclass, and control the population. In the case of Darlene Johnson and many other men and women who are sentenced to contraception or sterilization, this process "has turned the assertion of guilt into a strange scientifico-juridical complex" (Foucault

1977, 19). The body emerges as an instrument of the expression of state and other third-party power. The body is instrumentalized through a complex synthesis of analysis and manipulation. It is within this context that analyses of growing black poverty can comfortably conclude with policy recommendations of Norplant as a necessary condition for receiving welfare payments.

Foucault presents the partitioning of space and the organization of time as a means of dividing/creating populations and maximizing time. Norplant does not, formally speaking, fit Foucault's definition of partitioning (prison is one obvious example), but I consider it to be a more *flexible* form of partitioning. He writes on partitioning: "Avoid distributions in groups; break up collective dispositions. . . . Disciplinary space tends to be divided into as many sections as there are bodies or elements to be distributed. One must eliminate the effects of imprecise distributions, the uncontrolled disappearance of individuals, their diffuse circulation" (ibid., 143). The goal here is to monitor and master the uncontrolled. In the case of Norplant, the dilemma of direct observation of the "unruly" subject is eliminated through the convenience of a subdermal implant that can be removed only by trained experts. Vision and external surveillance become less important as the panopticon is literally internalized. The implant regiments the time of the disciplined body into five-year increments/sentences. Moreover, the productivity of nonpregnant women (no sicknesses, interruptions, weight gain, days lost at work) dramatically increases. Radical feminist critics of new reproductive technologies, such as Gena Corea and Robyn Rowland, have uncovered masculinist biases and power relations in contemporary medical practices. But Norplant is also an effect of a larger drive toward rationalization and efficiency through disciplinary mechanisms. By "enabling" Johnson to go "free" (and this argument could be generalized to many forms of parole sentencing), a more *productive* individual emerges— one who can (often must) participate in the workforce and live a lifestyle that is in accordance with dominant norms of conduct.

Norplant emerges as an expression of the power/knowledge nexus. In Johnson's examination, her gender, class, ability to rehabilitate, and potential for drug use (despite having *no* recorded history of drug use) all constitute her as a "case" or an effect and object of disciplinary power. Although this notion of disciplinary power is illuminating, it does not approach the complexity of power relations in these cases. Thus, it would serve us well to return to Foucault's discussion of power from his *History of Sexuality,* volume 1 (1990, 12–13). The decision to force Johnson to have Norplant implanted by the court would be, in the context of Foucault, an instance

in the development of *contending force relations.* This institutional crystalliza-
tion is not the sole "cause," but the result of confrontations, struggles, and
reversals that are part of a "multiplicity of force relations."

For Foucault, there is no cause for nihilism because even within au-
thoritarian power relations, there are countervailing resistances. Are there
forms of resistance to the types of power that this new reproductive technology represents? How have they contributed to ruptures in the state apparatus and to what extent have they reified it? Female midwifery, "natural"
(noninvasive) birthing methods, women's health organizations and networks, feminist legal discourse, feminist methodologies that give priority
to the experiences of women over "experts," and citizens' groups can all
be considered forms of resistance in this context. To many (including myself), it is cold comfort that legislation mandating the use of Norplant has
lost in all the states where it has been introduced. However, at the core of
these losses is a vague recognition of the viability of women's experiences
and the inviolability of women's bodies. Some of this has been produced
through the above-mentioned resistances. Conversely, participation in
the liberal state apparatus does to some extent legitimate the state as a
politically viable entity. Although this essay cannot adequately answer
these questions, it is hoped that their presence can reveal the utility of a
Foucauldian treatment of new reproductive technologies within the context of "political technologies of the body" (see also Sawicki 1991).

I have discussed mostly the anatomo-politics of the human body as
manifested in disciplinary power. However, this is wed to biopower, a
kind of power that produces forms of life that are considered healthy or
socially desirable. Although it is not the focus of this essay, a trend toward
biopower predominates in discourses of genetic technologies, especially
in the cases of new reproductive technologies. Such a discourse is also
present in attempts to prevent minorities and the poor from producing
children under the assumption that these children somehow would be less
than others or that it would be better for them not to exist given the conditions of poverty they would face (Kimmelman 1990; Gilliom 2001).

Here the subjects of the state are rendered calculable in a controlled,
rationalized, and now internalized environment. The regimens of scientific discourse and knowledge contribute to this production of the docile
body in that the very standards of scientific discipline and positivism
(control of exogenous variables, quantification, and rational or logical cohesion) mirror the regimen that the state has imposed on welfare mothers,
criminals such as Darlene Johnson, and other women who do not conform
to the norms. Although many feminists believed that increased knowledge

and information would logically result in a lessening of political and social oppression, knowledge is constituted by (and constitutes) power relations.

Revitalizing the Web of Human Relations and the Necessity of Public Spaces: Action and Natality in Hannah Arendt's Work

Foucault may be correct in asserting that power is both everywhere and nowhere, but power also is corporeally based. As Maxine Sheets-Johnstone notes, there is a tendency in Foucault's work to consider both power and the body only in the abstract. This abstraction of the human body is particularly evident in Foucault's inability to explain the origin or cause of resistance. He merely asserts that wherever there is power there is resistance. For Foucault, there is something in us that inexplicably resists: "there is something in the social body, in classes, groups and individuals themselves which in some sense escapes relations of power . . . an inverse energy, a discharge . . . a plebeian quality or aspect" (Foucault 1980, 138). Perhaps the reason Foucault never could adequately answer the question of the genealogy of resistance is that he did not examine how the social is born directly out of the conditions of living, breathing human bodies. The capacity for anyone (that is to say, an actual human) to dramatically alter what Foucault calls social hegemony frequently seems random at best.

Sheets-Johnstone (and Arendt via Montesquieu) presents a way in which human experience (as opposed to behavior) has dramatic impacts on sociopolitical relations. It is what both Sheets-Johnstone and Arendt term "I can's." These "I can's" are the very structure of our capabilities that inform our common capacities to take certain actions. Part of the atomization that has occurred within the rise of the liberal state is the withering away of these "I can's" through a simultaneous breaking down of what binds us together along with an obliteration of our actual differences. The atomization of the liberal state assumes and produces subjectivities, unencumbered not only by the world they live in, but the world of which they are a part. Common physical matters of corporeality (that we eat, that we sleep, that we share "the same binary patterning on our feet," that we live in the same biosphere) enable us to think and act intersubjectively, in a manner that is not entirely foreign to others (Sheets-Johnstone 1994, 328–29). Simultaneously, the structure of our "I can's" prevents us from overlooking the palpable differences that do separate men and women because we *are* different. Combined with Foucault's critical insight, these differences and commonalties provide a potentially fruitful politics of resistance.

However limited, a politics grounded in imaginatively comprehending bodily grounds of commonality and difference contains the possibility of adhesion to the world. In this light, the "I can's" are always posited inter-subjectively (Merleau-Ponty 1968). Foucault's crucial contribution in this context is in underscoring the ways in which disciplinary liberalism works to articulate and institute subjectivity, effectively disassembling the corporeal matrix of intersubjectivity. Sheets-Johnstone writes: "Our differences must be equally understood in bodily terms. Male and female bodies *are* different. Their corporeal differences give rise both to different experiences, including different experiences of power, and to different possibilities, *including different possibilities of power*. . . . We must fathom what it is to be the bodies we are not. We must, in effect, ask ourselves, what is it like to be female? What is it like to be male?" (ibid., 329).

In this consideration of what it is like to be the opposite sex, the possibility for compassion for what sets us apart both socially and physically emerges. Foucault provides a framework for social and political critique, but fails to offer an activism rooted in action through plurality. The "I can" is not a biological fact in Foucault, but a social inscription. In reaching to express all the ways in which the physical body can be written, Foucault has lost touch with the opposite—the ways in which the social is corporeally inscribed (Grosz 1994, 146–47).

In her concept of action, Arendt asserts a notion of plurality that resonates with Sheets-Johnstone in that it is *men* (or people, as I would say it), not *Man*, who inhabit the earth. She also links plurality and action to natality. Natality, for Arendt, is defined by the physical act of birth but inclusive of the human capacity to begin anew. Political freedom is contingent on our existence as natal beings, for without it we lack the capacity to initiate the new. As Arendt (1958, 9) puts it, "Action has the closest connection with the human condition of natality; the new beginning inherent in birth can make itself felt in the world only because the newcomer possesses the capacity of beginning something anew, that is, of acting. In this sense of initiative, an element of action, and therefore of natality, is inherent in all human activities. Moreover, since action is the political activity par excellence, natality, and not mortality, may be the central category of political, as distinguished from metaphysical, thought."

In this context, natality includes the endless possibilities that accompany the insertion of word and deed into the world (ibid., 176). Such an insertion emerges not out of necessity, but is often "stimulated by the presence of others" (ibid., 177). Arendt's contribution marks a great distance from the mutually constitutive relationship between power and resistance or the abstract "swarm of points of resistance" that haunt Foucault's work on social change. Coming into the world anew is followed by a "second birth" that is "word and deed." The bringing of our words and deeds into the world is significant because they are both new and distinct. Yet, we share a commonality in that all of us are distinct. The emancipatory promise of Arendt's theory of action is rooted not only in the potential for some messiah, but in the messianic potential for transformation that we already embody. Arendt highlights the interrelatedness of speech and action, noting that we cannot even dismiss the potency of one word. Arendt's accounts of natality and action are not diametrically opposed to Foucault's notion of resistance, but complementary in that her concepts help explain the ways in which the mechanisms of resistance have a possibility of working.

Yet, little has been said about the willing or actualization of word and deed. Whereas natality signifies the possibility of resistance, the power to resist is located in plurality—in spaces where people can act in concert with and distinction from one another. Such "spaces of appearance" can only emerge where people are present and always disappear upon their dispersal (ibid., 199–207). The political power to resist is distinctly relational and intersubjective. It is not that all of Darlene Johnson's problems (or anyone else's) would be solved if we had a town square where we could talk it over, but that such spaces would serve as avenues for difference and commonality. As Seyla Benhabib put it, "once in action, one can make things happen" (Benhabib 1990, 194). Debate and conversation on the harm and damage caused by new reproductive technologies are not "merely words" but possibilities for new articulations and understandings of the limits of contemporary politics. Spaces for speech and action can also provide a sense of *durability* to resistance by constructing what Arendt terms "a web of human relationships" (Arendt 1958, 183). Efforts to create feminist spaces of appearance (e.g., women's resistance to Norplant trials in Brazil) can and do provide powerful resistance with an enduring character. Such efforts to construct vibrant public spaces are a crucial source for new beginnings.

Natality, the possibility of a new beginning, is a threat to anyone invested in previous beginnings. These "previous beginnings" help constitute the hegemonic suture that holds structures of domination in place (Laclau and Mouffe 1985, 47). Because of the dependence of the technology on its provider, Norplant often functions as a disciplinary apparatus, rendering the unpredictable calculable. Norplant can (and does) serve to discipline women in developing nations, minorities and the poor in the United States, and others ("deviants") who do not behave properly. Whenever and wherever the state—or any external party—eliminates or regulates a woman's power to reproduce, a very significant part of the spontaneity inherent in natality (i.e., its necessary condition) is occluded.

Whereas Arendt's "prescriptions" are valuable, they are only valuable in this context when balanced with a feminist perspective that rejects the essentialist components of her theory. For Arendt, the social realm had no place in the political because it was related to the "realm of necessity" rather than the realm of freedom. Contrary to Arendt, I assert that *the realm of necessity* (what Arendt terms *the social*) *must be brought out into the spaces of appearance above all else.* This against-the-grain reading of Arendt may provide a reworking of political theory and praxis that does not relegate the realm of necessity to a "secondary" status, something she was not willing to do.

Conversely, although Foucault's contributions on power and discipline may help to explain the disciplinary construction of the social relations of reproduction, his treatment of resistance is incomplete. We are provided with a myriad of ways to understand how the body is acted upon and disciplined. But how can women and men under these conditions initiate responses and new beginnings? A turn toward Arendt is also problematic. Arendt's framework remains troublesome because she was very wary of bringing "private" household matters (including relations of reproduction) into the political realm. In much of her writing, this "realm of necessity" must be left outside the political in order for words and deeds to flourish in a free public realm. This societal appropriation of the realm of necessity (what she terms "the social") has produced a conformist public sphere devoid of distinction and difference. Put differently, for Arendt, the only public matters that are valued in modern society are those "connected with sheer survival" (ibid., 46). Such a position can only be spoken from a social location of privilege (Norton 1995). I present the rise of the realm of necessity as a required precondition for the emergence of any inclusive space of appearance where equality and distinction are respected. Arguably, "private" issues (e.g., domestic violence, homelessness) are socially constructed as matters that are not for public discussion as a result of hierarchical political relations. An egalitarian politics of distinction and difference can only emerge where such "private" matters are put squarely in the public arena.

In conjunction with her concept of natality, Arendt's analysis of the discovery of the Archimedean point also provides a viable supplement to feminist accounts of the patriarchal components of new reproductive technologies. Galileo contributed to the devaluation of *the human body itself.* Through his telescope, Galileo provided empirical proof of the unreliability of human sense perception. This technology has contributed greatly to

> the modern astrophysical worldview, which began with Galileo, and its challenge to the adequacy of the senses to reveal reality, have left us a universe of whose qualities we know no more than the way they affect our measuring instruments, and in the words of Eddington—"the former have as much resemblance to the latter as a telephone number has to a subscriber." Instead of objective qualities, in other words, we find instruments, and instead of nature or the universe—in the words of Heisenberg—man encounters only himself. (Arendt 1958, 261)

For Arendt, when we build nuclear reactors or "attempt to initiate in a test tube the processes of cosmic evolution," we "handle nature from a point in the universe outside the earth" (ibid., 262). Arendt links these processes to Descartes, whose philosophy eventually has done great violence to plurality and natality. The remoteness of the scientific and medical gaze can do violence to the realm of plurality by disconnecting what lies between us (Arendt's inter-est) and reassembling it from a universalizing standpoint (ibid., 182). From the Archimedean point of objectivity, new truths produced between people are statistically insignificant conversations and opinions. It is within such a perspective that living and breathing people become populations and the merits of contraception are measured less often by user satisfaction or health than by "effectivity." The conclusion that our own apparatuses of sense perception are "subjective" and secondary to the true and neutral Truth is often an act of violence against ourselves—who we are as embodied beings.

In this realm there is a muting of the spontaneity and unpredictability inherent in natality. Arendt closes *The Human Condition* with a gloom that matches the unbridled optimism of Francis Fukuyama's reflections on the end of History:

> The last stage of the laboring society, society of jobholders, demands of its members a sheer automatic functioning, as though individual life had actually been submerged in the over-all life process of the species and the only active decision still required of the individual were to let go, so to speak, to abandon his individuality, the still individually sensed pain and trouble of living, and acquiesce in a dazed, "tranquilized," functional type of behavior. The trouble with modern theories of behaviorism is not that they are wrong but that they could become true. (Ibid., 332)

Philip W. Jenks

≈ 30 ≈

Thus, for Arendt, the hyperrationalization of behaviorism is not just an "idea," but a powerful ideology that severely limits human potential. Those who can act in freedom do not channel their creative actions into revelation through the plural web of human relations because they view humans from a perspective outside the earth itself. Such a perspective overlooks two crucial contingencies of human existence: that we are birth- and earthbound creatures. As natal newcomers on the earth, a vibrant potentiality resides between us through our words and deeds.

"Truths" that are produced and agreed on between people in freedom are crucial in Arendt's vision of an egalitarian politics. The attempt to view the political and social realms "objectively" inhibits our capacities to create and re-create communities that are durable (through pact and promise), yet also capable of change (through the spontaneity of natality). By excluding natality, we run the risk of never *creating and holding* "self-evident" truths, but rather being *"held by them"* (Honig 1993, 107). Arendt "perpetually reminds us that we are not nature's creators" (Curtis 1995, 173). We are earthbound creatures and our more dramatic attempts to act into nature (e.g., the atom bomb, clear-cutting, new reproductive technologies, the Human Genome Project) are grounded in a perspective that views "nature" from a standpoint outside the earth. As people who are not nature's creators, but with possession of a great capacity to create, humankind acts into nature with a limited sense of the unpredictability of consequence. To what extent have Arendt's dire predictions about (post)modern human relations been realized? I close with a consideration of postmodern identity and the potential for democratic resistance.

Denying the Body, Erasing the Body Politic: Postmodern Antidemocratic Trends and the Liberal Suppression of Anecdotal Experience

How exactly have we managed to detach ourselves from the painful, bodily facticity of new reproductive technologies? It is by way of this question that I seek to reflect on how the corporeal self is mediated within the context of global capitalism, for it is through this context that some troubling developments in postmodern identity are realized. A general process of desensitization not only is evident in relation to new reproductive technologies, but also lies at the heart of how knowledge and identity are mediated in postmodern societies. Postmodern identities emerge out of a particular aspect of post-Enlightenment positivism, which in its manic attempt to annunciate progress pushes all evidence to the contrary to, or beyond, the margins of awareness. In this hegemonic cultural logic, experiences of those who are stigmatized as different or deviant are commonly explained either as "the price of progress" or simply denied. In the United States, both denial and minimization of corporeal experience are achieved in a culture that prizes a particular form of empiricism—one that categorizes persons at the margins as "statistically insignificant."

This phenomenon forms the foundation for what may be termed, by way of Thomas Dumm's contributions, "disciplinary liberalism" (Dumm 1987; see Foucault 1979). This form of liberalism flourishes wherever face-to-face human interaction is lacking for the simple fact that the lived experiences of others are treated with a level of high abstraction: "To the Enlightenment, that which does not reduce to numbers, and ultimately to the one, becomes illusion; modern positivism writes it off as literature" (Adorno and Horkheimer 1990, 70). Although the logic of disciplinary liberalism depoliticizes the lived experiences of subordinate groups, it is precisely these experiences that disciplinary liberalism defines itself against. Just as the Enlightenment is defined by the unenlightened, so disciplinary liberalism depends heavily on the "undisciplined" for its corrective progress. The utilitarian, positivist discourse of reforming the unruly "welfare mother," for example, is buttressed not only by the rhetoric of scientific, liberal political progress, but also by an overarching appeal to the rhetoric of individual, autonomous choice.

In these ways, problematic experiences (such as the death, pain, and suffering of many women) are overlooked in favor of an overarching telos (such as the management of the population). It is this process of negation and affirmation that both produces a subject and renders her own bodily experiences insignificant. This relation of the self to the body is crucial because it denies the self full access to the public sphere. Hence, the assumption of the validity of each person's corporeal experiences—the simple assertion that one's lived existence is real—is a necessary condition for egalitarian social relations.

In the case of Norplant (or many other reproductive technologies such as the Dalkon Shield, other IUDs, the Pill), the ideal progress of the disciplinary state overshadows the actual experiences of women who have used the device. Some legislators have proposed at the state level to make Norplant mandatory for welfare recipients while putting no provisions for Norplant removal in their bills. Such a move hails the general telos of more disciplined individuals and a "better" society while ignoring the fact that leaving Norplant in longer than five years can cause ectopic pregnancy, which can be deadly. Such thinking excludes the fact that

47 percent of women with Norplant experience steady menstruation, while labeling "spotting" as an inconvenient "side effect."

I have dealt primarily with what Foucault terms the "anatomo-politics of the human body." This "pole" is "centered on the body as a machine: its disciplining, the optimization of its capabilities, the extortion of its forces" (Foucault 1990, 139). Yet, in the case of new reproductive technologies, there is an equivalent tendency toward the second pole that Foucault describes: "The second, formed somewhat later, focused on the species body, the body imbued with the mechanics of life and serving as the basis of the biological processes: propagation, births and mortality . . . with all the conditions that can cause these to vary. Their supervision was effected through an entire series of interventions and *regulatory controls: a biopolitics of the population*" (ibid.). Norplant and many new reproductive technologies, in marking the transformation of birth control into population control, are technologies of the species body. The history of birth control is integrally connected to women's health movements, which emphasize each woman's autonomy through the assertion of embodied subjectivities. Population control emphasizes the *species character* of women (and men), putting a premium on controlling life forces at any cost, including the denial of women's experience, suffering, and agency.

This Archimedean shift toward the species character of the human world has enormous ramifications in the construction of our bodies. This transformation is not merely an abstraction, but a development that can have particularly dire consequences—from the disappearance of female babies in China to eugenic policies in Indonesia to the international abuse of Norplant and Depo-Provera (Hartmann 1995, 93–221). In its most extreme form, the emergence of biopolitics of the population (the bomb, concentration camps) puts human existence at the center of the political realm: "For millennia, man remained what he was for Aristotle: a living animal with the additional capacity for a political existence; modern man is an animal whose politics places his existence as a living being in question" (Foucault 1990, 143). In this perspective, perhaps it is not the accumulation of capital that drives "global capitalism," but the drive to maintain hegemony over the life process itself. Thus, it is not surprising that a significant strand of postmodern thought is profoundly skeptical about the emancipatory potential of critical thought. I turn now to the dangers posed by this trend in postmodern thought and conclude with a consideration of the value of Arendt's work to the ontological foundations of embodied democratic resistance.

While the tendencies of postmodern culture are toward fragmentation and the dissolution of metanarratives, the contours of postmodern culture remain sharply delineated by consumer capitalism. In this context, shifting identities and multiplicities not only are possible sites of resistance but easily revert to a comfortable affirmation of the autonomous consumer. The shift toward denaturalization in many intellectual communities risks losing any grounding in material, corporeal existence. If Foucault is correct in asserting the rise of biopolitics of populations, then oppositional thought that eschews corporeality cannot fully address the impact of this transformation. As Kathleen Jones writes:

> Denaturalization easily slips into denial; the refusal to be given, or even to give one's self, a "name" shades over into fantasies of autogenesis (Vergès 1991). The fantasies with which feminist post-structuralists in the United States have become mesmerized are imaginative narratives that promise the possibility of escaping the constraints and responsibilities of a specific location in time and place by avoiding being caught in a specific corporeality: if I can dress my body up in the costumes of the unexpected, then I can refuse to have a shape limited by the meaning that my body is supposed to have. (Jones 1993, 9)

Jones notes later that "power refuses to disappear with the wave of the deconstructionist's magical wand" (ibid., 10). Physical horror exists. The socially constructed components of that horror do not take away from its corporeal existence. The refusal to have a shape limited by bodily constraints is not disconnected from the eagerness to dissociate oneself from basic economic conditions through excessive consumption. This capacity to make the body disappear and to deny corporeality works hand in glove with a similar trend toward abstraction and denial of corporeal situatedness in positivism. This merely means that poststructural, postmodernist, and deconstructivist thought and action are not necessarily oppositional. Moreover, given the cultural, economic, and political contexts from which postmodern identities emerge, oppositional thought is truly the exception. Just as Adorno reflected on the limitations imposed on oppositional intellectuals by instrumentalism, postmodern resistance faces similar constraints vis-à-vis positivism: "When oppositional intellectuals endeavor, within the confines of these influences, to imagine a new content for society, they are paralyzed by the form of their own consciousness, which is modeled in advance to suit the needs of this society. While thought has forgotten how to think itself, it has at the same time become its own watchdog" (Adorno 1997, 197). But, given these circumstances, do we stop at this juncture and assume that embodied oppositional actions are impossible? What are the possibilities of democratic action? Moreover, how are these possibilities hindered by our location in postmodern culture? I shall answer the last of these questions first, focusing on two more trends in postmodern identity formation.

In the first case, it is critical to address a particular tendency in postmodern academic culture toward epistemic relativism. In this strand of postmodernism—whether it is Jean Baudrillard's collapse of material reality into simulacra or some "positivist" claims in Foucault's archaeological accounts—in both cases the corporeal self often appears as an afterthought, if at all. This is not to assert that the rise of postmodern thought is resulting in a decline in embodied subjectivities. Rather, I argue that postmodernism is a continuation of, rather than a radical departure from, the long-standing tradition within Western thought running from Plato through Descartes to the present that relegates the body to a secondary status. This refusal carries with it the likelihood of an uncritical attitude to the material grounding of the postmodern self within the world political economic system, or within the community for that matter (Norris 1992).

Thus, positivists and some postmodernists alike risk writing off the lived experiences of marginalized groups as "literature." Here, postmodern critiques of the subject ironically reconfigure existing power relations. To whatever extent the body is bifurcated from "the mind" or from "images," the lived experiences of that body are not fully recognized. Nor is this purely a matter of understanding human suffering. Conversely, this particular tendency in postmodern thought may have difficulty recognizing corporeal potentiality. Beginning anew is not only a discursive matter. Meaning may be polysemic and infinitized, but the same cannot be said of the capacities and limits of our bodily and material potential. We are birth- and earthbound creatures with demonstrable bodily distinctions *and* similarities. To some extent, postmodern theorists risk forgetting our adhesion to the world and to one another.

That being said, one might argue that this criticism is unfair. Neither Foucault nor Baudrillard is making strong claims to a counterhegemonic system of thought. However, I concern myself here with the consequences or effects of their arguments. Perhaps a more convincing argument can be put forth from a postmodern thinker who attempts to construct an oppositional political "ontology." Poststructuralist feminism, for example, works to examine and challenge the "constructedness" of gender and identity. Judith Butler's contributions to this discourse include an attempt to establish that both gender and sex are constructed categories. Sex is a "regulatory fiction" for the operation/performance of gender. "Gender is the repeated stylization of the body, a set of repeated acts within a highly rigid regulatory frame that congeal over time to produce the appearance of substance, of a natural sort of being. A political genealogy of gender ontologies, if it is successful, will deconstruct the substantive appearance of gender into its constitutive acts and account for those acts within the *compulsory frames set by the various forces that police the social appearance of gender"* (Butler 1990, 33). Butler's notion of gender as the stylized repetition of the body is deeply indebted to Foucault's works on sexuality but, like Foucault's formulation, it describes processes by which the body is inscribed by the social, and overlooks the ways that the social is enabled and shaped by the corporal.

The finest analysis of many of these poststructural quandaries is Susan Bordo's *Unbearable Weight,* particularly her chapter titled "Feminism, Postmodernism, and Gender Skepticism." Like Foucault and Arendt, Bordo is difficult to neatly categorize. She not only turns toward multiplicity and fragmentation, but also returns to the contributions of earlier feminist theories with new insights drawn from her study of Foucault. Bordo asserts that there are four currents contributing to "gender-skepticism": (1) a concern that to speak of women potentially obliterates race, class, ethnic, and other differences; (2) a deconstruction of the Archimedean point of view where meaning and interpretation are entirely indeterminate and unauthoritative; (3) as women have gained access to male-dominated institutions, they have been "under the gun" to *not* be feminine, to *not* be wholly other; (4) all of these currents are part of a postmodern complicity with liberal neutrality. The poststructural critique of the category of "woman" as wholly essentialist (and therefore needing to be abandoned) is manifested in rejections of "classic" feminist accounts of women's distinctive differences of the 1960s and 1970s. Such rejections, though not without merit, ignore the strategic value of such categories (Bordo 1993, 242). The "generalist" critique of women's differences carries pragmatic value in a wide variety of institutional settings from the Senate to the classroom, settings where men and masculinist ideologies often do hold great influence. Put differently, although contemporary poststructural projections on gender construction are of great value, the vast majority of Western political and social institutions are barely beginning to adopt the contributions of feminists from the 1960s, 1970s, and 1980s.

Bordo notes that liberation movements questioned the neutrality of Reason, Truth, and Tradition by asking *whose Reason* and *whose Truth* were represented as neutral. Indeed, feminists of the 1970s introduced the idea that a neutral "view from nowhere" (or Archimedean point) "may itself be a male construction on the possibilities for knowledge" (ibid., 220). This was followed by internal critiques within feminism where various racial and ethnic exclusions were exposed. Bordo's most significant contribution is her critique of the rhetoric of certainty behind Butler, Nancy Fraser, Donna Haraway, and others in that their "deconstruction" of the Archimedean point produces a new point of certainty, which she terms "the dream from everywhere."

A consideration of Bordo's argument here is crucial not only for this essay but for a more general understanding of the dangers of state and corporate involvement with human reproduction. Bordo cites Foucault's observation that "everything is dangerous," even the dream of diversity (ibid., 223). Both Foucault and Bordo successfully navigate their way through the dangers of poststructuralism by anchoring their pursuits in corporeal and material reality. And, it seems to me, both are responding in their own ways to what Arendt called "the frailty of human affairs." Whereas Arendt is writing on the dangers of the "dream of nowhere," Bordo feels compelled in the era of postmodern identity politics to attend to the ensuing "dream of everywhere." What is significant is that both thinkers critique the certainty and positivity with which this dream is greeted.

The dream of positivism fails to include the perspectives of women and men on the margins of society. It is a dream of an episteme located in the nowhere of a space outside the earth itself, the dream of a perspective that is not a perspective. Because all knowledge is perspectival, positivist claims to neutrality end up reifying a certain set of perspectives as yielding the Real and the True (Brown 1989, 1998). But the dream of "everywhere" also carries dangers because knowledge is *still perspectival*. Even when this is acknowledged through counterhegemonic postmodern narratives of inclusivity, the postmodernist self does not thereby become more inclusive or less perspectival or less prejudiced. Whether it is the certainty that objective truth is ultimately ascertainable or the certainty that nothing is ultimately true, certainty itself can be intellectually and politically disastrous. It deadlocks the vibrant web of human relations, turning the natal interchange of word and deed into a narrative with a certain pre-given ending. By knowing more than it does not know, the politics of certainty puts the potentiality of new beginnings between political actors in jeopardy.

A synthesis of Arendt and Foucault allows for a viable critique of the production of subjectivities, while providing a richer reflection on the sources and possibilities of resistance. When read in tandem with Sheets-Johnstone's and Bordo's writings on the body and corporeality, a theory of intersubjective corporeal egalitarian action also is introduced. Narrated embodied experiences of women and men are the stuff of lives that are human, and they take on a particular importance in a cultural framework that frequently writes off those experiences as statistically insignificant or merely anecdotal. The delineation of a public space for the sharing and validation of such discourse might enable us to disclose rather than imprison difference. Such disclosures can flourish within an understanding that confronts the masculinist, classist, and racist components of any space of appearance. It is this web of relationships that may, if only for a brief time, enable women and men to take embodied action that is politically meaningful. I strongly believe that we must create spaces that enable stories and accounts that have been elided by the patriarchal structures of society and knowledge in order to break the power of denial that inhabits and produces who we are and what we can do. Such spaces may be physical or nonphysical, although the viability of face-to-face interaction is underrated in contemporary political culture. In so doing, I arrive at no grand solution, but what I hope is a contribution toward egalitarian democratic action in a world political economy that often seems to negate it.

References

Adorno, Theodor. 1997. *Minima Moralia: Reflections from Damaged Life.* London: Verso.

Adorno, Theodor, and Max Horkheimer. 1990. *Dialectic of Enlightenment.* Trans. John Cumming. New York: Continuum.

Alexander, Amy. 1991. "Judge's Old Cases Get Scrutiny." *Fresno Bee,* January 10.

Allen, Amy. 1998. "Power Trouble: Performativity as Critical Theory." *Constellations: An International Journal of Critical and Democratic Theory* 5.4 (December): 456–71.

Appellant's Opening Brief. 1991. *The People of the State of California v. Darlene Johnson.* No. 29390. State of California. April 24.

Arendt, Hannah. 1994. "Social Science Techniques and the Study of Concentration Camps." In *Arendt: Essays in Understanding, 1930–1954,* ed. Jerome Kohn. New York: Harcourt, Brace and Company. 232–47.

———. 1958. *The Human Condition.* Chicago: University of Chicago Press.

———. 1965. *On Revolution.* New York: Viking Press.

———. 1972. *Crises of the Republic.* New York: Harcourt, Brace and Company.

———. 1993. *Between Past and Future.* New York: Penguin Books.

Benhabib, Seyla. 1990. "Hannah Arendt and the Redemptive Power of Narrative." *Social Research* 57.1 (spring).

Bordo, Susan. 1993. *Unbearable Weight: Feminism, Western Culture and the Body.* Berkeley: University of California Press.

Brown, Richard Harvey. 1989. *A Poetic for Sociology: Toward a Logic of Discovery for the Human Sciences.* Chicago: University of Chicago Press.

———. 1998. *Toward a Democratic Science: Scientific Narration and Civic Communication.* New Haven: Yale University Press.

Butler, Judith. 1990. *Gender Trouble: Feminism and the Subversion of Identity*. New York: Routledge.

Corea, Gena. 1985. *The Mother Machine: Reproductive Technologies from Artificial Insemination to Artificial Wombs*. New York: Harper and Row.

———, ed. 1987. *Man-Made Women: How New Reproductive Technologies Affect Women*. Bloomington: Indiana University Press.

Corrêa, Sonia, in collaboration with Rebecca Reichmann. 1994. *Population and Reproductive Rights: Feminist Perspectives from the South*. London: Zed Books.

Curtis, Kimberley F. 1995. "Hannah Arendt, Feminist Theorizing, and the Debate over New Reproductive Technologies." *Polity* 28.2 (winter).

Derrida, Jacques. 1994. *Specters of Marx: The State of the Debt, the Work of Mourning and the New International*. Trans Peggy Kamuf. New York: Routledge.

Dryzek, John. 1994. *Discursive Democracy: Politics, Policy, and Political Science*. Cambridge: Cambridge University Press.

Dumm, Thomas. L. 1987. *Democracy and Punishment: Disciplinary Origins of the United States*. Madison: University of Wisconsin Press.

———. 1996. *Michel Foucault and the Politics of Freedom*. Thousand Oaks, Calif.: Sage Publications.

Fish, Stanley. 1992. *Doing What Comes Naturally: Change, Rhetoric, and the Practice of Theory in Literary and Legal Studies*. Durham, N.C.: Duke University Press.

Foucault, Michel. 1972. *The Archaeology of Knowledge (and The Discourse on Language)*. Trans. A. M. Sheridan Smith. New York: Pantheon Books.

———. 1977. *Discipline and Punish: The Birth of the Prison*. Trans. Alan Sheridan. New York: Vintage Books.

———. 1980. *Power/Knowledge*. Trans. Colin Gordon, Leo Marshall, John Mepham, and Kate Soper. New York: Pantheon Books.

———. 1990. *The History of Sexuality*, vol. 1, *An Introduction*. Trans. Robert Hurley. New York: Vintage Books.

———. 1994. *The Birth of the Clinic: An Archaeology of Medical Perception*. Trans. A. M. Sheridan Smith. New York: Vintage Books.

Gilliom, John. 2001. *Overseers of the Poor: Surveillance, Resistance, and the Limits of Privacy*. Chicago: University of Chicago Press.

Gramsci, Antonio. 1971. *Selections from the Prison Notebooks*. Trans. Quintin Hoare and Geoffrey Nowell Smith. New York: International Publishers.

Grosz, Elizabeth. 1994. *Volatile Bodies: Toward a Corporeal Feminism*. Bloomington: Indiana University Press.

Hansen, K. V., and I. J. Philipson, eds. 1990. *Women, Class, and the Feminist Imagination: A Socialist-Feminist Reader*. Philadelphia: Temple University Press.

Haraway, Donna. 1990. "A Manifesto for Cyborgs: Science, Technology, and Socialist Feminism in the Last Quarter." In *Women, Class, and the Feminist Imagination: A Socialist-Feminist Reader*, ed. K.V. Hansen and I. J. Philipson. Philadelphia: Temple University Press. 580–617.

Hardon, Anita. 1994. "Norplant: Conflicting Views on Its Safety and Acceptability." In *Issues in Reproductive Technology*, ed. Helen Bequaert Holmes. New York: New York University Press. 11–30.

"Hardware, Software, Humanware." 1984. *Independent School* 43 (May): 39–42.

Hartmann, Betsy. 1995. *Reproductive Rights and Wrongs: The Global Politics of Population Control*. Boston: South End Press.

Holmes, Helen Bequaert, ed. 1994. *Issues in Reproductive Technology*. New York: New York University Press.

Honig, Bonnie. 1993. *Political Theory and the Displacement of Politics*. Ithaca, N.Y.: Cornell University Press.

————, ed. 1995. *Feminist Interpretations of Hannah Arendt*. University Park: Pennsylvania State University Press.

Jenks, Philip. 2000. "Foucault, Arendt, and the Norplant Condition in Liberal America: New Reproductive Technologies, Public Bodies, and Disciplinary Liberalism." Dissertation, University of Kentucky.

Jones, Kathleen B. 1993. *Compassionate Authority: Democracy and the Representation of Women*. New York: Routledge.

Kaeser, Lisa. 1994. "Public Funding and Policies for Provision of the Contraceptive Implant, Fiscal Year 1992." *Family Planning Perspectives* 265.1 (January/February). Washington, D.C.: Alan Guttmacher Institute.

Kansas State House of Representatives. 1991. *State House Bill No. 2089*. Representative Patrick.

Kenney, Martin, and Richard Florida. 1998. "Beyond Mass Production: Production and the Labor Process in Japan." *Politics and Society* 16 (March): 121–58.

Kimmelman, Donald. 1990. "Poverty and Norplant: Can Contraception Reduce the Underclass?" *Philadelphia Inquirer*, December 12, 4-C.

Laclau, Ernesto, and Chantal Mouffe. 1985. *Hegemony and Socialist Strategy: Towards a Radical Democratic Politics*. London: Verso.

Merleau-Ponty, Maurice. 1968. *The Visible and the Invisible*. Trans. Alphonso Lingis. Evanston, Ill.: Northwestern University Press.

National Women's Health Network. 1991. "Population Council Press Release." Washington, D.C.

Norris, Christopher. 1992. *Uncritical Theory: Postmodernism, the Intellectuals and the Gulf War*. London: Lawrence and Wishart.

Norton, Anne. 1995. "Heart of Darkness: Africa and African Americans in the Writings of Hannah Arendt." In *Feminist Interpretations of Hannah Arendt*, ed. Bonnie Honig. University Park: Pennsylvania State University Press. 247–62.

O'Brien, Mary. 1981. *The Politics of Reproduction*. Boston: Routledge and Kegan Paul.

Reid, Herbert G., and Betsy Taylor. 1999. "Merleau-Ponty's Philosophy and the Practical Tasks of Ecological Citizenship." Presented at Goucher College Conference, "Merleau-Ponty and the Culturing of the Body," November.

Ribbens, J., and Rosalind Edwards, eds. 1998. *Feminist Dilemmas in Qualitative Research: Public Knowledge and Private Lives*. London: Sage Publications.

Roberts, Dorothy. 1997. *Killing the Black Body: Race, Reproduction and the Meaning of Liberty*. New York: Pantheon Books.

Rowland, Robyn. 1992. *Living Laboratories: Women and Reproductive Technologies*. Bloomington: Indiana University Press.

Sawicki, Jana. 1991. *Disciplining Foucault: Feminism, Power and the Body*. New York: Routledge.

Schatzki, Theodore, and Wolfgang Natter. 1996. *The Social and Political Body*. New York: Guilford Press.

Schuster, Heather. 1999. "Reproduction and the State: Between Bodily Performance and Legal Performativity." *Angelaki: Journal of the Theoretical Humanities* 4 (May): 189–206.

Scott, James C. 1990. *Domination and the Arts of Resistance: Hidden Transcripts.* New Haven: Yale University Press.

Sheets-Johnstone, Maxine. 1994. *The Roots of Power: Animate Form and Gendered Bodies.* Chicago: Open Court.

Smith, Lynn, and Nina J. Easton. 1993. "The Dilemma of Desire." *Los Angeles Times Magazine,* September 26, 24–42.

UBINIG. 1988. "Norplant: 'The Five Year Needle,' an Investigation of the Bangladesh Trial." *Radical Journal of Health* (March).

Womack, James, Daniel Jones, and Daniel Roos. 1990. *The Machine That Changed the World.* New York: Rawson Associates.

Women's Global Network for Reproductive Rights (WGNRR). 1988. "Press Release." Amsterdam.

Yanarella, Ernest J., and Herbert G. Reid. 1996. "From 'Trained Gorilla' to 'Humanware': Repoliticizing the Body-Machine Complex between Fordism and Post-Fordism." In *The Social and Political Body,* ed. Theodore Schatzki and Wolfgang Natter. New York: Guilford Press. 181–219.

3

Genocide or Assimilation:

Discourses of Women's Bodies,

Health, and Nation in Guatemala

This essay explores relationships between health, women, and the nation-state that emerge from a national discourse that gravitates around the education and appropriation of the bodies of Mayan women.[1] My analysis draws on data that I collected between 1989 and 1991 in Guatemala City, when the Guatemalan state was still operating under a military regime that conducted a politics of genocide against Indian people in spite of the elected civilian government (1986–90). This is the background of my discussion of the role of health discourse in the formation of a "new" consciousness among women, and of efforts to create a body politic for the Mayas. But it also is framed within the politics of ethnicity and modernization during President Vinicio Cerezo's civilian government. I focus on the relation between health development programs sponsored by government agencies and the constitution of Mayas as modern citizens. Specifically, I analyze ways in which the nationalist ideology of ladinos, or the mixed-blood Guatemalans, has been able to maintain an image of the Mayas as irreducibly Others.

The emergence of a medical discourse focused on women, and on Mayan women in particular, raises the following questions: Why has the concern for women's health only recently been addressed by governmental and nongovernmental development agencies? Why, after destroying indigenous organizations by slaughtering their male leaders, was the government promoting local associations charged with raising women's consciousness about their roles as mothers and spouses? Why, after centuries of impoverishment and exploitation, has there recently emerged a humanitarian concern for the indigenous population, which is centered on issues of health and sanitation? Further, how does the newly discovered dignity of Mayan women fit a nationalist agenda? Can health be considered an institution of the nation-state that hinges on the manipulation of women's bodies and on their consciousness for constituting a new and fit citizen?

The Dis-eased Body

Since the Conquest, Mayan people have been present and represented as a potential subversive force for the state. The state's ideology toward the Indians underlies the massacres of the 1980s and the superimposition of the notion of the Indians as ignorant, uncivilized, and "cannibals."[2] The maintenance of Indians at the subsistence level also has been part of the politics of the Guatemalan nation-state, insofar as extreme poverty both reinforces and is justified by their image as a people whose lives are formed around only the most basic animal instincts. This applies in particular to Indian women in the context of national discourse of health and sexuality. In Guatemala, Indian women are often portrayed by ladinos as promiscuous and overtly sexual. The Mayan people are characterized by the dominant ladino culture as primitives, not being able to exercise self-control, responding only to basic needs such as their food supply—in a word, deviants who need to be controlled. As deviant, the Mayan body represents a form of social pollution that needs to be contained. Mary Douglas (1966, 7) has discussed the body as a natural symbol of society, and thus an indicator of a society's functioning. Scheper-Hughes and Lock also affirm that "The body in health offers a model of organic wholeness; the body in sickness offers a model of social disharmony, conflict, and disintegration" (1987, 7). Given such an image of the body, and particularly of Mayan women's bodies, state control is deployed not only openly by violent repression, but also implicitly by health and medical practices and development programs. The goal of control, when not to exterminate, is to normalize the individual in order to create obedient citizens.

The concept of the individual body reflecting the social body, and more specifically the right functioning of society, is clearly present in Guatemala and may provide one explanation for various campaigns of violence, the victims of which have been overwhelmingly Mayan people.[3]

Violence justifies itself by reducing the body of the victim to a dirty, rotten, and hence polluting and potentially subversive space that needs to be neutralized. From the interviews of individuals who survived the violence, it can be inferred that survivors seem to undergo "healing" techniques of control and discipline that are administered by health professionals who are direct or indirect agents of the state. The "healing" discourse that generates and authorizes such techniques is presented to women as a form of emancipation that can be achieved through their subjection to medical practices informed by the values of the dominant culture that aim at controlling the sexuality of Mayan women.

The creation of widows during the dictatorships of General Romeo Lucas García (1978–82) and General Efraín Ríos Montt (1982–83) attests to the "cannibalization" of women's bodies through the actual killings and mutilation of their bodies, or the murder of their men and relatives, and the dispossession of their lands and homes—either by destruction or by forced migration. All this sets up the premises for a new constitution and conception of the body of Mayan women. The acquisition of consciousness becomes one of the main discourses that link the process of modernization to the socially reconstructed female body. At first, the infliction of pain radically centers individuals to their own bodies. One effect of the embodiment of pain is silence, which is also the effect that the torturer or murderer wants to achieve (cf. Scarry 1985). When the energy from this implosion gets released under the form of rage, resentment, and even fear, it must be controlled and channeled. This is sometimes achieved by ladino medical discourses that aim to neutralize the threat of revolution, and by different indigenous discourses that aim to propagate the potential for revolutionary changes. In other words, the body becomes a battleground, only now there is a historical shift in the struggle that is waged. The first struggle corresponds to war in the literal sense. The second corresponds to "peace," and entails the effort to reconstitute the subject within a newly emerging and highly contested civil society. The military repression continues, not as war, but now as routine development and law enforcement. The struggle over the body becomes a question of the internalization of the social values derived from, or the hegemonic notions of the "citizen" of, a repressive state, or from the counterhegemonic, oppositional values of ethnicity and gender.

The Health of the Nation

The present discussion is based on participant observation in family planning programs directed at Mayan women. The focus is on the program and activities of ASECSA (Health Association of Community Services), a private health organization, and on interviews with Mayan women and doctors. Although ASECSA is only one program that promotes health in Mayan communities, its rationale is common to that of other organizations that propogate methods for the control of fertility and for the improvement of hygiene within the family. The underlying rhetoric of health programs—governmental and nongovernmental—centers on the education of Mayan women and their perceived ignorance and inadequacy to reproduce "healthy" behavior within their families. The objectified body is both that of Mayan women and of Mayan people as a whole. I argue that prevalent discourses make these bodies the objects of normalizing practices and the targets of techniques of control whose goal is to shape Mayan women into docile bodies that fit into the ideology of the repressive nation-state.

Existing family planning programs in Guatemala echo the philosophy and practice of eugenics, especially in their sterilization of Mayan women. According to article 40 of the Declaration on Social Progress and Development, family planning needs to be responsible, free, and voluntary, that is, emanating from the rights and choices of the people. It has been reported that the number of women who have freely opted for sterilization is much less than the overall number of sterilized women (Citgua 1989, 30). Morever, many women who ostensibly agree to be sterilized do not understand that this practice is irreversible.[4] This practice of sometimes involuntary sterilization is carried out on women who live in extremely poor conditions and do not have access to education, in part because of sexism, poverty, lack of government services, or the remote location of their homes.

National and international policies, including U.S. intervention in Guatemala's governance and its contribution to the "dirty war," also have invaded the social body of the Mayas, especially its internal structures such as the family, by encouraging violent and dehumanizing techniques of control. The massive killings perpetrated by the government have been especially directed against Indian men who were accused of insurgency against the government. This has left many widows and orphans with a disruption of family structures and traditions. Apparently, the purpose of the brutality against Indians was to generate an attitude of fear, suspicion, and distrust among the entire population so that they would withdraw support and sympathy for the guerrilla movement.[5] The Commission on Human Rights of the Organization of American States in 1986 estimated that forty thousand people had disappeared and another hundred thousand had been assassinated during the preceding fifteen years. More than 90 percent of these killings were caused by the government (Kinzer 2001).

Women were the targets of several forms of physical and psychological violence. They were forced to witness brutalization of their relatives, to betray their dead (to pay homage to them was understood by the army as an act of disobedience), and to deal with the disjuncture that occurred in their lives when one of the men in the family was "disappeared." Even more, the violence waged against women undermined their sanity, integrity, and self-identity. Widows have had to face new responsibilities, often move away from their family homes, change the focus of their work and their lives. Rape and the killing of children, even the "unborn," have been common acts of violence against indigenous women. As a consequence, these women experience shame and guilt, and are often left without family or support. Even within their own communities, these women have been treated as though they were contaminated. The surviving "children of rape," usually rejected even by their mothers, often become wandering and suffering reminders of the oppressive conditions in which these people live. Women's bodies therefore have carried an intense symbolism, because they constitute the place of communication and expression of violence at its deepest level.

Even before the Law of Population and Development was approved by President Jorge Serrano in 1992, it was condemned by the church and directors of popular organizations, such as CONAVIGUA (National Committee of Guatemalan Widows).[6] Many interpreted this law as a prelude to the legalization of abortion. The law was the result of the public condemnation of women who "conceive without any control," and of the need to improve the means of subsistence of the Guatemalan population and to fight the endemic conditions of "underdevelopment" and overpopulation of the rural, mostly Mayan population. In January 1993, the Guatemalan government accepted the donation of $7.5 million from AID (Agency for International Development) to the Association for Voluntary Surgical Contraception. However, deputies of the Guatemalan government, in a public declaration, insisted that the Law of Population and Development does not promote or assist either abortion or mass sterilization policies (Hernández and Paiz 1993, 19).

Contributions to the public debate on practices of regulation and control of fertility were published mainly in the Guatemalan periodical *Crónica*. Its participants were the state, the church, and the purported representatives of Mayan women and various Mayan groups. The state and APROFAM (Association for the Well-being of the Family) supported the law on abortion as a "humanitarian law that allows Guatemalans to improve their health specifically in the area of maternity," and the church was in favor of only natural contraceptive methods. Nonetheless, CONAVIGUA approached the debate from the point of view of Mayan traditions. As the director of CONAVIGUA, Rosalina Tuyuc, affirmed, "Mayan principles demand from women the acceptance of pregnancy as a form of dignity, as something sacred" (ibid., 20). For the Mayas, Tuyuc asserted, procreation was linked to cultural identity because it represents the "essence" or the "essential role" of Mayan women. Tuyuc's position, however, was perceived even by the Guatemalan representatives of the ladino feminist movement as being induced by a political agenda rather than by thoughtful consideration of women's health. *Crónica,* which aims at a liberal and progressive audience, was also critical of her position: "With this declaration, Tuyuc seems to be more concerned with increasing the numerical force of the ethnic groups. By maintaining this position, the indigenous leader keeps distance from any organization that defends the rights of women and attributes to her gender merely the role of reproduc-tion of the species" (ibid.).

In short, Tuyuc was considered irresponsible by many liberals and even leftists for perpetuating an essentialized role of Mayan women as procre-ators. However, in maintaining this position, and thus reaffirming the most traditional function and image of women as linked to their bodies, Tuyuc also engaged in an act of resistance by affirming the position of Mayan women as subjects and an active presence within their own culture. Thus, both sides—the ladino feminists and CONAVIGUA—claim maternity as a "natural" biological condition, but with one crucial difference. Whereas ladino feminists conceive of biology as a field of science that can be modified with the conscientious scrutiny of the expert, Mayan culture defends the sacredness of mother earth and its self-regulating rhythms. The Mayan position reflects not only a stubborn essentialism, as many middle-class women perceived it, but, more important, a cultural image of women's bodies as "natural" that provides a site of protest, or at least of understanding, to those women who have suffered from violence on their bodies; that is, the traditional image serves as a means of rationalization of their "disconcerting sensation of disjuncture," a way to turn their sense of guilt and shame into a matter of "continuing humanity" within the natu-ral role of women (Zur 1998).

Article 5 of the Guatemalan Congress specifies rules for the National Council of Population and Development. The fifth paragraph addresses the responsibilities of the Council toward women and establishes that women's participation in national institutions and activities needs to be promoted at the educational, economical, and social levels with equal rights, opportunities, and responsibilities. These rules are implemented by health organizations and address women as the bearers of tradition and continuity because the "natural" role of women is to procreate the future of the nation. In effect, the norms for the control and development of the population aim to regulate women's reproductive functions and affirm women's role as guarantors of the continuation of the Guatemalan nation. This discourse not only defines women's bodies as the repository of values embodied by the nation-state, but also seems to imply that the violence inflicted on the bodies of Mayan women is redeemed through their role in the restoration of the essence of the Guatemalan nation. Here *mestizaje* is conceived not as a fusion of races, but rather as a primordial rape, the rape of the Indians that confers power to the dominators.

Women and the State

In spite of defending the most traditional of the roles, Mayan women also acknowledge that they have traditionally been subjected to the authority of men and confined within their roles of reproduction and transmission of cultural values. As one Quiché Mayan woman put it, "We come from the Mayas. The Spaniards labeled us indigenous and the abuse started. A man demands that his woman works at home, as he is always abused so he too abuses his woman . . . A woman is like an animal, she is worth the same . . . some strange men come to our country and took away everything we had here, the land . . . Abuse is like a big chain. Men are powerful" (personal communication, Guatemala City, May 12, 1990). Mayan women's bodies have always been the objects of discourses based on regulation and control, and the violence of the last several decades that has been perpetrated against them continues this domination.

Like women's bodies, children also belong to the constituted authorities of the community, the church, and the state. Thus, the debate on abortion and population control also reveals deeper cultural meanings and relations between the body and its reproductive functions and social institutions. Mayan women in popular organizations perceive abortion and sterilization as a form of ethnocide against Mayan culture. After their men have been killed and the social role of women has been constituted as that of widowhood, the state enforces a politics of death against the Mayas through women's bodies. The term frequently used by women to talk about this violence is invasion. Invasion is a disease that, like violence, has penetrated the victim's bodies. Other terms used to express this violence are plague, deluge, and illness. These extend the idea of invasion to include such tactics as forced hospitalization of pregnant women where the unborn are surgically aborted.

For the dominant society, images of Mayan women shift between the figure of the prostitute—reinforced by the repeated assaults and rapes by the military—and of the poor, ignorant "Indita" who, like a child, needs to be indoctrinated. Modern health practices require Mayan women to abandon the traditional values of their culture in order to better fit into the national, ladino-dominated society. The nuclear family, of parents and children only (with perhaps one grandparent), which is typical and also normative of middle-class ladino families, is taken as the model for the Maya to follow. Women are thought to be the instruments for implementing this model, the ones therefore responsible for the correct functioning of society. Thus Mayan women are expected to function as a link for the two major ethnic groups—the ladino and the Indian—by reshaping themselves for the health of the nation. At the same time, ladino medical discourses, even when not based on abortion and sterilization, impose and propose a way to destroy Mayan culture by advancing this alien model.

One irony in the proposed programs and perspectives on health and hygiene for Mayan women by national organizations is that, when Mayan women decide to not adopt the changes, they are represented as being totally anachronistic and irrational. This, for example, was the view of ladino feminists represented in *Crónica*. Such advocacy of a new, assimilationist identity for Mayan women, however, can be seen as a disguised form of ethnocide or ethnic degradation; that is, if Mayan women do not comply and identify with the new rules, indigenous people are once again castigated as "cannibals" or "savages" by the ladino and white-dominated nation-state.

From observation of the Guatemalan government's practices of control of the population, and of Mayas in particular, it appears that the body is a sign, a repository of images and practices that belong to the nation-state. The body of the citizen is inscribed by the larger social body; it is a "field of political practices" (Foucault 1980, 140) regimented and regulated by the state and its institutions. Citizenship is a matter of appropriation by the state of the population and also a matter of contract between the citizens and the nation-state. In Elaine Scarry's words, "This centering of the body in citizenship provides a doorway for the continual entry of political philosophy into medicine . . . The emphasis on the body . . . is almost equally characteristic in political philosophy: the social contract comes into being by the act of consent by the population, and the fundamental logic of this consensual act is the protection of persons" (Scarry 1990, 872, 874). Citizens consent to be protected by the state; in exchange, they have to confirm their own presence and visibility as objects of state intervention.

In the case of Mayan women, their cooperation with the health organizations symbolizes a form of consent by which individuals delegate their well-being to the power of the institution. This consent is a kind of symbolic contract signed by the individual through her body. In exchange for the adherence to a medical contract, individuals and their families are promised improved health and living conditions. Ultimately, these health programs are integrated into a kind of internal colonial discourse as political practices of domination through integration. Consent can be required or imposed. In the case of Mayan people, techniques of displacement, segregation, and torture at first, and practices of subtle normalization aiming at creating "docile bodies" later, have been used to these ends.

Health development agencies should be understood in the context of the nationalistic plan of assimilation and/or extermination of traditional Mayan culture, because they partake of a discourse of control that includes the institutions of the family and of women's sexuality, among others. From the perspective of the interests of the nation-state as defined by the ladino and white elite, Indians are viewed as the cause of the nation's slow economic development, lack of homogeneity, and backward culture. While Mexico colonized, or rather "cannibalized," its internal Others, Guatemala exterminated them in attacks led by the militaries. Thus, unlike Mexico, which has used a strategy of incorporation of the Indians in the creation of the nation-state since the Revolution in 1910 and even more since 2001, Guatemala has perpetrated a steady brutal war against the Mayas without any basic change in the politics inherited from the Spanish conquerors. These two modes of repression, cannibalization and extermination, are in moral but not semiotic opposition in that they both reaffirm dominant social categories and practices.

Women are the main symbols of tradition and the core of traditional institutions. This is in part the reason why communities resist changes that involve women. In some Guatemalan villages, for instance, while men have opened to the ladino world, women still speak exclusively Maya and wear *huipiles*, the traditional embroidered blouse that visually identifies the wearer with her village of origin. Yet, language and dress are markers of identity not just for the women, but for the whole community, because women's space, the home, is a sanctuary for family and tradition, a space that the state cannot violate (see Franco 1985). But in Guatemala, this space has been deterritorialized; like women's bodies, the spaces of home and church have been invaded, desacralized by the military, and appropriated by national politics.

The bodies of Mayan women become a place in which the two main traditions, that of Mayas and that of ladino elites, contest their authority. Whereas Mayan social custom reifies tradition and essentializes woman as its bearer, the ladino-nationalist discourse evokes values of abstinence and sacrifice and the legitimization of women's sexuality. In both, though, women are treated as transcendent emblems of culture and privileged sites of tradition. The woman's body in both discourses is manipulated as a space for foreseeing and restoring the well-being and correct functioning of society through scientific discipline (see Stolcke 1981). Thus our reading of the health politics of the Guatemalan nation-state reveals elites' concern for the formation of a modern nation and a homogeneous national culture, as well as the ideologies and technologies of control that shape old and new roles and practices of reproduction of Mayan women.[7]

The challenges faced by the government during Vinicio Cerezo's presidency (1986–92) included the ethnic problem and social development, two concepts that for most Guatemalans are linked in opposition. The "beneficiaries," or targets, of health and development projects are mostly poor ladinos and Mayan women, fragments and yet pillars of the nation-state who, as such, need to be re-formed and reshaped according to modern canons. One of the efforts of the government to rehabilitate the Mayas is to reeducate Mayan women about their domestic responsibilities. Through such programs, the institution of the family suddenly became something valuable and in need of protection by the government. Traditional Mayan practices of having and raising children came to be considered irresponsible and out of place in a modern or modernizing country. Instead, the ideal middle-class family is presented as the model to which all women should aspire. All this, along with the politics of health and reproduction, represents a rhetoric of assimilation. Within this paradigm, the indigenous Other becomes even more anomalous or anachronistic and therefore out of place. The language of development programs infantilizes Mayan women, thus reproducing a paternalistic order that reinforces the stereotype of the savage child of colonial times.[8] Although the official ideology of the assimilationist practice of health organizations is one of self-improvement—a transformation of the self that is deemed necessary to develop the country's resources—the underlying assumption is paternalistic. It is an assumption of the defectiveness, inadequacy, and childlike character of the people to whom these programs are directed.

The project of ASECSA (Association of Health Community Service) stresses the idea of becoming responsible mothers and of raising consciousness. Although this suggests empowerment of women, it requires for its implementation a crucial role for men, who are viewed as responsible for raising women's consciousness and guaranteeing the unity of the family. The only role that women are required to fulfill is that of responsible procreators of a healthy and dignified generation. In return, women are promised freedom from the long-endured conditions of poverty, disease, and mistreatment by their men. The logic of this organization is the protection and assistance of those "in need of knowledge and assistance, to become capable," or *capacitación*, which I translate literally according to the Guatemalan understanding and usage of the term. This tacit contract in which women, health organizations, communities, and the state tacitly collude also represents the reiteration of the deployment of power by the same agencies. Thus, the state delegates to the organization, which in turn delegates to the community, to form a group of the most capable women who will be trained to educate the others. The realm of women, that is, the home *(hogar)*, becomes the area of activities and the ground of the organization, while the midwives, or *comadronas*, assume the role of cultural brokers in this process of modernization. The hierarchical pyramid, with the church and the state as directors of the entire structure, is ideologically reconstituted and imposed within the local communities.

The education of women parallels the concept of *superación*, or transculturalization. Within the discourse of health organizations, this condition can be achieved by consent to control. Thus, the condition for the functioning of the system is women's participation in such programs as subjects responsible for the correct functioning of their sexuality. In other words, women's participation in such programs is the means for the cleansing and health of the nation-state. The woman's body is first objectivized and then transcended, for it represents the locus of reproduction of another body. This is the social body of the Guatemalan nation-state, where Indians are the labor force on which rests the Guatemalan political economy. Therefore, what could be seen as a promise of empowerment for Mayan women can also be understood as an act of manipulation in which the most capable women in the community, the ones who could really break through ladino segregation and use their knowledge to improve the conditions of their own people, are taken away from their own communities. Their "reeducation" or *capacitación* fails to be an instrument of empowerment for their communities because it disconnects potential leaders from their shared communal, traditional knowledge, such as, for instance, the particularities of medicinal plants, which has always been part of women's culture among the Mayas.

The program of ASECSA mirrors and reproduces the politics of the state toward Mayas and poor ladinos. The demarcation between those who are fit and those who are not ready yet to be integrated within the nation-state is marked by classes. Ignorance and poverty and lack of education are terms used to refer to those in need of *capacitación.* Thus the stress is not so much on racial or ethnic differences between Mayas and ladinos, but more on gender and cultural and economic capital for improvement and modernization. It is as if the intention of these development programs was to replace old discriminatory categories with new ones. In a would-be democratic society like the Guatemalan, class, rather than ethnicity, constitutes and is constituted as the unifying yet discriminating discourse that allows institutions to incorporate "less developed" groups within the nation-state and the new society. The new main identity is poor and "woman," understood in ladino and modern terms. Hence "ethnicity" is replaced with class and gender, which are taken to adequately describe minority, underprivileged, or needy parts of the population. This appears to be democratic. No discrimination seems to exist toward Indians by ladinos. The ethnic problem is eliminated thanks to a change of terms, but it remains deeply ingrained in the society.

The Constitution of a Gendered Subject

"You are the ones who are going to work, not ASECSA." In this quotation, the women to whom the program is directed are encouraged to take charge of themselves as subjects and agents of change. However, despite such encouragement, they are supposed to be agents of the ideology behind the organization, its emissaries, not its authors. Women become the "middle persons," because the main project of ASECSA and other development organizations is to use selected women as purveyors to other women of a set of rules and practices established by the organization. The feeling of hopelessness and susceptibility to illnesses plays an important role among women—especially those who were widowed by the war—in their decision to adhere to the organization. For Mayan women, the death of elderly people because of the war cut their ancestral roots and the traditional support of their communities. Thus, the isolation in which they live, not only physical but also psychological and temporal, often opens them to embracing new tasks and functions, such as migrating to a new place, initiating a profession, working the land, or becoming part of an organization in which they feel represented. Thus, an organization might offer women an opportunity to have more control over their lives and teach them new skills and knowledge that might go beyond their traditional roles. Often the organization replaces the immediate relatives who died in the war. Hence, the awareness of health, hygiene, and the necessity to control births generates among some women another type of consciousness, mainly an awareness of their condition of subjugation within a patriarchal society. The rhetoric of control of the body is augmented by a rhetoric of liberation from the old, traditional, and oppressive systems.

The discourse on health represents a principal preoccupation, especially within the populations in the *aldeas modelos* or *caseríos*, that is, settlements created by the army and administered by military commissioners for those people whose houses or villages had been destroyed. In these settlements people live in enclosed, limited spaces that, along with dislocations of the war, breed ill health, promiscuity, and venereal diseases. A doctor who has worked in health programs in Baja Verapaz, the northeastern area of Guatemala, articulated some of the problems of Mayan people displaced in the area:

> The violence has originated apathy and a sense of hopelessness. More often than before the violence, people complain that they do not have food. These people need medicine more than ever; before, they made use of medicinal plants, but with the phenomenon of displacement the knowledge of traditional medicine got lost. In addition, their condition is such that anything can affect them; they are particularly sensitive in their stomachs. People often describe stomach pain as a heart-burning feeling, but it is mostly the stomach that is in pain, since the main problem of these people is to eat to survive. The rural population always lived in subhuman conditions. But the violence made it worse and caused apathy and insecurity among the people. During the violence, the majority of the women, especially the young ones, were raped and many aborted. Although abortion is not a traditional practice of Mayan women, after the violence several women did it. Also promiscuity increased; it might sound bad, almost grotesque, but many women who go to work in the capital become prostitutes; others start going out with soldiers and policemen who get them pregnant and then leave them. (Personal communication)

These words stress the manner in which violence has both uprooted people morally and made them more receptive to any program that might bring them resources. The politics of health can be seen as one of the strategies of the capitalist state, because the population needs to be healthy in order to be productive.

The plan of social and economic change of the Guatemalan nation-state partially includes a shift from agricultural to factory work, as in most Latin American countries.[9] Such a plan also has been facilitated by MINUGUA (United Nations Mission for the Verification of Human Rights in Guatemala) and the ratification of the Peace Accord, in May 1996. The accord included "The Socioeconomic and Agrarian Situation," which calls for procedures to solve conflicts in the use of lands and to alleviate poverty. This part of the accord has been the most difficult one for the parties to agree on. Owners of large lands did not want to relinquish them, and the state could not count on enough lands to meet the needs of the population. Further, in terms of productive resources and profit efficiency, small subsistence farms cannot compete with large export farms. Also, as a consequence of the violence, many rural people migrated to the city to escape the risk of having their villages destroyed and their lands burned.[10] Thus, an increasing number of Mayan people are part of the urban labor force, working in factories and sweatshops, or *maquilas*. Hence, Indian people, who once were an indispensable source of labor for the seasonal work on the large ladino landholdings, are becoming proletarianized.

The overall plan of assimilation of indigenous cultures has been undertaken through several forms of repression and indoctrination. With the disappearance of a majority of men and the destruction of productive lands, the old communities often disintegrated as the sense of collective solidarity and communal economic support were lost. Moreover, many women migrated, along with other survivors. Displaced indigenous people who now occupy roles in development projects often say they would not go back to their communities even if they could. Many people have gotten used to living under the strict control of the army and to being dependent on government assistance. Changes in the mode of subsistence also may entail estrangement from some of the tenets of Mayan culture, because food, religion, social organization, and gender distinctions all rotated around agricultural work.[11]

Nonetheless, despite the sufferings inflicted on the Mayas, a distinct Mayan social movement has emerged since the early 1990s that aims to recover Mayan identity in spite of the many changes and adaptations that Mayan people have had to endure. However, the followers of this movement are mostly educated and professional Mayas who are conscious of their resistance to a process of assimilation into the ladino or modern culture. Other Mayan people, pressured by poverty and unhealthy living conditions, and living in extreme passivity and fear, have been abandoning their traditions and rejecting the authority of shamans and elders. Many Mayas who observed Catholicism, within which a syncretic tradition between Catholic and Mayan religion was tolerated, join the Evangelical churches out of fear of being labeled "subversives" by the army. Families often send male children to the army because soldiering represents a sure income. Yet when these young men return home, they do not want to go back to work on the land even though they lack any other useful skill. This situation induces passivity as well as resistance. In other words, while indigenous people become easy targets of manipulation, they also adapt to and resist their situation by creating different identities, dislodged yet freed from the constraints of tradition.

Strategies of production parallel strategies of reproduction within the logic of capitalism. In the traditional Mayan agricultural economy, reproduction was a means of increasing the labor force available for small agricultural holdings. Mayan children were part of this labor force, because their work contributes significantly to family subsistence. The campaign for abortion and sterilization implemented by the Guatemalan government and supported by the United States is therefore contrary to the traditional interests of the rural population, but it does serve the interests of the oligarchy that largely controls the nation-state. In this sense, the appropriation and conquest of Mayan women can be seen as a reenactment of the Conquest—an attempt by the nation-state to subjugate the Mayas and reconstitute their bodies, their reproduction, and their myth of origin. Mayan women are now made to symbolize the roots or the matrix of the nation and its state apparatus. In other words, the Mayas—their bodies and wombs—are sacrificed once more for the constitution of another body with which they will be identified only if they largely cease to be Maya. The incorporation of Mayan women into development projects thus represents a shift in the strategies of the nation-state toward the Indian peoples, mainly from a policy of extermination that visibly punishes the body to a discourse of normalization that takes possession of the self and shapes it according to its needs. Once the Mayan body is incorporated, disciplined, and "dignified," the Guatemalan nation-state hopes to have a wider source of docile bodies as politically nonresistant and efficiently functioning labor resources rather than obstacles to the achievement of modernization and development. Indeed, the new nation—premised on the cannibalization of the Other through the control, possession, and transformation of women's bodies—is presented to the Mayas as a politics of liberation.

This strategy of domination by the Guatemalan government has often dictated the terms of the struggle for emancipation facing Mayas and particularly Mayan women. This is recognized in a document on the Second National Encounter of Indigenous People and People in Resistance: "The struggle for emancipation of indigenous people . . . as a part of any process of emancipation and national liberation, must begin with the recognition of the demands related to gender; of the values, experience, and contribution brought by women as women and as a part of the population in general. Therefore, it is important that women work together in their own organizations at the grassroots level to gain their own space, while it is also necessary that women and men struggle together in this, beginning with their common interests . . . Discovering and rescuing women's identity, as a generator of culture and an example of an untiring search for liberty, is a challenge to our campaign." Here the claim of liberation is advanced by a program based on female emancipation but, at the end of the manifesto, the role of women is blurred into the whole population. Also, the place advocated for women is converted into the space for the organization and given up for a common cause. The discourse of resistance and emancipation is based on women's role as procreators, but it shifts later toward a discourse centered on the unity of classes. Women—or rather, the space of women's bodies—are once again utilized as the medium for the establishment of discourses that transcend the physical body.

Radio announcements, midwives, nuns, and nurses also are used as means of access to women who live in isolated communities. In particular, midwives become cultural brokers. Their new role is to refer women to doctors by convincing them to go to hospitals and local health centers that often amount to extensions of the government's program of abortions for Mayan and poor ladino women. The emissaries of the organizations are in charge of "capacitating" the women, literally making them capable, educating and instructing them on the habits they have to adopt in relation to health, hygiene, and sexual behavior. In sum, indigenous movements of resistance, as well as development organizations, use gender, and in many cases ethnicity, as the foundational concept of their programs.

Courses on consciousness-raising imparted by leaders of social organizations make awareness appear to be necessary for manipulation. The input from the recipient of the *capacitación* is the essential condition for the functioning of the organization. The irony is that agency is entirely inverted in the whole discourse of consciousness-raising, because the women who are the objects of instruction are to be transformed into subjects or agents of change; that is, Mayan women need to be objectified in an alien discourse in order to be able to function on their own. Dignity is the goal to be achieved by women, but the notion of dignity to be earned is defined according to dominant paternalistic discourse. Women are incorporated, literally, into the dominant discourse; that is, women are discursively invaded and conquered in order to cure the "sick" body of the Mayas.

There is, however, resistance to this broad strategy of repressive assimilation. For example, intellectual Mayan women base their social critique on the legacy of colonization and identify themselves within ethnic categories. They understand their present conditions and their own repression to be a legacy of colonialism. Both cultures, they insist—the colonizer and the colonized, or ladinos and Indians—have subjugated and thus silenced Mayan women, but the real origin of domination lies in the imposition of Spanish and ladino values on Mayan men. For this reason, such Mayan women claim a revision of the historical past and utilize an ethnic discourse, rather than the gender one, in order to demand rights for Mayan women. In other words, such Mayan women perceive the basis of their exploitation as women as primarily rooted in the colonization of the ethnic Other, which includes Mayan men as well as women. Claims of exploitation in terms of gender raised by Mayan women are extended to men also in order to lay the basis for definition and revitalization of Mayan culture as a whole. Thus, in contrast and in resistance to state-sponsored programs, gender essentialism is used by Mayan women and men alike as a primary step toward ethnic essentialism.

This discursive strategy of resistance has its dangers. If the redefinition of the role of Mayan women is inscribed within the form of a cultural essentialism, the result might be a construction of an "ethnicized" gender. The ethnic discourse, by this essentialization of identity, is close to becoming hyperreal, where the Indian is converted into an empty image, devoid of content and floating between the mirror work of representation set by the nation-state. In the long run this could neutralize the power of resistance that the Indian discourses of gender and ethnicity aim to convey, symbolize, and propagate. On the one hand, the construction of a homogeneous Mayan culture through historical criticism of the role of Indian women could lead to the constitution of an isolated entity paradoxically trapped in its own totalization. On the other hand, the emancipatory value of this opposition cannot be overlooked. Against the negative qualities essentialized by the superordinate groups, a positively valued nature is created in the reappropriated space of the Mayan woman, as Rosalina Tuyuc, CONAVIGUA's director, points out.

Both interpretations of this essentializing, perhaps hyperreal, discourse entail the use of the body of women. In other words, women initiate a critique, and construct their selves as subjects, but later they step aside to lend this self to the project of a general redefinition of gender-sponsored Others. Among several grassroots organizations, for example, women are still the ones who are assigned the most menial tasks, while men are generally the coordinators and the authorities in the group. The body of women seems to be fetishized and cannibalized in that it is used as a foundation for new discourses. A different but parallel form of women's liberation and acquisition of consciousness is represented by Indian women who are mostly widows and displaced from their rural communities. They have experienced violence in its most brutal and direct forms. Assuming class, not gender, as the primary critique of society, their ideology is primarily Marxist, not feminist. Ironically, though, their adoption of a unifying theory to explain their status and their search for a cohesive social critique also opens up the possibility for co-optation. For example, those organizations composed exclusively of women posit women's struggle for their rights within a wider context of human rights. Therefore, the space for women and, more specifically, for Indian women in Guatemalan society, becomes entangled with struggles and claims that unify the victims of terror of any gender and ethnicity. Such a politics of alliance with other groups obviously has its advantages, but the direct violence and widowhood suffered by women become absorbed by a discourse of class, thus deferring and displacing the attention away from women once more.

Projects of emancipation of women are generally characterized by an accent either on class or on ethnic revitalization, but not on gender alone, as if women's bodies are used as a channel for political action and then displaced onto a separate sphere, deprived of any value by and in themselves. Both class and ethnic approaches subvert the notion of women's emancipation. The pragmatic and political difficulties of Guatemalan women find a parallel in two strategies that have been debated in Anglo feminism: a politics of difference based on theories of gender and a politics of sameness based on feminist empiricism (see Nicholson 1990). The Mayan use of feminist empiricism and models of gender fails because in both, gender is converted into an essentialized form of either ethnicity or class.

Mayan feminism in Guatemala has close affinities with what Gayatri Chakravorty Spivak defines as an "epistemic violence" (1988, 281–83). This refers to the colonial constitution of the Other, of the subaltern—that is, the impossibility of self-representation of the subaltern within the hegemonic colonial discourse. However, as Spivak recognizes, "strategic essentialism," which is expressed and practiced by Tuyuc, for example, might be one successful means for subalterns to represent and perhaps emancipate themselves. Within Guatemalan grassroots organizations women are allowed to express themselves only through a dependence on authorized male or ladino voices. It seems that the voices of Indian women are restricted to their bodies and that the constitution of a whole social body out of these women becomes a means to create a facade of social unity. Women represent the subordinate within a subaltern social group and their position as such is continuously re-created. Thus, the formation of organizations of women might be interpreted either as a space of resistance appropriated by women or, paradoxically, as the formation of an "event" that designates the woman as the body upon which practices of domination are inscribed.

Conclusions

Just as the Mayas are recognizing and rejecting old practices of domination, new medical practices, which are inserted in a discourse of modernization and state formation, operate to reappropriate the Mayan body. Programs of health care, maternity, food preparation, and hygiene target indigenous women. These present the unwritten rules prescribed by a nationalistic discourse for the Mayas in order to insert the physical body and corporal practices of Indian women into the modern Guatemalan nation as a social body. As such, Mayan women are being reconstituted as the new subjects who will make Indians law-abiding citizens, or perhaps merely subjects, of the state.

From the silence imposed through violence, the body becomes a new terrain for struggles of power. A new speaking subject is created as a gendered, ethnic, and subordinated body that can function as a citizen of the new society: a civilian with a newfound dignity. This dignity is simultaneously that of the individual and of the nation emerging from illness into health. Nonetheless, within these new discourses, silence is again imposed on the subaltern.

Notes

1 Whereas the term *ladino* is used in reference to the Guatemalans of Spanish descent, the term *Maya* agglomerates the indigenous population. Although there are twenty-two distinct Mayan groups in Guatemala, each with their own language, indigenous intellectuals use it as the general term to designate Maya-speaking people. In short, it homogenizes the distinct indigenous groups in order to distinguish

them from the ladinos, or the Spanish-descended group. In the words of a Mayan leader: "Guatemala is culturally a nation, but it is politically divided, atomized, so that all the indigenous people in Guatemala are Maya, and so is their collective memory. We are alive, but we need symbols because we do not have a community yet since the governments divided us as Mayan people" (Cojtí 1991). The term Maya is problematic because Mayan peoples do not constitute a homogeneous identity. Maya, rather, has become a strategy of self-representation for the Mayan movements and its followers. The official Academia de Lenguas Mayas de Guatemala (ALMG) finds twenty-one distinct Mayan languages.

2 At the time of colonization, the Spaniards referred to the Indians as cannibals and used this image in part to justify their crusade against the Indians in the name of civilization and Christianity. I believe that this image persists today (see de Certeau 1986; Greenblatt 1991; Hulme 1986; Pagden 1982).

3 Guatemala experienced thirty-five years of civil war that ended only with the signing of the definitive peace agreement on December 29, 1996. The repression and violence experienced by the Guatemalan population was devastating, and that experienced by Mayan people was even worse, owing to their scarcity of land, unemployment, poor health and education, and generally low standard of living. Further, Mayan people, who make up 56 percent of the Guatemalan population, have always been the target of continuous and massive discrimination. For example, in the first phase of the state's counterinsurgency program, hundreds of rural communities, mostly Indians, were falsely thought to be the heart of rebellion, and so were destroyed.

4 Mayan women are subjected to a double exploitation—as women and as Indians. Within Mayan culture, women are highly appreciated and venerated for their capacity to procreate. Because of poor health conditions and the many births that Mayan women experience, they are more exposed to malnutrition, diseases, and death. Patriarchy has not allowed contraception, and high illiteracy and the lack of knowledge of Spanish on the part of most Mayan women limit their access to information and other resources that could help them to curb the frequency of pregnancy.

5 In the 1980s, when the violence reached its peak, the army suspected every Indian of cooperating with the resistance movement. This "culture of fear" (see Carmack 1988) was not only characterized by killings and disappearances, but also by more subtle forms of repression, control, and psychological warfare. An example of this were the so-called model villages or hamlets to which the army removed and reunited survivors of distant, destroyed villages. Another example is the civil patrol system in which Indians were both actors of the military repression and objects of the violence generated by this instrument of control. The patrol system undermined social trust by creating spies in every village. Also, it was not uncommon for many Indians to have their Mayan names changed into ladino names in order to disguise their ethnic identity, or to go into exile.

6 Jorge Serrano was again elected president in January 1999, a neoliberal rightist who was supported by only 30 percent of the electorate. He undertook the first dialogues with the revolutionary movement and took the lead in the delicate operation to convert years of military dictatorship into a civilian government. He had the burden of bringing economic growth to the country and of making neoliberal

dreams come true. He also had the difficult task of restoring social peace and dealing with autonomous popular movements, such as CONAVIGUA. The integration of Mayan people into the new society was also part of his discourse. However, Serrano, in his effort to establish a modern society, denied not only the difference in the composition, demands, and needs of the population, but also the still lingering memories of violence among the majority of Guatemalans (see Jonas 1991).

7 Culture, class, and race are interrelated and grounded in the female body. This is especially true in Guatemala as a nation that aspires to what many whites and ladinos conceive as the European model, that is, not only economic advancement, but also "purity of blood." But, because even the middle and upper classes of Guatemala are more "mixed" than "pure," purity of race, although desired, remains unattainable: elites are already established in their hybridity. Unlike Mexican national identity, founded on the concept of *mestizaje*, Guatemalan national identity refuses to face itself as hybrid.

8 Modernization and development also have served U.S. efforts to maintain a Guatemalan nation revolving around U.S. dictates, and as a cover for U.S. support for repressive military actions and regimes. U.S. educators and missionaries have been sent to Guatemala since the 1960s, following the overthrow in 1954 of the liberal government of President Jacobo Arbenz in a U.S.-assisted coup that initiated decades of military rule. Civic works in Guatemala begun in 1966 by the U.S. civic team provided engineering, medical, social, religious, and educational assistance, but were essentially part of the U.S. ideologies of "national security," "anticommunism," and, more recently, "antinarcotics" (see Jonas 1991).

9 Even by Latin American standards, Guatemala has been an extremely underdeveloped country. The 1995 GDP per capita of $1,340 placed Guatemala in the World Bank's classification of middle income–lower middle income nations. Such figures, however, say nothing of the distribution of wealth or income *within* countries. Indeed, in rural areas where 60 to 70 percent of Guatemalans live, the poverty percentage rises to 85 percent. Efforts to reduce poverty and promote social reforms generally have failed. Two of the four actors that were key in the process of signing the Peace Accord (the government and the CACIF [Chamber of Agricultural, Commercial, Industrial, and Financial Associations]) viewed the peace process as an opportunity to modernize the state apparatus, gain access to international finance, and launch a neoliberal political economy. In contrast, the other two parties, the Assembly of Civil Society and the URNG (Guatemalan National Revolutionary Unit), wanted to take measures against the extreme inequality of land and wealth distribution that have existed since the colonial era.

10 The government's scorched-earth campaign in 1981–83 depopulated vast areas, displacing an estimated 1.5 million people (then 20 percent of the population). Some fled to Mexico, Canada, and the United States, while others moved to other parts of Guatemala, especially to Guatemala City, where they might find jobs. There are no census data on the internally displaced, because many of those displaced within Guatemala remained dispersed and anonymous. However, organizations of displaced people and government agencies estimated that in 1997 some fifty-five thousand *families* had been internally displaced.

11 The repression of the 1980s was deployed under the dictatorship of Efraín Ríos Montt, who seized power in a coup in 1982. He escalated the counterinsurgency

campaign and also promoted evangelical Protestant sects. These were used as an instrument of assimilation and counterinsurgency, and to combat liberation theology, which informed many radical Catholic priests.

References

Carmack, Robert, ed. 1988. *Harvest of Violence: The Mayan Indians and the Guatemalan Crisis.* Norman: University of Oklahoma Press.

Citgua (Ciencia y Tecnología para Guatemala). 1989. "Situación de la Mujer en Guatemala." *Publicaciones Especiales* (Mexico), no. 2.

Cojtí, Cuxil Demetrio. 1991. *La Configuración del pensamiento político del pueblo maya.* Guatemala City: Asociación de Escritores Mayances de Guatemala.

de Certeau, Michel. 1986. *Heterologies: Discourse on the Other.* Trans. Brian Massumi. Minneapolis: University of Minnesota Press.

Douglas, Mary. 1966. *Purity and Danger.* London: Routledge.

Foucault, Michel. 1980. *The History of Sexuality,* vol. 1, *An Introduction.* Trans. Robert Hurley. New York: Vintage Books.

Franco, Jean. 1985. "Killing Priests, Nuns, Women, Children." In *On Signs,* ed. Marshall Blonsky. Baltimore: Johns Hopkins University Press. 414–20.

Greenblatt, Stephen. 1991. *Marvelous Possessions: The Wonder of the New World.* Chicago: University of Chicago Press.

Hernández, I., and M. O. Paiz. 1993. *Crónica* (February): 16–20.

Hulme, Peter. 1986. *Colonial Encounters: Europe and the Native Caribbean 1492–1797.* London: Routledge.

Jonas, Suzanne. 1991. *The Battle for Guatemala: Rebels, Death Squads, U.S. Power.* Latin American Perspectives Series, no. 5. Boulder, Colo.: Westview Press.

Kinzer, Stephen. 2001. "Guatemala: The Unfinished Peace." *New York Review of Books* (June 21): 61–63.

Nicholson, Linda, ed. 1990. *Feminism/Postmodernism.* Albany: State University of New York Press.

Pagden, Anthony. 1982. *The Fall of Natural Man: The American Indian and the Origin of Comparative Ethnology.* Cambridge: Cambridge University Press.

Scarry, Elaine. 1990. "Consent and the Body: Injury, Departure, and Desire." *New Literary History* 21: 867–96.

Scheper-Hughes, Nancy, and Margaret Lock. 1987. "The Mindful Body: A Prolegomenon to Future Work in Medical Anthropology." *Medical Anthropology Quarterly* 1.(1): 6–41.

Spivak, Gayatri Chakravorty. 1988. *In Other Worlds.* New York: Routledge.

Stolcke, Verena. 1981. "The Naturalization of Social Inequality and Women's Subordination." In *Of Marriage and the Market: Women's Subordination in International Perspective,* ed. Kate Young, Carol Wolkowitz, and Roslyn McCullagh. London: Routledge and Kegan Paul.

Zur, Judith. 1998. *Violent Memories: Mayan War Widows in Guatemala.* Boulder, Colo.: Westview Press.

4

The Ludic Body:

Ritual, Desire, and Cultural Identity in the

American Super Bowl and the Carnival of Rio

In his now famous analysis of the birth of tragedy, Nietzsche argued that behind the Apollonian cults of harmony and self-discipline were those of Dionysus that celebrated bodily indulgence in wine, song, dance, and frenzied passion. A short time later, perhaps without reading Nietzsche, Émile Durkheim illustrated the centrality of the body in religious ritual. Every year, he noted, otherwise dispersed clans of Australia came together to celebrate the sacred, that is, the power of the social. The body was imbricated within a complex system of rituals of song, dance, and relaxations of a number of dietary and sexual taboos. The intensity of sacred rituals, bodily indulgences, and close physical proximity evoked an "efflorescence of feelings" and emotional contagion that dramatized the power of the social, served to maintain solidarity, and celebrated collective identities based on lineage to totemic progenitors.

If fostering and expressing Dionysian frenzy informed one theme of social theory, so too did the demand for Apollonian control of the body and bodily desire inform another. For Freud, "rational" civilization demanded guilt-based renunciation of the instincts. For Max Weber, such rationality was manifested in ascetic Protestantism, disciplined work, bureaucratic administration, and even rule-bound music and sports. Reason as renunciation stood apart from—if not opposed to—the affectivity and hedonistic indulgences of traditional communal society and its carnival culture. Norbert Elias (1978) complements Weber in showing that a "civilizing process" mediated between sociocultural changes and internalized controls. Rituals of manners and politeness fostered constraints upon the bodily and the impulsive, even while suppressing the carnival and recasting its vulgarity, its grotesque and sensual bodiness, as the denigrated and excluded Other. The repression of bodily desire, sublimated in work that was akin to a religious calling, led people to endlessly productive effort and thereby to accumulate far more than they needed for immediate consumption. Thus, repression enabled the "spirit of capitalism" to flourish.

From this brief sketch, we can see that, though rarely made explicit, the body, whether working (Marx, Weber), desiring (Freud), playing (Huizinga), creating the sacred (Durkheim), or being civilized (Elias), has long been a central moment of social life and a focus of sociological interest. I would further note that, following Durkheim, the body is the site of basic social classifications. For example, age and gender are the most fundamental and universal ways of classifying people. These categories are not only "marked" on the body, but also inscribed in the ritual practices that usually are limited to young or old, male or female, especially as these may relate to birth, sexuality, coming of age, or warriorhood. Thus in adolescent *rites de passage*, only after circumcision and initiation does a boy or girl become an adult who may engage in sexual relations or marriage.

By the end of the twentieth century, popular culture had valorized the body and become concerned with health, beauty, fashion, and vigorous, if not Viagrous, sexuality. The postmodern cultural logic of late capitalism also encourages ludic consumption in which the body is a site of commodified *pleasure*. In turn, recent sociological concerns with identity, embodied desire, and corporeal subjectivity have renewed academic interest in the body. In this context, Foucault's analysis of the disciplining of the body as the means of inscribing identities and control has found a receptive audience (Grosz 1994). The work of Turner, Featherstone, and Shilling, among others, also makes the body a central focus of sociological study.

Just as there has been a renewed concern with the body, so too have there been interrogations of identity. These two themes are interdependent, because many of the questions of identity also concern bodies that may be gendered, racialized, nationalized, erotized, surveilled, and disciplined. The current sociological interests in identity reflect the increasingly problematic character of selfhood in contemporary society. This can be seen in various debates over social fragmentation, identity politics, youth cultures, or generations X, Y, and Z. In many youth cultures, body markers such as dress, tattoos, rings or posts, hairstyles, and the like are badges of identity and markers of social belonging and exclusion. The following analysis brings together concerns with identity, ritual, and embodiment. More specifically, I show how certain ritualized forms of body display and performances become essential moments of identity.

Rituals of Identity

A crucial moment of every culture is its construction of the body, body images, ideals of beauty, and rules and norms of cleanliness and body care, culinary manners, and, above all, of bodily exposure and display, fashion and adornment, and standards of sexuality and gender. These norms influence how the body is experienced in everyday life and celebrated also in ludic rituals in which fantastic articulations of the body and liminal expressions of bodily desire affirm distinct cultural identities. In these ways, social constructions of embodiment are intrinsic components of cultural identity.

Every culture also constructs reflexive narratives, stories, and images of itself that form its collective identity. This is a story of collective roots that proclaim who the people are, their difference from others, and their continuity over time. This often involves myths of ancestry and origin or historical legends that link the past with the present, and offer promises of a utopian future. Identities often include stories of gods, heroes, and heroines who personify cultural ideals and values. Finally, narratives of identity allow one to be recognized. In this sense, cultural identities are not just collections of myths and stories, but scripts that are expressed in the ritual performances of embodied actors who sustain solidarity and affirm distinctive roles and personae. But, as Nietzsche and Durkheim suggested, these rituals also often permit the expression of otherwise submerged identities and usually tabooed desires.

Despite the differences between premodern people and modern nation-states located within a system of globalized capital, and notwithstanding the secularism of modernity, Durkheim's analysis of rituals still offers profound insights. Social relationships, commitments, attachments, and identities tend to wane over time. Thus, for a society to endure and reproduce itself, it must continually dramatize the power of the social, renew bonds of solidarity, and affirm collective identity. Every society fosters rituals in which people come together at times and places deemed sacred, special, and distinct from the profane or ordinary. As Durkheim argued, religion was the prototypical form of collective rituals, which range from everyday dietary restrictions or demands for prayer to annual "high holidays" such as Easter, Dewali, Passover, or Aid el Kebir. These holidays, much like the yearly gatherings of the aboriginal clans, typically include special songs, dances, foods, drinks, and often intoxicants that, in turn, evoke powerful feelings and emotions. In some cases, participants may go into trances or other ecstatic states.

Societies provide positive feelings that encourage certain acts and use fear, anxiety, and shame to control conduct that might bring the person gratification but impose excessive social costs. Most societies limit aggressive acts, sexuality, and unbridled hubris. In some societies, social control may depend on guilt over wishes as well as controls over deeds. At the same time, social structures, as the organization of external constraints, dialectically foster alternative realms that stand apart from the quotidian with its constraints and restrictions. Insofar as such controls generally limit thought and conduct for the sake of preserving the regularities of social life, societies create alternative sites and moments of antistructure, liminal times and places of resistance, inversion, and repudiation in which social norms can be safely flaunted (Turner 1969). Such liminal realms are often ones of freedom, equality, spontaneity, and role reversals. These are the realms of agency, empowerment, and license insofar as their own codes of conduct overturn the official or dominant ones. Here inversions of norms are tolerated or even celebrated, and otherwise proscribed acts are valued.

The spectacle, an extraordinary public display, has long been part of complex societies. Parades, rallies, and commemorations draw people together in nonordinary larger groups and experiences. Like religious rituals to affirm faith, elites have long created dramatic pageants, circuses, games, or contests to celebrate power and entertain or distract subjects. These may involve athletic competitions such as chariot races, javelin tosses, or jousts that are closely associated with military prowess. Athletic spectacles may express cultural mythologies whose heroes articulate shared values and identities (Cummings 1972). Sports thus become a mythological realm in which heroes and heroines symbolically present a morality play wrapped in pageantry and laden with unconscious appeals. Thus, the political efficacy of sports and spectacles depends on their psychocultural functions, especially their articulation of collective identities and the realization of individual desires.

One form of spectacle is the carnival. Whereas most spectacles are sponsored by elites, carnivals generally come from the "people." The carnival emerged in feudal Europe as a moment of peasant folk culture (Bakhtin 1968), creating a liminal space for the ludic that granted feudal peasants pleasurable release. Carnivals were times and places of popular inversions, sanctioned deviance, and reversals of norms that stood opposed to the official feasts and tournaments that celebrated the power of the elites. The sacrosanct elites of church and state were typically parodied, mocked, hectored, and ridiculed. The transgression of moral boundaries was alluring at several levels from the political to the erotic. Carnivals expressed the Dionysian that Nietzsche claimed was suppressed by the Apollonian. These were times of indulgence in wine, song, dance, and sex. Typical patterns of hierarchy, deference, and demeanor were ignored, indeed repudiated, in favor of what usually was forbidden. Alternative meanings could be displayed as resistances to top-down impositions.

Thus, a more social theory of desire begins not with biology but with embodiment. Through socialization and identification, individuals learn and come to embody their "emotion culture" and "feeling rules"—that is, social rules and symbolic cues that elicit emotions, define their meaning, and guide their expression in various situations. People everywhere seek the positive emotional experiences that come with community and attachments, recognition, esteem and dignity, and a degree of empowerment. Conversely, people generally avoid the negative effects and adverse feelings of isolation, anger, shame, guilt, powerlessness, and, above all, anxiety and dread in the awareness of death (Langman 1992).

Indeed, despite his structuralism and antipsychologism, Durkheim's theory of religion depends on the evocation of emotions bordering on frenzy to dramatize and elicit collective sentiments. Thus, rituals, as scripted performances, represent an intersection between cultural demands and individual desires. Liminal rituals provide the subject with a number of emotional gratifications that she or he elects and enacts in various performances. If a social structure limits certain actions through fears, anxieties, and shame, the liminal may become a site where what is otherwise proscribed is encouraged.

In sum, societies necessarily bifurcate experience into two realms of structure and antistructure—a quotidian of the normative and moments of the liminal. The structural constraints foster antistructural releases that can only exist for fleeting moments in marginal, interstitial, or even imaginary sites for the expressions of acts, feelings, and identities that are usually forbidden or taboo. Such releases exist in "containment fields," much like the antimatter in the warp engines of the starship *Enterprise*, and cannot themselves endure on their own. Thus the liminal has a dialectical relation to structures. Whereas the liminal provides resistance, inversion, and repudiation, it also serves to secure the structure (on "ritual irony," see

Bahktin 1968; Brown 1989). The alternative realms of the liminal have often included the chiliastic, millenarian, and the carnivalesque such as the Roman Saturnalia and the medieval Feast of Fools. Such liminal moments can offer access to usually submerged identities and experiences whose pursuits are utopic experiences of an alternative reality (Bloch 1986). In the Western world, shaped by Greco-Roman and Christian traditions, structural imperatives of the Apollonian have elicited the antistructural and spontaneous frenzy of the Dionysian.

A comparison of festivals and ritual spaces suggests that the Carnival of Brazil and the Super Bowl in America both can be seen as rituals that construct and celebrate bodies and identities in relation to broader social norms and ideals. These performances show the radically different ways in which cultures construct the self and celebrate this construction in rituals that maintain solidarity even as they arouse and fulfill usually suppressed desires. Whereas Brazil celebrates the erotic body in a fantasized festival of equality, football celebrates the violent body of the male warrior in simulations of team combat. Just as Carnival is central to Brazilian culture and identity, the Super Bowl is a key trope of American identity. Indeed, these rituals are the most popular celebrations in each society and their participants and audiences number in the millions.

Carnival Comes to the New World

The American Super Bowl and the contemporary Carnival of Brazil, as ritualized performances of cultural identities, are rooted in historical legacies that have shaped character and culture. The legacies of the English Protestant colonization of North America now inform football, whereas the traditions of Portuguese Catholic settlers, melded with those of African slaves and indigenous tribes, dispose the Carnival of Brazil.

Brazil was colonized by Portuguese Catholics seeking fortunes for their king and for themselves. Early explorers described Brazil as a sexual paradise, an erotic Eden where the native people were without modesty or restraint; there was "no sin south of the equator" (DaMatta 1991). Brazil soon became a major agricultural producer—and much of that production was based on the slave labor of Africans. Precolonial legacies, with Portuguese Catholicism and African slavery, melded into a unique cultural identity celebrated in Carnival. The Catholics of southern Europe were far more likely to indulge the desires of the flesh and the spirits of the vine than were disciplined northern Protestants. Machismo and Marianismo first emerged in the *latifundias* of southern Europe—many of which had vineyards. Catholicism permitted the sensual and left a cultural space for bodily pleasure, with churches filled with icons, statues, incense, and paintings, and the possibility of cleansing through confession.

Brazil's myth of origin begins in the plantation owner's Big House that stood apart from the slave quarters. The free and open sexuality of the male owners and the seclusion and control of *their* women in the house were telling aspects of the myths and realities of Brazil's origins. Slavery was cruel and patriarchal and led to carnal indulgence by male owners and the ravishing of female slaves. But at the same time, the familiarity and often intimacy of master–slave relations produced a mixed race of Brazilians whose elites saw themselves as living in a peaceful, harmonious, multiracial society (Freyre 1986). This cultural identity is, of course, more mythic than real; Brazil remains a violent and racist society largely controlled by a small white elite.

Carnival, while rooted in the folk cultures of medieval Europe and West Africa, was transformed in the New World to become the major ritual celebrating Brazilian identity. Carnival expresses an alternative experience and tradition, a social history of the poor as opposed to the official history celebrated by elites in festivals of the state, such as Independence Day. It applauds the historical continuity and distinctiveness of the unique montage of Brazilian society. There are carnivals elsewhere, of course, but they differ in many ways from Brazil's, which is owned by the poor and in which samba is central. In the 1830s, Carnival was celebrated in the home with family and neighbors. It was only later that the *carnival de rua* (street) or *clube* (ballroom) appeared. Brazilian society sharply divides the home and the street. Whereas the home ideally is a world of order, calm, and control, the street is the site of passion, freedom, and even danger. Carnival is above all a festival of the streets and plazas during the night, with some streets blocked off to traffic. Carnival is celebrated in a variety of places, a vast public spectacle with millions of celebrants in which the boundaries of performer and spectator are blurred. Some of the samba parades and parties are scheduled far in advance, but other celebrations spontaneously occur. For the majority, who are poor and with little social opportunity or status, there are myriads of street festivals with informal musical groups and outbursts aided by large quantities of *cachaca* (sugar cane liquor). Although many of the festivals take place in the favelas, masses of poor celebrants meander throughout the city and many flow into the upscale beachfront areas such as Ipanema, Copacabana, and Vieira Souto. During Carnival, the poor lay claim to the public spaces, even those typically claimed by the affluent. As Carnival possesses the public places and the night, it repudiates the everyday home, work, job, and church—the dominated worlds of order and restraint.

Carnival is not a spectator sport viewed at a distance; instead, immediate physical, often erotic, contact and direct participation are part and parcel of the celebration. Members of southern cultures in general are more physically expressive and close than northerners, and proximate human contact more valued. Brazilians are very much a touching, hugging, kissing people. Carnival demands the crowds of celebrants be in constant contact with each other. The whimsically, elegantly dressed spectators are as likely to sing and dance as the singers, dancers, and local bands (*blocos*). Thus, the performers become audiences to the performances of the spectators.

The Carnival of the streets is a festival of huge crowds that come to drink, dance, sing, shout, prank, flirt, and sometimes make love (Linger 1992). It is a time and site of play and merrymaking; revelry abounds, barriers fall, and there are inversions of norms. Play (*brincar*) has a number of sexual overtones and meanings. Anything goes—and sexual indulgence is one of the central moments of Carnival. Carnival creates a realm of freedom from oppressed labor and coerced sexuality without restraints of race, class, or gender. Of course there *are* limits and codes. The sexuality tends not to be public but occurs discreetly in the shadows. The government may be insulted, but the many police and military guards maintain certain boundaries and prohibit open rebellion. Yet, during Carnival, the poor can live in alternative realms apart from the squalor and hardship of their usual lives. For a few days they can be kings and queens ruling the kingdoms of fantasy. That Carnival is a fantasy does not nullify its psychocultural force. On the contrary, Carnival proposes that one had better know how to delude oneself. It prescribes a self-conscious expulsion of burdens as a generalized antidote to fear and suffering.

From Football to Super Bowl

Most cultures have competitive games and sports that often celebrate the abilities and bodies of champions, either individually or collectively. With the rise of courtly society in the West, the nature of desire and the body changed. Indeed, part of the civilizing process was the evolution of team sports from regulation by local custom to rule-bound games, including competitions between distant teams. With modernity came nationalism, which, much like a religion, served as a collective culture with shared beliefs and rituals, commemorations, and military parades that celebrate the Nation and patriotic union with it. The popularity of participatory sports

and spectatorship-based fandom became an inherent part of state formation, as seen today in competitions of national teams. Likewise, preparation for "citizenship" came to be associated with training or schooling of
the embodied self in order to instill identification with the larger social
order as well as loyalty to particular organizations, schools, teams or corporations. With industrialization and the expansion of leisure time, the
growth and commodification of spectator sports brought large crowds
together, and sports became collective rituals that affirmed national identities. Certain sports events then served as entertainment, commerce, and
patriotic celebration.

Whereas the Super Bowl is a recent creation, the particular dispositions to football as a violent game of male teams seeking territorial power
and control were foretold in the earliest moments of American culture (see
Langman 1992). American identity is rooted in the aggressive aspects of
American character embedded deep in the Puritan sensibility, a hostility
to untamed nature, and a more explicit urban tempo (Cummings 1972,
104). A crucial moment of both early Puritanism and later "muscular
Christianity" was the increasing economic power of the male qua economic actor as opposed to the clan, family, or guild. As the anthropologist
Lloyd Warner once argued, the Protestants threw the indulgent Mary out
of the house just when the father, as the worldly head of the family, gained
in economic power. Thus, Protestantism reflected the world of masculine
asceticism that displaced female emotion. At the same time, of course, this
economic power came at the price of highly disciplined behavior in the
marketplace or in bureaucracies. The legacy of this dual heritage has been
the ritual celebration of violence and the symbolic elevation to mythic
status of warrior heroes who enact in sports-spectacles the aggressive, competitive nature of corporate life.

Baseball and football, though American innovations, were rooted in
earlier European traditions. Football seems to have actually originated in
Mardi Gras festivals in which oval leather balls represented eggs. Early
colonists played some sort of team game using an inflated bladder for a
ball. Although the roots of football might also include soccer and rugby,
it became a highly distinct and, indeed, uniquely American game. Indeed,
football came to celebrate a general allegiance to an American conception
of self. Thus, it is not surprising that football emerged among the new
national elites as they were attempting to forge an inclusive national identity that would valorize masculine aggression during the period of brutal
industrialization during and after the bloody Civil War.

Moreover, with urbanization and industrialization there was a decline of small farming and its physical labor and an increase in professional and managerial work. A great fear among the upper-middle and elite classes was a growing "effeminacy" in face of the changing nature of work and changing roles of women. There were anxieties over masculinity, passivity, and ill health. "Muscular Christianity" was as much a part of the response to this as was the introduction of healthy foods from Kellogg's cereals to Graham's crackers. This was also a time when growing numbers of women were entering college. In the 1870s, 21 percent of postsecondary students were women; by the 1920s it was almost 47 percent, after which female enrollments declined until the 1970s. The "New Woman," more assertive and androgynous, raised questions and fostered anxieties about gender identity (Oriard 1993; Dworkin and Wachs 2001). In this context, the rise and growth of football served to affirm a masculinity facing challenges.

At the same time, given the social dislocations of industrialization and urbanization, amateur athletics were promoted as a stabilizing force that would integrate immigrants, socialize delinquents, thwart radicalism, and foster the values required by the industrial order—namely, discipline, teamwork, and aggressiveness (Schwartz 1998). After industrialization and the factory system severed work from home and craft, people increasingly turned to sports for a positive sense of self (Cummings 1972). Professional baseball grew in popularity as a blue-collar sport. Football became organized into a college sport with formal rules for the elite few who went to schools such as Harvard, Princeton, Columbia, or Yale. Teams were primarily recruited from the upper-class student population.

The growth of football as an elite sport was aided by the efforts of one of the first Yale players, Walter Camp, who later became the president of the New Haven Clock Company. His approach to football was influenced by Frederick Winslow Taylor's view of "scientific management"; thus he saw football and corporate life as essentially one and the same. "Team play" might require the sacrifice of individual brilliance to achieve organizational goals (Oriard 1993). Football came to embody the same principles of management in which positions are organized on the basis of function and ability. By the beginning of the twentieth century, it was believed that young men educated in college and in football would become business, professional, and political leaders of the future, because the keys to (white) manhood, Christian character, and the managerial attributes of the corporate executive were forceful personalities offering knowledge and leadership (ibid., 211ff.). Teddy Roosevelt was an incarnation of and cheerleader for these values that would ensure that the elite Anglo-American classes would remain real men with masculine prowess in the face of declining patriarchal control of the family and challenges of a new immigrant working class.

Changes in typography facilitated mass circulation, and thus media coverage of sporting events. Those sports with entertainment value flourished and were reported by newspapers owned by Pulitzer and Hearst. This encouraged the rapid growth of fandom—especially among elites. By the end of the nineteenth century, football, as a uniquely American game and intially a sport of the "gentlemen" of elite schools, had quickly spread throughout the country from eastern colleges to urban sandlots (Schwartz 1998). Football would soon become an important financial aspect of college life as alumni donated more money to football-related aspects of their schools and to schools with winning teams. By the late 1960s, television viewing had greatly expanded and football games were watched by growing audiences who were not college educated. Football overtook baseball in popularity after the rapid postwar growth of managerial and professional groups for whom football spectatorship had been an integral part of college. As collegiate sports became more commodified, players were more likely recruited from minorities.

Whereas football has been professionalized for a long time, only recently has it become a big business, culminating in the creation of the Super Bowl. In little more than three decades, the Super Bowl became the most widely celebrated annual event of American popular culture, far surpassing the World Series or the Academy Awards and Miss America contests, with more than 100 million viewers and global corporations paying some five hundred thousand dollars for a thirty-second TV spot. To achieve such popularity, the Super Bowl taps long-standing cultural legacies and deeply rooted desires. It both draws on and reproduces the historical construction and performance of identities, only now in an age of globalized consumption. Just as Carnival reflects much in the cultural identity of Brazil, the Super Bowl is a unique expression of American (male) identity.

Football's principal early booster, Walter Camp, compared football not only to business but also to war, with football armies, artillery batteries, and generalship (Oriard 1993). Teams were like platoons, lines were engaged in hand-to-hand combat. The players in the trenches were directed by generals (coaches) whose locker rooms were war rooms. The groans, screams, blood and injuries, stretchers, and medics simulate a battlefield—but without actual death. "It is an aggressive strictly regulated team sport fought between males who use both violence and technology to win monopoly control of property for the economic gain of individuals within a nationalistic, entertainment context" (Rapping 1987, 84). Thus, war and commerce as rationalized combat find their ultimate ritual performance in a Super Bowl that celebrates the male warrior/spectator and affirms that they are "real" men who enjoy violence and power, and not sissies or pussies (McBride 1995). Football valorizes the phallic aggression of war but without death and destruction. Moreover, though wars eventually end, in the Super Bowl aggressive identities are confirmed and constantly renewed in celebrations of violent male performances. Following Georges Bataille and René Girard, the taboos against in-group violence are sustained and the ritual sacrifice of the enemy enables both the experience of the taboo and its transgressions. As in war and business, winning is everything. The identity of the fan, short for fanatic, is invested in the team to which he owes allegiance. "Fans thrill to the moves of players with whom they identify . . . and find euphoria in victory . . . humiliation in defeat" (ibid., 85).

The violence of men in combat, whether football or war, is not irrational; it is clearly oriented toward goals and bound by rules, with well-planned strategies and practiced tactics. It also bonds males together, provides them with recognition and a sense of empowerment, and, especially for those inflicting pain and not seriously hurt, violence feels good. The planned yet still mystical bonding of males through the pain and violence of war or football and the struggle for victory overcomes separation and alienation and for brief moments provides wholeness and completion. As Bataille might suggest, violence enables transcendence of the mundane through a descent into excess and degradation. Like the mystics, berserkers, or dervish dancers described by Weber, combat can provide ecstatic experiences. In this way, football acts as a cathartic in which the domination and symbolic castration of the Other serves to displace that violence from everyday life and preserve social order. Whereas religion fails to provide the redemption it promises, football *does* deliver its promised violence. Larger than life mythic heroes clash on the fields of battle, some opponents are hurt, cheerleaders dance, and hierarchical gender relations that favor powerful males are affirmed and secured.

Football's cultural power derives in large part from the collision of the modern and the antimodern, one aspect of which was a dialectical embrace of competing notions of manliness. For middle-class males in the nineteenth century, the new industrial and commercial order meant a redefiniton of work in terms of mental rather than physical activity, with a consequent uncertainty about the masculinity of mental work. Physical power became a mark of the lower classes, yet its rationality in industry kept it tied to middle-class definitions of masculinity. Thus, football could represent a union of the physical and the mental that was difficult for middle- and upper-class men to find elsewhere in modern America (Oriard 1993, 201). As one male former athlete put it, "A woman can do the same job as I can—maybe even be my boss. But I'll be damned if she can go out on the football field and take a hit from Ronnie Lott" (Messner 1988, 168).

The male players use instrumental aggression to combat each other, while the expressive cheerleaders foster a solidarity through a shared male gaze of the powerful warriors and the males who identify with them and the women who desire them, thereby reproducing gender domination. Thus, although most men are not overtly violent to each other and do not abuse their wives or children, domination through violence is valorized by the football player who acts out the erotic/aggressive fantasy desires of many spectators and implicitly reinforces the gender privileges of males, their monetary advantages, institutional power, and feelings of superiority.

Football can be seen as a Nietzschean moment of a will to violence and refusal of bourgeois civility that yet remains encapsulated within the substantive rationality of bourgeois society that must realize repressed violence that otherwise would return as self-hate. Just as Weber noted the battlefield superiority of Cromwell's disciplined Protestant Iron Men, so football violence is subjected to rules that make it a site between "the unreason of desire and the rational order of civilized society. . . . As a form of character ethics, football inculcates a virile asceticism of fortitude and discipline that will serve men well in the society at large in much the same way as does the military" (McBride 1995, 82). Football in its uniquely American form thus can be seen as a hypermasculine war game over territory in which primitive violence is subsumed under rational codes that carefully locate combat within a clearly measured site, at definite times, regulated by strict rules in which technological rationality attempts to regulate the violence of war and commerce in simulated fashion.

Desire and Liminal Identity in Carnival and the Super Bowl

Why did such radically different celebrations of the body as Carnival and Super Bowl become crucial collective affirmations of identity? Each celebration can be seen as a unique constellation of its respective cultural heritage. Further, the celebrations foster a number of emotional satisfactions and compensations. The participants can partake of otherwise submerged liminal identities that are not and cannot be parts of the quotidian. Just as Carnival celebrates an egalitarian erotic of bodily indulgence and illusory luxury of inclusion, football affirms an aggressive phallic identity and boundary of national and gender exclusion.

In the context of patriarchy, Brazilian women attempt to realize male criteria of beauty. The cultivation of the beautiful body is a major theme in Brazil. Rio alone has thousands of gyms and health clubs. Breast enhancement or reduction is one of Brazil's most common medical procedures. But the butt is equally valued; the Brazilian *thonga* may well be the smallest bathing suit in the world. Yet as Carnival creates an antistructure of ludic equality that empowers women and gives them erotic agency, the aesthetic of Carnival valorizes female sexuality in relatively egalitarian mass festivals, symbolized by scanty erotic dress and fully exposed breasts. Some feminists would argue that this partial nudity objectifies women, but in the context of the sexual culture of Brazil it is more of an inversion and celebration of the permissible collective eros of Carnival and a repudiation of male standards that realizes agency and empowers women (Parker 1991). Female modesty and reserve typical of everyday life in the home wane as exhibitionism and desire become "normal" aspects of doing Carnival. For a few days, women take charge of their own sexuality and express the submerged side of the Virgin not only as male fantasy but for their own pleasure. The desiring woman, the angel whore who flaunts her erotic body, now takes center stage in the streets, the parades, and the ballrooms. "The naked body is one that moves, revealing its reproductive potentialities . . . the body cries out for its complement, for its 'other' always alluding to the sexual act, that most essential form of the confusion and ambiguity of the grotesque when two bodies are transformed into one. . . . The naked, seductive women mark the transformation of public space into one big house" (DaMatta 1990, 106).

Doing Carnival can be seen as a cultural game with rules of time, space, conduct, and successful outcomes. But it is also a site of desires fulfilled. These are closely intertwined; both come out of the social conditions of subordination. Carnival creates realms that allow emotions and experiences apart from the typical; as a *festa popular*, it values life over death, joy over sadness, poor over rich. Carnival is an intersubjectively shared framework for the ritual performance of a social life that dramatizes both real and fantasied identities that elsewhere are negated. It is a respite from the fears, woes, and anxieties of "normal" lives.

Carnival is a time of spontaneous community in which the *blocos*, samba schools, or tribes can most openly express ties as neighbors, relatives, or colleagues (DaMatta 1990). Carnival provides moments of community, recognition, and dignity that are little found in the daily lives of the impoverished. It is a realm where the poor can realize "microspheres of empowerment," where the janitor may be a great dancer, the maid a fine singer, and the factory worker a songwriter-musician. Brazilians leave aside their hierarchical, repressive society to live more freely and individually. Indeed, in the context of Carnival we can now understand sexuality and aggression, not as Freudian motives, but as realms of selfhood and expressions of agency. One could suggest that Carnival is so intrinsic to most Brazilians because, given the structuring of everyday life around gross inequalities of wealth, race, and gender, it is a momentary release from the not so hidden injuries of class.

Carnival is primarily a public festival of the poor (povos) from the shantytowns (favelas) teeming with the unemployed and those who work in low-wage jobs—especially in hotel, restaurant, and domestic services that cater to the affluent. Indeed, though Brazil has the greatest inequality in Latin America, most of the festival takes place in the streets and the intermingling of classes is quite typical. Yet Brazil being a highly stratified society, there also are a number of private celebrations that are highly homogeneous by color and class. Thus, the balls and festivals of the yacht clubs and country clubs and swimming clubs may rival the festival of the streets and stadiums in passion and excitement; moreover, class segregation ensures that even anonymous sexual encounters occur within class boundaries—and these boundaries are highly racialized. Yet Carnival is produced by the people of the favelas, samba schools, carnival associations, and blocos. It is a festival without elite owners. Carnival is a time of ironic inversions and reversals of the "normal" hierarchies; the poor can experience luxury, they can dress in fantasied splendor and for a moment be dukes and ladies, rogues, and villains, men can dress as women, women as men, and drag queens can publicly flaunt their regalia. Indeed, cross-dressing is widespread. The patriarchal legacy of the colonial era, as it intersected with the race and gender systems, created a sharp duality between men and women; the master had several slave mistresses and concubines, and the passive wife/mother was the eternal virgin. But during Carnival, women in a patriarchal society can be assertive, the virgin of the house can become the whore of the street. Spouses criticize each other and everyone criticizes the government. The entrudo (an aggressive provocation, a common expression of frivolity) becomes a ritualized form of empowerment of subordinates who gain symbolic equality by throwing cornstarch, water, confetti, or mud on one another and on superiors.

Elaborate dress, costumes, and masks that may be erotic, grotesque, or satirical are essential aspects of Carnival. The costume is a conjunction of domains, a synthesis of people, their roles, and who or what they would like to be. The costumes, especially of women and drag queens, often combine whimsy with eroticism. Women in skimpy or highly revealing clothing are rarely aggressively approached; the otherwise *machoa* men appear timid. Whereas Carnival is licentious, it does not give license to assault. Whether erotic, grotesque, or absurd, the party clothes or the fantastic costumes (*fantasosias*) of the samba parade are sites of inversion or reversal of what are usually separate domains. Beings, roles, and categories that are typically separated are brought together; thief and cop, prostitute and lady of the house, transvestite and *machoa* all dance together (DaMatta 1991).

The unpleasant, perilous consequences of warehousing bad emotions can be avoided by means of expulsion (*desabafo*), a controlled release of internal pressures that can be realized in many ways—including by drinking, dancing, shouting, and relatively open displays of aggressive and sexual impulses. Thus, Carnival constitutes the healthful, equiliberating *desabafo* that, "like a restorative ritual, at once signals a problem and resolves it" (Linger 1992, 23). In this way, doing Carnival repairs the self and provides a degree of recognition and in turn dignity, honor, and power to those who otherwise have so little.

But on the other side of Brazil's structural inequality are the indignities and degradations that subalterns experience in their dealing with superiors (e.g., gross economic inequalities, rituals of subordination and deference, neglect of one's welfare by the state). Poor people receive brutal treatment by state authorities—including paramilitary death squads that sometimes kill poor youths. *Briga*, a disposition for aggressive displays to defend honor that often do lead to injury and murder, is an expression of violent *desabafar* that signifies the smothered resentments and frustrations. Yet such emotions can be revealed within the limits permitted by Carnival without danger of rupturing cordial interactions and the social order (Linger 1992).

Self-esteem derives crucially from one's position on the social ladder, however differently those ladders have been built; *briga* is fueled by the usually suppressed bitter emotional residues of hierarchy and domination in Brazil. Such resentments accumulate more heavily in society's lower reaches, because socially and politically incapacitated individuals suffer most the arbitrary exercise of power. What becomes valued when living within such a system, not as something necessarily "good," but as a premoral affirmation of the self, is the ability to withstand impositions by others and, conversely, to impose one's will on them. Much of such negative energy can be released in Carnival, which makes it one of the central moments of Brazilian identity. Thus, Carnival, *briga*, and *desabafo* compose a tightly integrated cluster. Carnival and *briga* signify, respectively, "good" *desabafo* and "bad" *desabafo* (ibid., 239).

Carnival celebrates the sensual, if not sexual, body in a society of patriarchal values. Many, often most, of the floats in the samba parades feature bare-breasted women. There are highly codified rules governing a "parade" of the song, dances, and costumes and if, when, and where the bare-breasted *mulatas* appear. Moreover, the relaxed sexuality takes place in beaches, alleys, alcoves; Carnival is not a sex orgy in the streets. Extremely revealing clothing is typical, but this is more a celebration of the aesthetics of femininity and female empowerment than a prurient voyeurism or exhibitionism. What is more salient is that egalitarian sexuality, in a masked form, is part and parcel of the festival. The streets and beaches become meeting grounds for all kinds of lovers, straight and gay, black and white, rich and poor; liaisons occur between strangers who wear masks and, often, little more. To the normal world of work, Carnival is play; to the hierarchy of gender, there is an equality of desire because females can initiate eroticism as equals. To the norms of restraint, indulgence is the rule. In the liminal polysemic antistructures of ironic inversion and sensual indulgence, a good time is had by all. Whatever the status of "contagion" in contemporary social movement theory, all who view and participate in Carnival become swept up in its music, passion, and excitement.

In contrast to the sensuous female body of Carnival, the ideal football body is a hyperreal male warrior who dons armor to join a legacy of warriors now instantiated as teammates fighting to control territory. These differences can be seen as the bare breast versus the armored shoulder, a difference between eroticism, connection, and Dionysian sensuality in contrast to competition, aggression, and Dionysian violence. Warriors with big shoulders are juxtaposed against slight women. It may not be coincidental that battering of wives or partners rises in Super Bowl season. The shoulder motion that throws the ball mimics the use of the club, battle-ax, sword, or spear. In modern armies the shoulder supports the rifle and rocket launcher, and in football it throws the "bomb" or "missile." The football player moves from civilian to warrior as he dons his helmet, massive padded shoulders, and extensive body armor—icons of masculinity that exaggerate male angularity and musculature (Oriard 1993). As such, the football player joins with the legacy of the centurian, gladiator, armored knight, or samurai, seeking control and mastery in violent combat on the field of battle.

Football is a realm where masculine independence reigns, female dependency and passivity are elided, the phallus is affirmed, and male solidarity is sustained. Thus, while football celebrates the aggressive arm-shoulder, players and fans have an ambivalent obsession with breasts. The protruding breast is an obvious visual marker of bodily difference, and the hypermasculinity of football needs the woman's breast to mark difference in order to affirm itself. The objectified breast affirms the superiority of the phallus. The larger the breast the greater the visual difference between real men and real women. The castrated woman can never be a true and equal buddy who bonds through violent territorial games, but she does serve as the perpetual antifetish whose very existence as a curvy castrata celebrates the superiority of penis power (Irigaray 1985). Thus, most of the choreography for cheerleaders can be seen as ways to either bounce breasts, raise short skirts, or preferably both at once. Pom-poms can be taken as symbolic exaggerated breasts to be viewed and cheered as modes of defining and affirming hypermasculinity. Breasts are objects of a male gaze that empowers the voyeur through visual domination. The concern with the breast is not for warmth, nurturance, intimacy, or relationship. More so than most societies, the United States frustrates community, attachment, and dependency and thus abhors those who embody these qualities—for example, women and traditional peoples, who become objects worthy of violence and whose existence alone is cause for anger. The woman is not a person but a pastiche of breasts and orifices to be penetrated, dominated, and denigrated, thereby dramatizing masculinity as superior.

Just as Roland Barthes saw wrestling as an allegory of good versus evil, American football can be seen as an ideologically constructed group of disciplined, instrumental warriors working together to compete over property against a similar group to score a victory. Sports in consumer capitalist societies are both an economic enterprise and an ideological mirror of the system. In most of our lives, there are few clear winners and losers in the short term; in sports, there are clear winners at the end of each game. In this sense, football is an alternative realm of male territorial competitive violence that stands in dialectical opposition to the quotidian of corporate life where violence is neutralized. Thus football is more than an athletic competition; it also is a boundary-maintaining male subculture that mythically glorifies hypermasculine identities as warrior-heroes who do bodily violence. Although identities are created by culture, for the person, identity performances are impelled by desire. Football, for players, managers, owners, and of course fans, is not understood abstractly as a cultural ritual, but as the occasion for "real men" to get together and express who they truly are.

In the United States' traditional gender stereotypes, masculine power stands above and against feminine passivity. Although football celebrates phallic aggressive masculinity, it is an anti(hetero)erotic practice. Indeed, as a cultural fiction that re-creates the psychological dynamics of war, football is the struggle of two male teams for the exlusive possession of the phallus. It reiterates the boundaries of the homosocial community by defining sexual differences based on victors and vanquished, winners and losers. And whereas the defense attempts to sack the quarterback and strip the ball, the quarterback attempts to penetrate the defense through the use of his surrogates—the ball carriers and receivers. When the defense is successful in either stopping the offense's drive or in forcing a fumble of the ball/phallus, the siege undergoes a transformation. The offense becomes the defense (ball-less) and the defense is now the offense in possession of the ball/phallus. Although the defense is in the more vulnerable position, ascribed in sexual difference to the female, the defensive players attempt to undo this disadvantage by acting with even greater aggression, trying to do to the other team's offense what has already been done to their own. But whereas war frequently illustrates the loss of the phallus, even literally by death in the most horrifying ways, football spares the spectator the unpleasant reality of war even while simulating its primary emotions in the safer spectacle of sports. The teams with their totemic emblems (uniforms, mascots, names) enact rituals of solidarity that draw in the spectators and bring all together to affirm an inclusive group identity of warrior males or their cheering consorts. Communities of pride and dignity are created in (observing) violent combat that cements male bonds through misogynist denigrations of women and the conversion of the enemy into "pussies." Whatever else, football affirms that men are not the women they fear and desire (McBride 1995, 164).

Football as a spectator sport has become a basis for relaxed, easy communication between males, be they bosses and workers or salesclerks and customers, so that even total strangers can relate to each other through it. In the mundane quotidian of de-skilled work in impersonal organizations, knowledge of sports and discussions in "sportuguese" demonstrate shared "stocks of knowledge" and individual expertise that become realms of sociality and recognition. Sports knowledge has become a central trope of identity for real men that differentiates them from women, children, and what Vice President Spiro Agnew called "effete intellectuals." Indeed, the "Super Bowl party" now ranks close to Thanksgiving as the most important secular ritual. Typically, males gather around the television set and bond through the consumption of intoxicants and the exchange of "sports talk" laden with frequent obscenities and a sexual imagery of phallic power and domination by penetration and degradation. If present, females, aka "football widows," dutifully serve beer and food and embody the excluded subaltern Other whose breasts, castration, and supplication forever bar her from the mysterium of the phallus, save by being penetrated.

Just as football first emerged as a celebration of a threatened masculinity, the Super Bowl, a spectacular game dependent on television, began in the era that gave rise to feminism and more women moving into professional and managerial positions. Indeed, the growing popularity of football in recent years may in part be a response to the growth of the service sector and of emotional labor, and hence the growing feminization of the workplace in which workers with "denigrated genitals" *can* do and *do* men's work, often outperforming the males. But no matter how well men and women work together in the office, hospital, courtroom, or university, football remains a sport reserved for men that affirms phallic aggressive masculine identities. Although some women find male violence erotic and desire submission to the warrior, they will never fully bond with those whose identities are based on possession of the powerful, intrusive phallus. As a kind of compensation for men, the female Other can never enter the sacred temple of the phallus and delight in its rituals of violence.

Conclusion

The body is central to gendered identity, desire, and other expressions of selfhood. Identities are more than cultural narratives that become part of one's "internal" psychic organization. More, identities are performed in the many everyday presentations of self through which embodied actors negotiate daily life. But the orderly performance of that same quotidian requires that certain identities remain submerged—either through individual repression or through isolation to marginal sites. Thus, the structure creates antistructural, liminal sites where rituals allow the repressed to return in ways that serve to maintain stability through controlled violations. In this way, cultural celebrations can be seen as times and sites in which ritual performances mark the intersection of long-term cultural legacies and individual desires to impel identity performances that dramatize the power of the social. For a few moments, often denied desires may be realized and subjects allowed to find pleasures, even as a repressive social order is preserved.

Carnival in Brazil and the Super Bowl in the United States exemplify cultural rituals that celebrate distinctly different expressions of bodily based identities. Although both were rooted in feudal Christianity and the European colonialization of the New World, with the Reformation there was a rift and growing bifurcation between the ascetic Protestantism of entrepreneurial North America and the hedonist Catholicism of neofeudal Brazil that flourished in the multiracial land "without sin." The radically different histories and legacies of Brazil and the United States have led to substantially different cultural identities and different idioms for their (counter)expression—sensuality on the one hand, aggression on the other. The social and cultural legacies of the respective colonial periods shaped the subsequent postcolonial societies and now provide the respective contexts for ritualized articulations of collective identity. These two radically different expressions of the body and bodily desire both dramatize the power of the social and sustain solidarity by proclaiming continuity with the past and validating current distinctions. These rituals of identity are idealized moments when otherwise submerged aspects of the self can be celebrated, and hidden desires fulfilled.

But this antistructure, this liminal toleration for the forbidden, this "repressive desublimation," nonetheless sustains the dominant system. In this sense, Carnival and Super Bowl can be considered moments of hegemonic processes in which the identities realized in cultural consumption sustain relations of rule. Yet each celebration is shaped by specific historical and material factors, and each has its own cultural logic. Brazil was a feudal colony long before it became an industrial power, and its inegalitarian social structure and cultural legacies have endured. Carnival is a Dionysian moment of compensatory liminality for the poor that repudiates the dominant culture and celebrates an alternative egalitarian erotic that comes from "the people" who are the entrusted caretakers and producers of the event. Carnival is a symbolic revolt, a joyous expression of outrage against injustice by the weak and scorned who have been degraded by the powerful, but it is *not* an overthrow of the structure of inequality per se (DaMatta 1991). It provides a kind of ritual or safety-valve irony of the established order, not a "mastered irony" in the creation of a new order and new values (Brown 1989). The rules of erotic propriety, modesty, gender relations, sobriety, and deference are suspended as the millions of "poor" can become "rich" for four days. But at the end of Carnival, the poor look forward not to social change, but to next year's Carnival. Thus Carnival, while repudiating cultural norms, serves to secure the structures of social and political power that ensure that Carnival takes place, and continues to be needed, rather than to foster a just society.

By contrast, if Carnival is a festival of the poor, football, though a legacy of economic elites, has become a symbol of both middle-class status and American national identity. Football is a celebratory ritual that seeks to affirm in spectacular forms the dominant culture and its mythical heroes who enact its exemplary identity performances in phallic aggressive simulations of war. In spectatorship, the otherwise restrained and sedate docile bodies of fans can, through projective identification, bond with other warriors in the safety of a stadium or living room. Just as Carnival allows the expression of a submerged egalitarian erotic, football affirms hypermasculine identites and male bonding through ritualized aggression.

Let me conclude with a note on the carnivalization of the world of global capitalism. One of the defining features of the current age has been the transition of the economy from the production of goods toward the production of information and sign values expressed in rituals of consumption. Although carnival was once part of traditional folk culture, its essential moment, ludic indulgence of the bodily, has been recovered by advertising and has now been appropriated by late capital as part of the universalization of commodified spectacles. The lure of the carnival, a place for otherwise submerged desires and identities, has been renewed in the form of commodified simulations of carnival. More specifically, promises of "forbidden pleasures" have become an integral feature of mass marketing. Consumerism now depends on the production and diffusion of carnivalesque "dreamworlds," fantastic realms that promise and often provide more pleasurable moments of bodily gratification than does the constraining rationalized quotidian. Consumption, as a site of otherwise denied pleasures, freedom, agency, and *jouissance*, serves to sustain late-capitalist society. Carnival is now globally diffused as consumerism that not only provides emotionally gratifying identities in the new liminal spaces of capitalism but, at the same time, has become the legitimating ideology of that system. But as this same capitalist system produces ever more inequality, we see not only a resurgence of neofeudalism, but also the carnivalization of the modern world, which, like its earlier incarnations, promises Dionysian pleasures to sustain its growing inequality.

References

Bakhtin, Mikhail. 1968. *Rabelais and His World.* Cambridge: MIT Press.
Bloch, Ernst. 1986. *The Principle of Hope.* Oxford: Blackwell.
Brown, Richard Harvey. 1989. *A Poetic for Sociology: Toward a Logic of Discovery for the Human Sciences.* Chicago: University of Chicago Press.
Cummings, Ronald. 1972. "The Superbowl Society." In *Heroes of Popular Culture,* ed. Ray B.

Browne, Marshall Fishwick, and Michael Marsden. Bowling Green: Bowling Green State University Press.

DaMatta, Roberto. 1991. *Carnivals, Rogues and Heros*. Notre Dame, Ind.: University of Notre Dame Press.

———. 1995. "For an Anthropology of the Brazilian Tradition." In *The Brazilian Puzzle: Culture on the Borderlands of the Western World*, ed. David J. Hess and Roberto DaMatta. New York: Columbia University Press.

Durkheim, Emile. 1965. *The Elementary Forms of Religious Life*. New York: Free Press.

Dworkin, Shari Lee, and Faye Linda Wachs. 2001. "Size Matters: Male Body Panic and the Commodification of Masculinity in Mainstream Health and Fitness Magazines." Paper presented to the American Sociological Association, Anaheim, Calif. August 16–19.

Elias, Norbert. 1978. *The Civilizing Process: Sociogenetic and Psychogenetic Investigations*, vol. 1, *The History of Manners*. Oxford: Basil Blackwell.

Freyre, Gilberto. 1986 [1936]. *The Masters and the Slaves (Casa-Grande and Senzala): A Study in the Development of Brazilian Civilization*. New York: Alfred A. Knopf.

Geertz, Clifford. 1973. *The Interpretation of Cultures: Selected Essays*. New York: Basic Books.

Grosz, Elizabeth A. 1994. *Volatile Bodies: Toward a Corporeal Feminism*. Bloomington: Indiana University Press.

Hess, David J., and Roberto A. DaMatta, eds. 1995. *The Brazilian Puzzle: Culture on the Borderlands of the Western World*. New York: Columbia University Press.

Hochschild, Arlie. 1983. *The Managed Heart: Commercialization of Human Feeling*. Berkeley: University of California Press.

Irigaray, Luce. 1985. *Speculum of the Other Woman*. Trans. Gillian C. Gill. Ithaca, N.Y.: Cornell University Press.

Langman, Lauren. 1998. "Identity, Hegemony and Social Reproduction." In *Current Perspectives in Social Theory*. Greenwich, Conn.: JAI Press.

———. 1992. "From Pathos to Panic: American Character Meets the Future." In *Critical Theory Now*, ed. Phillip Wexler. London: Falmer. 86–116.

Linger, Daniel. 1992. *Dangerous Encounters*. Stanford, Calif.: Stanford University Press.

McBride, James. 1995. *War, Battering and Other Sports*. Atlantic Highlands, N.J.: Humanities Press.

Messner, M. A. 1998. "Sports and Male Domination: The Female Athlete as Contested Ideological Terrain." *Sociology of Sport Journal* 5 (197–211).

Oriard, Micheal. 1993. *Reading Football*. Chapel Hill: University of North Carolina Press.

Parker, Robert. 1991. *Bodies, Pleasures and Passions: Sexual Culture in Contemporary Brazil*. Boston: Beacon Press.

Rapping, Elayne. 1987. *The Looking Glass World of Nonfiction TV*. Boston: South End Press.

Schwartz, Dona. 1998. *Contesting the Superbowl*. London: Routledge.

Turner, Victor. 1969. *The Ritual Process: Structure and Anti-Structure*. Chicago: Aldine Press.

Warner, Lloyd. 1959. *The Living and the Dead: A Study of the Symbolic Life of Americans*. New Haven: Yale University Press.

Timothy W. Luke

5

From Body Politics to Body Shops:

Power, Subjectivity, and the Body

in an Era of Global Capitalism

An Opening

As the focus of power and locus of subjectivity in our world markets, the psyche and physique always are being built. No bodies issue forth on their own without the mediations of intentional action and disciplined interpretation in both the body politic and the body shop. Much of global capitalism's politics and economics pivots upon these mediations, and no critical ontography of the present can ignore the history of practices behind the built being of the body.

Bodies are built in the body politic and body shop, not only by design, but also by accident. As Foucault put it, "truth or being do not lie at the root of what we know and what we are, but the exteriority of accidents" (1977, 146). Returning to the scene of those accidents leads to the body today, and testimonies from key witnesses, such as Thomas Hobbes or Adam Smith, need to be considered again more closely. Something has been missed, even though it never has been missing, in the bodybuilding routines of global capitalism. This analysis, then, joins Tierney (1993) by critically rereading technology in society, in order to investigate how the body, as psyche and physique, mediates the machinic force of states (the body politic) and markets (the body shop). Thus, I examine, much like

Gramsci's "Americanism and Fordism" (1971, 272–318), how vast social forces, such as capital, technics, science, and markets, become embedded in the psychophysical nexus of individual human bodies so thoroughly that machinic performances become close to instinctual operations.

One view of the many accidents "that gave birth to those things that continue to exist and be of value for us" (Foucault 1977, 146) can be found in contemporary celebrations of the forces for bodybuilding in today's world marketplace. William Greider, for example, asks us to

> Imagine a wondrous new machine, strong and supple, a machine that reaps as it destroys. It is huge and mobile, something like the machines of modern agriculture but vastly more complicated and powerful. Think of this awesome machine running over open terrain and ignoring familiar boundaries. It plows across fields and fencerows with a fierce momentum that is exhilarating to behold and also frightening. As it goes, the machine throws off enormous mows of wealth and bounty while it leaves behind great furrows of wreckage.
>
> Now imagine that there are skillful hands on board, but no one is at the wheel. In fact, this machine has no wheel nor any internal governor to control the speed and direction. It is sustained by its own forward motion, guided mainly by its own appetites. And it is accelerating. . . . The metaphor is imperfect, but it offers a simplified way to visualize what is dauntingly complex and abstract and impossibly diffuse—the drama of a free-running economic system that is reordering the world. . . . Everything seems new and strange. Nothing seems certain. (1996, 11)

Greider's metaphorical inscription of global capitalism as "a wondrous new machine" anchors his anxieties about its implications for our everyday life: it is running faster, while getting closer to some unknown abyss, entirely out of control. More important, he concludes: "Before the machine can be understood, one must first be able to see it" (ibid., 12).

We might be able to see this wondrous new machine, and thereby understand it, by looking at its operations over several centuries. Ready or not, the capitalist world has been being made into one world by its manic logic of commodification for half a millennium, but it is neither seen nor understood in all of its entirety. Under this horizon, Lyotard's vision of performativity can help interpret this wondrous new machine and its manic logic. Today, "the State and/or company must abandon the idealist and humanist narratives of legitimation in order to justify the new goal: in the discourse of today's financial backers of research, the only credible goal is power. Scientists, technicians, and instruments are purchased not to find truth, but to augment power" (Lyotard 1984, 46).

In their own odd fashion, Hobbes and Smith anticipate how the manic performativity of capitalism has been coevolving with the body politic's compulsive logic of sovereignty. Like Hobbes's, then, this analysis of body shops and body politics sets down its "own reading orderly, and perspicuously" of a bodybuilding material world in which one can read what it takes "to govern a whole nation," and for which everyone "must read in himself, not this or that particular man; but mankind . . . for this kind of doctrine admitteth no other demonstration" (Hobbes 1962, 20). And, like Smith, this analysis of the built body traces out its own account of "the productive powers of labor, and the order, according to which its produce is naturally distributed among the different ranks and conditions of men in the society" (Smith 1987, 105). The new resource-body of contemporary bioengineering as well as the techno-body of bodybuilding machines, such as Nordic Track, will be used as examples. These body forms will be reviewed here, even though their final forms remain obscured in the unfinalized empiricities of modernity. The interoperations of body politics and body shops manifest themselves in "machinations," or the fusion of technics with people in nations as social formations.

The social machines of the market, the technical machines of production, and the disciplinary machines of the state rarely are seen with the clarity that Greider expresses. His fears center on how world capitalism affects individual nations; yet, individual nations are more than those people who are born together, occupy a certain territory, share a language, or create a culture. They also invent and import machinic systems, which constitute a collective of acts and artifacts that create shared understandings and practices among their users. These "machinations," or machinic national communities, are in some sense artificial contrivances, or *Leviathan*-like entities, of artificial men made by men and women as artificers in states and markets. Some machinations work through broad transnational formations, like telephony, the World Wide Web, or fast-food outlets, while others manifest their operations more narrowly, like medicinal techniques, steel industries, or space programs.

John Stuart Mill nicely sums up the sense of collective action and common culture created by machinational sentiments:

> Our knowledge of the properties and laws of physical objects shows no
> sign of approaching its ultimate boundaries: it is advancing more rapidly,
> and in a greater number of directions at once, than in any previous age

or generation, and affording such frequent glimpses of unexplored fields beyond, as to justify the belief that our acquaintance with nature is still almost in infancy. This increasing physical knowledge is now, too, more rapidly than at any former period, converted, by practical ingenuity, into physical power. The most marvelous of modern inventions, one which realizes the imaginary feats of the magician, not metaphorically but literally the electro-magnetic telegraph sprang into existence but a few years after the establishment of the scientific theory which it realizes and exemplifies. Lastly, the manual part of these scientific operations is now never wanting to the intellectual: there is no difficulty in finding or forming, in a sufficient number of the working hands of the community, the skill requisite for executing the most delicate processes of the application of science to practical uses. From this union of conditions, it is impossible not to look forward to a vast multiplication and long succession of contrivances for economizing labour and increasing its product; and to an ever wider diffusion of the use and benefit of these contrivances. (Mill 1909, 696–97)

This union of conditions, of course, is also a condition of union: the (con)fusion of men and machines is what enables certain nations to be (re)born(e) by using their machinic marvels. Physical knowledge and power are channeled by practical ingenuity into machinational movements, or "a vast multiplication and long succession of contrivances for economizing labour and increasing its produce."

Time and space, sex and power, work and knowledge, even the market and the state are not natural givens; they are, instead, names given to historical constructs "in which the stimulation of bodies, the intensification of pleasures, the incitement to discourse, the formation of special knowledges, the strengthening of controls and resistances, are linked to one another" (Foucault 1978, 105–6) in the bodybuilding regime of global capitalism. Their psychophysical nexus in human beings is where body shops overlap with bodies politic, and this fusion of operational agendas in everyday life merits further investigation. Ultimately, this investigation of the body and bodybuilding dynamics is an exercise in "deep technology," which, in turn, explores the "onto-political" assumptions (Connolly 1992) underpinning modern nation-states and markets.

Modernity and the Body

Bruno Latour claims that modernity has nothing to do with the invention of humanism, the emergence of the sciences, the secularization of society, or the mechanization of the world. Instead, the unprecedented power and uncommon originality of modernity in his ontographies come from the conjoined generation of new Nature/Society/God constructs in an onto-graphic series of checked-and-balanced pairings between transcendence and immanence. Simultaneously, those who are modernizing or modernized can believe that

> They have not made Nature; they make Society; they make Nature; they have not made Society; they have not made either, God has made every-thing; God has made nothing; they have made everything. . . . By playing three times in a row on the same alienation between transcendence and immanence, we moderns can mobilize Nature, objectify the social, and feel the spiritual presence of God, even while firmly maintaining that Nature escapes us, that Society is our own work, and that God no longer inter-venes. (Latour 1993, 34)

Accepting these constitutional principles permits the proliferation of hy-brid collectives, or "the association of humans and nonhumans" (ibid., 4). Hybrids are the fabric of our lives, those good things corporations bring to life, or where science and technology get down to business, even while they deny the very existence of these mediated possibilities in conven-tional Enlightenment fables about live human subjects dominating dead nonhuman objects through science and technology. "The essential point of this modern Constitution," Latour maintains, "is that it renders the work of mediation that assembles hybrids invisible, unthinkable, unrepresent-able" (ibid., 34).

Modernization, as Latour frames it, runs on two sets of ontographic practices: *translation*, which "creates mixtures between entirely new types of beings, hybrids of nature and culture"; and *purification*, which denies the mixtures of translation as it "creates two entirely different ones: that of human beings on the one hand; that of nonhumans on the other" (ibid., 10–11). As long as everything and everyone treats these practices as separate and distinct, then we can think and be "modern." Translation builds networks of quasi subjects/quasi objects between "a natural world that has always been there, a society with predictable and stable interests and stakes, and a discourse that is independent of both reference and so-ciety" (ibid., 11). An effective analysis of modernity, then, must confront the "quasification" processes of making hybrids, because clearly "objects are not the shapeless recreatables of social categories neither the 'hard' ones nor the 'soft' ones. . . . Society is neither that strong nor that weak; objects are neither that weak nor that strong. . . . Quasi-objects are much more social, much more fabricated, much more collective than the 'hard' parts of nature, but they are in no way the arbitrary receptacles of a full-fledged society" (ibid., 55). Objects in motion within Hobbes's geometric universe and subjects motivated by Smith's trucking self-service cannot be understood fully as discrete objects or autonomous subjects, because these subjects make objects and the objects help define subjects. Without seeing how these quasifications underlie the purifications of discourse and disclose their translations in actions, one will miss the processes of bodybuilding.

Because of the wondrous new machine of global capitalism, as Donna Haraway claims, "the boundary between science fiction and social reality" has become, in many ways and at most times, "an optical illusion" (1991, 148), as Latour's quasifications indicate. As the boundaries dividing fact and fiction waffle and warp, a new life-form enters our time and space. This is the cyborg, or hybridized organisms that (con)fuse man and organism, animal and apparatus, physical matter and nonphysical information in new quasified forms of agency and structure. However, we must recognize how the cyborg materializes, and enters our time and space, in part, out of things creating a new order that makes "thoroughly ambiguous the difference between natural and artificial, mind and body, self-developing and externally designed, and many other distinctions that used to apply to organisms and machines" (ibid., 152). As she contemplates quasification in Nature/Society/Divinity, Haraway argues, "we are all chimeras, theorized and fabricated hybrids of machine and organism; in short, we are cyborgs. The cyborg is our ontology; it gives us our politics" (ibid., 150).

Because the setting of these shifts is so expansive, we also must accept Jameson's (1992, 418) assignment "to name the system" at work in the wondrous new machine, and thereby begin "systematizing something that is resolutely unsystematic, and historicizing something that is resolutely ahistorical." We may not yet understand the historicity or systematicity of global capitalism, but its cyborganizing power over the body clearly does reshape space, reconstitute power, and rediagram territoriality in new configurations through deep technology.

An Ontography of Bodies: Hobbes and Smith

Much of what ordinarily is accepted as modernity boils down to naturalizing the artificial action of quasi-subjective technical practices and beliefs through new quasi-objective rhetorics of mechanization, mobilization, and metrification. Freeing bodies to move, capturing the work of bodies in motion, or measuring mobility and mechanism all preoccupy anyone who is modern, particularly anyone interested in how this mobility and mechanism add to economic production and political power. None express the fascination of these psychophysical preoccupations better than Thomas Hobbes and Adam Smith.

At some point in modern time and space, whether one credits Galileo or Newton, "the Universe," or at least the purifying metaphors by which our universes are shaped, changed from a static great chain of being into a grand dynamic mechanism of becoming. Spiritual salvation gained by keeping a rightful position within this static world, and, in turn, was eclipsed by the corporeal cultivation of wants attained through proper motion in this worldly dynamism. Amid these epistemic shifts, Hobbes proclaims that "the end of science is the demonstration of the causes and generations of things" (1994, 206), and his logical demonstrations confirm the drift of his greater ontological vision:

> The *Universe*, that is the whole mass of all things that are, is Corporeal, that is to say, Body; and hath the dimensions of Magnitude, namely, Length, Breadth and Depth: also every part of Body, is likewise Body, and hath the like dimensions; and consequently every part of the Universe, is Body; and that which is not Body, is no part of the Universe: and because the Universe is all, that which is no part of it is nothing; and consequently *no where.* (Ibid., xxv)

Corporeality, then, becomes a first principle. To suggest otherwise is to be "no where," and the more scholastic world picture of medieval utopia must be replaced by this mobilized/mechanized ontotopia. Its whereabouts, heretofores, or whatnots can be tracked back to "one universal cause, which is motion . . . and motion cannot be understood to have any other cause besides motion" (ibid., 197). Bodies are built out of that which is forever and always either in motion, "a constant relinquishing to one place, and acquiring of another" (ibid., xxvi) or "at rest in place, *place is that space which is possessed or filled adequately by some body*" (ibid., 197) and soon returning to motion *"the privation of one place, and the acquisition of another"* (ibid.). Applied science, in turn, is a "compositive" practice, using geometrical methods of analysis, through which "we enquire what motion begets such and such effects; as, what motion makes a straight, and what a circular, what motion thrusts/what draws, and by what way; what makes a thing which is seen or heard, to be seen or heard sometimes in one manner, sometimes in another" (ibid., 197–98).

Human life for Hobbes is constituted out of the motions by individual subjects to attain or accumulate objects of desire. "Felicity is a continual progress of the desire, from one object to another; the attainment of the former, being still the way to the latter" (Hobbes 1962, 80). Hobbes anchors everything in his vision of the body politics to one initial principle: "A general inclination of all mankind, a perpetual and restline desire for power after power, that ceases only in death" (ibid.). The social essence of *Leviathan* is contractarian arrangements between desiring agents to construct a civic macrostructure to manage the desires, power seeking, and appropriated spaces of individuals in motion. Hence, as Deleuze and Guattari (1983, 29) assert, "The truth of the matter is that social production is purely and simply desiring production under determinate conditions." Sovereign authority and market exchange in modern capitalism are mutually dependent conditional determinants that remediate desire as social production in body politics and body shops.

With regard to humans and society, there are no exceptions to this cosmic mechanism. Hobbes has everyone observe their particular and universal motions, tracing out how their lines, lengths, and points constitute effects on one another. Indeed, his political philosophy is but a study of bodies in motion, allowing us "to observe what proceeds from the addition, multiplication, subtraction, and division, of these motions, and what effects, what figures, and what properties they produce" (1994, 198). Much of this motion is work, or the labor needed for satisfying desire and avoiding a lack of satisfactions. In turn, as the frontispiece of *Leviathan* depicts, these bodies will ideally collaborate in their civic conventions so that all might work more effectively. This fixation on the body politic also permits all bodies in motion to be seen and heard in ways that create covenants. Yet, many other exchanges and agreements obviously are at play in the covenants of individuals in bodies politic, namely, the motions, figures, effects, and properties of buying and selling in the body shop, which Smith celebrates in the figure of markets.

Smith celebrates the market as liberation, as a structure and location in which all men and women in any nation are free to truck, barter, exchange, and trade as they see fit "one thing for another" in "a fair and deliberate exchange" (Smith 1987, 117–18). Yet Smith's enthusiasm must be balanced by his sense of markets as deliberate, as the practices and dislocations in which all men and women are forced to weigh, evaluate, price, and calculate the use of "most dissimilar geniuses" to one another by "the different produces of their respective talents" (ibid., 121). In the inert practices of labor's division in every particular nation, then, one perhaps can see how the division of labor articulates the workings of all "machinations."

The wondrous new machine of global capitalism is celebrated by

Adam Smith in 1776 in his epic account of how, first, market-ready bodies are built, and then how their motion is captured as desires reach equilibrium in the marketplace via the division of labor:

> Observe the accommodation of the most common artificer or day-labourer in a civilized and thriving country, and you will perceive that the number of people of whose industry a part, though but a small part, has been employed in procuring him this accommodation, exceeds all computation . . . if we examine, I say, all these things and consider what a variety of labour is employed about each of them, we shall be sensible that, without the assistance and co-operation of many thousands, the very meanest person in a civilized country could not be provided, even according to what we very falsely imagine the easy and simple manner in which he is commonly accommodated. (Ibid., 115–17)

Here the hybrids that assemble and energize the wondrous new machine of global capitalism can be appraised without resorting to occult qualities, even though many writers have been content to celebrate this work as "the magic of the marketplace." The mechanisms of Smith's market are the same bodies in motion as in the *Leviathan*; out of many workers come one work, and one work sustains many workers.

Haraway argues that "a cyborg world might be about lived social and bodily realities in which people are not afraid of the joint kinship with animals and machines, not afraid of permanently partial identities and contradictory standpoints" (1991, 154). The world's most potent and enduring cyborganization is the market: what else so continuously, thoroughly, and finally crafts hybrids of machine and organism—human/animal, human/plant, human/mineral, human/machine—as lived realities? What other world-changing fiction can melt all that is solid into thin air and then conjure, once more, solid abundance out of that same thin air? Creatures who live as commodity futures, develop as human capital, or produce as cash cows are already ambiguously natural and crafted. Market mediations with their episodic points of valorization are nothing but permanently partial identities and contradictory standpoints in which social and bodily realities are necessarily nothing more than cyborg mediations of quasified hybridity. Haraway confirms these tendencies, but she is not the first to wonder why "our machines are disturbingly lively, and we ourselves frighteningly inert" (ibid., 152). Even though Smith celebrates our coexistence together through "the toils of the different workmen employed in producing those different conveniences," the market's animation of apparently dead matter with dead labor troubled Sartre, Nietzsche, Marx, and Rousseau long before Haraway.

The market as a mechanistic device fuses its machinic generation of worth, or the cost of a man's power in use, as price within other people's judgments of his worth. Honoring with payment or dishonoring through nonpayment adorns opinions of worth with actions on worth, while, at the same time, capturing and channeling the commodified power marked by this price toward some predetermined end in work for more exchange. Man in the market machine makes what he is worth and he is, in turn, worth what he makes. The machine made by men in markets is powered by the use of present means to obtain future goods, and the machine is, at the same time, sustained as a good for the future to obtain the necessary means of the present. The market machine gives men their prices for commodified powers, but men also make markets in valuing their powers as commodities with prices. What was free becomes necessity. Markets as machines place their trade, traders, and trade goods in an environment of deliberately determined spaces, surrounding and surveying them with power. The discovery of this mode of maintaining markets provided the means to obtain apparent goods, to make knowledge productive, and to maintain informed awareness of the consequences of one affirmation to another, to support the voluntary actions of men in commonwealths.

Environments are not Nature as such, but the denatured condition of Creation constructed artificially and deliberately in machinic ensembles. When Nature is submitted to the colonizing practices of performativity, men move in states and markets within vast new fishing machines, farming machines, mining machines, timbering machines, ranching machines. Their materials and energies flow through transport machines and communication machines via men in motion to manufacturing machines, managing machines, military machines, as well as living machines, leisure machines, labor machines where men exchange.

A more basic interpretation of the market's pervasive deliberated practico-inertness gives an apt reading of "the environment." The mobile ranges, where cyborgs roam amid markets, is not purely Nature or exclusively Culture, but rather it is their hybrid, denaturalized, quasi-subjective and quasi-objective englobing state: the environment. The "environment," as a concept, first enters English usage from Old French, and originally it was a term describing strategic action. An environment was the state of being produced by a verb: "to environ," and environing as a verb means to encircle, encompass, envelope, or enclose. It suggests the physical activity of surrounding, circumscribing, or ringing around something. Its various uses even imply stationing guards around, thronging with hostile intent, or standing watch over some person or place. To environ a place or a person is to beset, beleaguer, or besiege it.

Given this sense of "the environment," the practical effects of markets can now be read in a more useful fashion. Any market, in a sense, is already a rational set of maneuvers by men in motion, aiming to delimit some expanse in nature in a policing envelope of encircling deliberate control that can promote more exchange and work. Such an expanse might be a locale, a biome, a planet as biospherical space, or some city, any region, the global economy in technospherical territory. Within the enclosing rings of administrative, engineering, or scientific expertise, one finds well-intentioned marketeers, who stand watch over such surroundings in stationary sieges of men and women going through the motions of manipulation, domination, commodification. Thus enveloped, these environed spaces can meet new performative ends impelled by economic markets and state directives.

This renders moot all myths of redemption by returning to Nature, or recapturing organic wholeness. "No longer structured," Haraway continues, "by the polarity of public and private, the cyborg defines a technological polis based on a revolution of social relations in the *oikos*, the household. Nature and culture are reworked; the one can no longer be the resource for the appropriation or incorporation by the other" (1991, 151). Cyborgs confuse boundaries and make it futile to seek those responsible for their construction, because most existing ontological boundaries no longer divide what we think they do into that which we believe exists. Cyborgs and hybrids proliferate everywhere. They are "we." Nature is "environment," society is quasified collectives, and culture is cyborganizing principles. Bodybuilding builds psyches and physiques within these environments out of already decided necessities that once were always undecided freedoms. Here, in turn, are the origins of machinations.

Machination Building: Deep Technology

Behind the *dominium* of sovereignty over nations, something else burbles out and up from the *imperium* of performativity: the machination. Machinations represent quasified machinic collectives colonizing spaces with the hybrid agencies created by artificial contrivances. Every machinational movement reshapes deliberately the random motion of bodies in social space as an intentional assemblage of technical parts capable of transmitting forces, motions, and energies from one to another in some predetermined matter capable of serving some desired end. Machines, as Lewis Mumford asserts, are "combinations of resistant bodies arranged so that the forces of nature can be put to work through determinant motions" (1963, 9). A machination, then, might develop its complex coexistence of subject/object in the agencies and structures of some human society, whose history, economy, and culture are reshaped by the ends and means used "for converting energy, for performing work, for enlarging the mechanical or sensory capacities of the human body, or for reducing to a measurable order and regularity the processes of life" (ibid., 9–10).

Like Arne Naess's vision of deep ecology (1989), in which deep ecological thinking and acting are cast as nonanthrocentric paths to alternative ecological ethics, a "deep technology" accepts, for the purposes of this investigation, Latour's hybrids and Haraway's cyborgs as another sort of nonanthrocentric action in "the environment." Deep-ecological Self-Realization, at the same time, might point suggestively toward some intriguing forms of diversity, complexity, and symbiosis in nature, the self-realizing hybrid beings brought forth by coevolving technologies, biologies, and ecologies in the body politic and body shop as these collaborate in new symbiotic structures called "machinations."

One can establish the morphology of the machine by concomitantly mapping the morphology of the society it serves and by seeing this "techno-system" as ecosystem (Ihde 1990, 3). Machines, following David Nye, are not simply an assemblage of technologies with particular functions; they are integral parts of a social world that shapes, and in turn is shaped by, these larger life-worlds. "Each technology is an extension of human lives: someone makes it, someone owns it, some oppose it, many use it, and all interpret it" (Nye 1990, ix), but, at the same time, each human life rests on interpretations of any given mechanical extension as it makes someone, it possesses someone, it resists someone, and it translates someone within its determinant motions and design. Machination building in a Hobbesian and Smithian register turns anarchic motion in the universe toward polyarchic labors in the commonwealth, repositioning men from a state of nature into "technologically sublime" (Nye 1996) states of preternature that fuse the society with technics. Beginning with Hobbes's scientific visions of mechanization,

> The meandering energies of men, which had flowed over in meadow and garden, had crept into grotto and cave, during the Renascence, were turned by invention into a confined head of water above a turbine: they could sparkle and ripple and cool and revive and delight no more: they were har-

nessed for a more narrow and definite purpose: to move wheels and multiply society's capacity for work. To live was to work: *what other life indeed do machines know?* Faith had at last found a new object, not the moving of mountains, but the moving of engines and machines. Power: the application of power to motion, and the application of motion to production, and of production to money-making, and so the further increase of power—this was the worthiest object that a mechanical habit of mind and a mechanic mode of action put before men. As every one recognizes, a thousand salutary instruments came out of the new mechanics; but in origin from the seventeenth century on the machine served as a substitute religion and a vital religion does not need the justification of mere utility. . . . The impersonal procedure of science, the hard-headed contrivances of mechanics, the rational calculus of the utilitarians—these interests captured emotion, all the more because the golden paradise of financial success lay beyond. (Mumford 1963, 53–54)

A machination is organized by people carried along and created by machinic systems, but also machinic systems are contoured around people.

Often, the ultimate significance and motive force behind many national values, behaviors, or goals might be explained better by examining the dynamics of machinations. As the broad sweep of Mumford's vision in *Technics and Civilization* shows, machinations of many stripes are always contriving new plans and machinations for the psychophysical nexus of the societies and technics in bodies to employ the motion of people in the work of machines to serve power, profit, and prestige.

Bodybuilding Today in the Body Shop

The body shops in present-day global markets are continuously shaping the body, subjectivity, and power. Two characteristic forms of body development, however, are particularly interesting at this juncture: the resource-body of bioengineering and the techno-body of machinic bodybuilding. Here the wondrous new machine of global exchange imprints its current expectations of total commodification and relentless performativity upon the substance and forms of the body. In these forms, the corporeal connections of global capitalism lead out to Hobbes's bodies in motion and back into Smith's bodies for exchange. Their body ontographies focus power/knowledge on bodies of subjects, and subjects also willingly mobilize their bodies to accept such energies and ideas. Bodybuilding does not escape history; instead, it too is made and managed by historically contingent relations of culture, economy, government, and technology.

The resource-body in many ways simply brings full circle the beast-machine theories of Descartes in which animals are reduced to organic automata by systemic machine metaphors. Human agents in the animal kingdom are cast as machinic composites; their physiological subsystems are no less than machinic orderings for quasified energy accumulation, matter processing, or information storage. Like machines, they too can be disassembled and retooled at will to suit human purposes. Once animals are subjected to such resourceful thinking, human beings can be treated in a like manner. During the Enlightenment, La Mettrie articulated a key premise of modern life: "all scientists and competent judges" soon confess that "men . . . are, at bottom only animals and perpendicularly crawling machines" (cited in Kimbrell 1993, 242). The clockwork logics of disciplinary technics in modern armies, prisons, schools, hospitals, bureaucracies, and cities fragment human bodies into flesh to be trained, energies to be directed, mentalities to be normalized, and matter to be managed (Foucault 1978). Here is the machination-building project. The technics of modernity take the material human bodies, apply engineering principles, and extract energy, work, and intelligence to sustain the body politic and stock the body shop. In these reductions, much is perhaps lost, but more also can be gained as new ways of living beyond natural limits, on "artificial life support," extend and enhance the lives of those who otherwise would be lost.

What were once the sacred signs and substances of human corporeality are reified, instrumentalized, and commodified in the ideal resource-body of present-day global capitalism. Like the earth itself becoming reprocessed as environment, the human body is ramped up into "a free-running economic system that is reordering the world . . . Everything seems new and strange. Nothing seems certain" (Greider 1996, 11). The once essential signs of higher ends—such as the sacredness of blood, semen, eggs, bone marrow, skin, bone, and human embryos—have been priced as means in strange new circuits of supply and demand, along with babies, disease, bodies, organs, and fetal tissues. Of course, many ironies also develop here as such markets make life itself possible for many who would otherwise surely die or be harmed if such resources did not exist. Yet, something is also lost. These substances and essences no longer are sources of pristine transcendent meaning, but become material resources for a mundane trade in the body shops of bioengineered life. Just as the techno-body represents the mediations of performativity serving optimal form and function, the resource-body is the mediation of performativity responding to more diverse form and function with technified therapies, genetic reengineering, artificial cures, or spare parts to sustain its clients' power and subjectivity.

Plainly, the body shop here works upon the mobilization of others' self-interest to serve one's own interest, because, as Smith asserts, "it is not from the benevolence of the butcher, the brewer, or the baker that we expect our dinner, but from their regard of their own interest. We address ourselves, not to their humanity but to their self-love, and never talk to them of our own necessities but of their advantages" (1987, 119). The original trucking disposition, that gave rise to bowers and flechers trading bows and arrows to herdsmen and hunters for cattle and venison, now promotes the renting of wombs, harvesting of fetal nerve cells, purchase of blood plasma, and consignment of spare kidneys. The body shop can stock in common the common stocks of human bodies where—to rephrase Smith—every man/woman may purchase whatever of the produce of the other men's/women's bodies he has occasion for (ibid., 121).

Bioengineering life along the lines of a resource-body brings the uneasy gains of cyborganization out into full relief. No heart transplant recipient lives without transmutating into a cyborganism: a person plus a cadaver's cardiac muscle, a surgeon's skills, a drug company's antirejection drugs, an insurance firm's funding, and a managed care network's outpatient support system lives now as a quasified (re)source-body. Every test-tube baby has multiple machinic maters/paters, some have anonymous bought-and-paid-for genitors/genitrixes, and a few have fathers and mothers who were genetically counseled to extinguish less perfect embryonic siblings. The diabetic human hemophiliac, whose human growth factor, clotting factors, or insulin dosages are generated by transgenic sheep or pigs turned into bioreactors by drug companies, cannot escape his or her obvious cyborganization in resource-body management and design. A resource-body can, of course, be a comparatively underresourced body, but the disciplinary systems of technified power/knowledge do permit subjects to acquire greater resourcefulness with right expenditures of time, money, and effort. Whether it is gene therapy, bionic prostheses, artificial insemination, or plastic surgery, the resource-body serves as one more site for more rational resource management on an individual and collective level.

The techno-body, however, is perhaps an even more developed articulation of the resource-body than the transplant cyborgs. The ideal techno-body of transnational capital is imagined, following Greider's vision of the world marketplace, as "a wondrous new machine, strong and supple . . . huge and mobile . . . but vastly more complicated and powerful . . . ignoring familiar boundaries . . . with a fierce momentum that is exhilarating to behold and also frightening" (1996, 11). In a specialized workout apparatus, such as those from Nordic Track, machines are made to remanufacture men and women as machines by redirecting their animal energies into technified resistances. With a sufficient investment of time and energy, body forms and appearances morph into lean and mean android machines. The body shop sells the ideals of the techno-body, vends the apparatuses required to rebuild the body in these idealized mechanomorphic forms, and then markets specialized service sites, such as fitness centers or home gyms, where the ideals and apparatuses can be combined with time and energy to realize these techno-embodiments. With the percentage of all men in the United States "disenchanted" with their body image doubling to 34 percent since the late 1970s, and the percentage of American women with "body image dissatisfaction" rising to 38 percent, exercise machine makers are selling nearly a billion dollars a year in equipment (Kimbrell 1993, 249).

There are many mediations of the performative techno-body at play today, but some of the most expressive ones can be found in the Nordic Track exercise apparatus. The practices of the Nordic workout represent all of the body shop's most fundamental ends: efficiency, strength, wellness, flexibility, and tone all coaligned in the performative codes of fitness. Indeed, Nordic Track's corporate Web site (Nordic Track 1997) even goes so far as to package these attributes for corporations as "BeneFitness programs" to tune machinic capital and its human agents "in house" at work. Thus, one buys into fitness as a "BeneFit" from, but clearly also for, corporate capital.

The Nordic Track/Nordic Flex workout machines are the perfect working out of techno-body fitness rhetorics. Technified bodies are energized, compacted, hardened, trained, and perfected in alloys of animal/apparatus. The marriage of women/men to the machines is a superior design well suited to perfect the subject's body, workout, time, program, form, equipment, and investment in achieving "the well-defined, attractive body—washboard abs, shapelier legs, stronger, firmer arms and leaner hips" (ibid.). The bodies built by contemporary corporate capital are well represented by these machinic bodybuilders and bodybuilding humans flexing together in fitness on the Nordic Track.

The pursuit of such "programmed benefitness" on the Nordic Track in personal and business fitness programs is legitimated entirely as a performative maneuver. Corporations that promote fit employees soon are able to reduce health-care costs, reduce absenteeism, improve productivity and morale, reduce employee turnover, and enhance company planning of health and other benefits. Fitness is the product of these fitness products as Nordic Track shapes/sells/makes/manages/works/wins the body in its corner of the body shop. Hobbes may be correct, nothing else accentuates or adorns the "worthiness" of a man, or "the particular power, or ability for that, whereof he is said to be worthy: which . . . is usually named fitness, or *aptitude*" (1962, 79). The greatest benefit of Nordic Track fitness is the cultivation of many more performative aptitudes.

The operational logic of techno-bodies, then, finds a very definite expression in the values and practices of Nordic Track's mechanized physical fitness. Fitness regimes, for the functioning of human beings, incarcerate machinic expectations in the corporal discipline of corporeal conditioning. Exercise machines, workout tapes, and fitness centers all operate as performative packaging systems that discuss, discipline, and develop human bodies into packaged meat products with the valued attributes of performativity: fitness, strength, tightness, speed, wellness, survivability, leanness, or flexibility. Like the responsive flexible economies of scope that demand fitness to survive, bodybuilding machinery provides a Nordic Track to survival, first, by working out the body to be more responsive and flexible, and then rebuilding it around more performative embodiments in the machinic workout.

Nordic Track is a very special body shop devoted to selling the performative incarceration of discipline by/for/in/with machinic apparatuses. Nordic Track creates, and then re-creates, the Nordic Tracker as a Nordic Tracked performer. Voted by experts as "the most effective aerobic exercise," a machinic ski-simulator as machine environment surpasses natural outside skiing sites on its chrome steel crags and rubber runs. Customized, quiet, smooth, integrated, adaptable, comfortable, advanced: a Nordic Track envelopes bodybuilding subjects, placing them on the Nordic track to machinic superhumanhood. The *Übermenschismus* of flexible specialization gains corporealization on the apparatus: "Wider skis. More relaxed and in control. Firmer, sculpted arms. Trimmer, well-toned stomach and hips. Sleek, well-defined legs" (Nordic Track 1997). All of these indicators embody the new, unibody design of transnational postfordist exchange, featuring ironically a "quality base" and "more stability." In these devices, Hobbes's *meum* and *teum* become completely (con)fused, as Nordic Track claims, because "streamlining our parts" (global capital flows), makes "streamlining yours" (local corporeal bodies) "easier than ever" (ibid.).

Every Nordic Track ProPlus apparatus envelopes individual somatic space in the machinic discipline of social performativity. Capital can transfer its properties to an individual property owner, whose natural rights to property now are mobilized in the preternatural machinic rights of capital's propriety. It is the state-of-the-art technology best suited to support the art of the state with technology. Chronometrification, marketization, textualization, acceleration, and mechanization as states of machination-alized consciousness all are embedded in the quasifying designs of the ProPlus "5-Window Motivational Electronic Workout." This cybernetic monitor surveys and digitally displays such effects at this disciplinary site with multiple tracks of Nordic attainment: "calories burned, speed, distance (both miles and kilometers per hour), and elapsed time to chart progress and stay motivated" (ibid.). Programs of "BeneFitness" program the performative cyborg: at-a-glance readouts give you the focus you need to attain your fitness and reach your ultimate goals.

The man/machine fusion of Nordic Track, and other exercise machine apparatuses, positions the person as the driveshaft, mainspring, or animal motor of the device, pitting resistance, mass, or repetition against muscle to refine, enlarge, and harden the body (Rabinbach 1990). These stationary engines, in turn, reengineer human bodies at these stations of exertion in exhausting regimens of fitness to attain machinic ideals of performativity: shining, well-oiled, hairless, high-definition, hard surfaces. The machines work out the exercise, and the exercises work in the machines, ignoring the boundaries between soft fleshy tissue and hard disciplined stuff. The Nordic Track, like many other machines, leads ultimately, if the use of it is successful and sustained, to serious cyborganization: buns of steel, six-pack abs, biceps of iron.

The diffuse motion of ordinary organicity, then, is captured, concentrated, and contained in "the total-body workout," which reworks the totality outside of the body inside the ProPlus person/apparatus (con)fusion. Each streamlines the other's parts. Careful design takes the unproductive motions of walking, subjects them to an inventive plan, and fabricates a machinic contrivance to work out their forces and flows with a quasi-subjective/quasi-objective workout apparatus. Aerobic apparatuses—skiers, walker treadmills, weight machines—ensure performative outcomes for their users as streamlined parts in the machines streamline parts of their users.

Here the body shop exploits full tilt the uncommon powers of machinic multitude, producing uncommon peace, defense, and benefit for the Nordic Track man/woman over and above less Aryanized cyborg subjectivities. As capital outsources its constituent components, sheds unnecessary production lines and corporate divisions, tightens and flattens its hierarchies, cultivates its fiscal fitness, strengthens its balance sheets, and gains greater total productivity, so too does its performativity resonate through each of its apparatuses. Its discipline rebounds and recharges every body that in-sources new equipment to lose weight, shape and tone, refit cardiovascular efficiency, improve overall health, and strengthen muscle.

Body Politic/Body Shop: A Closing

How men, women, and machines interoperate in bodybuilding is a deci-sively important factor for securing profit, maintaining employment, exert-ing control, attaining benefits, keeping wealth, and sustaining technology in any particular place. Machinations, which are made by women and men coevolving with machines, can be subnationally divided or transnation-ally integrated, but most of them still coincide with national communities. Hence, world handbooks of political development or annual surveys of modernization still count the number of automobiles, televisions, radios, toilets, or computers per thousand people to gauge how machinationally advanced some territory or people has become in the body shops of the wondrous new machine. Within almost every nation, there are colonizing traces of machinations in which machinic forces are constantly recontriving human actions and practices in many determinate ways. Machinations work best in strong nations, but no nation becomes very strong without success-ful, stabilized, and secure machinational movements coursing through it.

Nevertheless, no machination is entirely unified, homogeneous, or set-tled within the confines of its various bodybuilding, subject-forming, and power-generating practices. Specific cutting-edge technologies always coexist with what might be regarded as established, orthodox, outmoded, obsolete, or outclassed techniques that still claim users, create loyalties, or capture supporters. Consequently, prior attachments to bicycles, type-writers, handsaws, or windmills will coexist with the willing acceptance of jet aircraft, personal computers, laser tools, and nuclear reactors. The bodybuilding of machinational movements creates a heterogeneous popu-lation of diverse cyborg subjects, who often all cling more closely to some machinic fusions rather than others. Counting the aggregate numbers of various technical apparatuses, appliances, or agencies therefore never begins to capture the real contours of cyborganization within any nation because it ignores the inconsistencies, complexities, and unpredictabilities of how hybridization actually works for any group of human subjects as they build their psyches and physiques out of a vast panoply of techni-cal alternatives. Coexistence with machines as the path to human power, knowledge, and progress becomes the common faith of those with access to the body shop and its machinationalist communities. Knowledge of the properties and laws of physical objects advances the power exerted by human subjects over their property and by their laws: this is the essence of quasification, cyborganization, hybridization.

Power—in bodies politic and body shops—marks new disciplinary interventions, coordinating events, discourses, practices, and values at the individual bodily level from the plane of larger collective consciousness and action. Within the confines of machinational movements, power works as "merely one element among others, working to incite, reinforce, control, monitor, optimize, and organize the forces under it: a power bent on generating forces, making them grow, and ordering them, rather than one dedicated to impeding them, making them submit, or destroying them" (Foucault 1978, 136). Machinationalist formations survey, manage, and channel a nation's body behaviors, coproducing them within their psychophysical regimens for knowing, controlling, and administering both individuals and collectives. The force fields of machinations have an immediate direct hold over the body: "They invest it, mark it, train it, torture it, force it to carry out tasks, to perform ceremonies, to emit signs. This political investment of the body is bound, in accordance with complex reciprocal relations, with its economic use; it is largely as a force of production that the body is invested with relations of power and domination" (Foucault 1977, 25–26). The machine retrains psyche and physique, but they, in turn, animate the mechanism. This psychophysical nexus is the crux of deep technology—technocentric systems that operate in symbiosis with organic life. Hence, people make machines, and machines remake people until nothing exists but popular mechanics in a machinic populace.

Very little of everyday life can be lived any day without technified support systems such as radio, TV, corporate foods, modern medicine, telephones, and automobiles: modernization really is in most meaningful ways cyborganization rather than modernity making. Therefore, any instance of successful modernization and development seemingly represents the fulfillment of a machination-building movement. Thus, modern economies and societies are integrated, centered, or homogeneous machinations in addition to being settled stable nations. Without this mass hybridization of people with performativity in technics, the main thrust of "modernization and development" does not happen. Still, machines are not simply a neutral system of technical objects carrying out uniform universal changes planned by subjects. They always are a key ontographic part of the larger culture, polity, and society.

The complete chaos being experienced in the Russian nation after the loss of the Soviet-style machination typifies these inconsistencies and interruptions. The new body shop of global capitalism has just opened in the Russian Federation, and its challenges are immense simply because so many Soviet machinationals survive. The Stalinist psychophysical nexus has yet to succumb to the Smithian variant. The machinational sense of time, mechanicity, speed, textuality, and exchange inherited from the Soviet era may take as many decades to change as they took to construct. Technification, scientization, mechanization, instrumentalization are not abstract, inexorable forces sweeping one certain swath of change through the history of all nations, but rather they are social shifts that vary considerably from one time and place to the next in the mostly accidental emergence of machinations. Furthermore, as Stalinist industrialization shows, not every path to machinationalization is the Nordic Track. Machinic bodybuilding sometimes involves personal construction, but, as the abysmal levels of personal and public health in the Russian case show, it also can mean considerable personal destruction as one machination crumbles and another organizes itself out of a new body politic and body shop.

To conclude this ontopolitical exploration, machinations unify national movements toward the collaboration, identification, or cooperation of human agents with machinic apparatuses. In these big technical systems, human bodies are politicized and shopped in the uneasy regimen of building bodies. Such invisible networks of influence must not be ignored, even though the purification discourses of modernity, as Latour maintains, try to efface the translations of human agency and machine structure into such hybrid networks. After what the social contract theorists present as a visible constitution of human government from organic realms in the State of Nature, there is always this less visible generation of synthetic environments within the State of Society.

Note

This essay was presented first at the annual meeting of the American Political Science Association, August 28–31, 1997, and parts from it appear in *Current Perspectives in Social Theory* 19 (1999).

References

Adas, Michael. 1989. *Machines as the Measure of Men: Science, Technology, and Ideologies of Western Dominance.* Ithaca: Cornell University Press.

Connolly, William. 1992. "The Irony of Interpretation." In *The Politics of Irony: Essays in Self-Betrayal,* ed. Daniel W. Conway and John E. Seery. New York: Routledge.

Deleuze, Gilles, and Félix Guattari. 1983. *Anti-Oepidus: Capitalism and Schizophrenia.* Trans.

Robert Hurley, Mark Seem, and Helen R. Lane. Minneapolis: University of Minnesota Press.

Foucault, Michel. 1977. *Language, Counter-Memory, Practice: Selected Essays and Interviews*. Ed. Donald F. Bouchard. Ithaca, N.Y.: Cornell University Press.

———. 1978. *History of Sexuality*, vol. 1, *An Introduction*. Trans. Robert Hurley. New York: Vintage Books.

———. 1991. "Governmentality." In *The Foucault Effect: Studies in Governmentality*, ed. Graham Burchell, Colin Gordon, and Peter Miller. Chicago: University of Chicago Press.

Gramsci, Antonio. 1971. *Selections from the Prison Notebooks*. New York: International Publishers.

Greider, William. 1996. *One World, Ready or Not: The Manic Logic of Global Capitalism*. New York: Simon and Schuster.

Haraway, Donna. 1991. *Simians, Cyborgs and Women: The Reinvention of Nature*. New York: Routledge.

Harvey, David. 1989. *The Condition of Postmodernity*. Oxford: Blackwell.

Hobbes, Thomas. 1962. *Leviathan: Or the Matter, Forme and Power of a Commonwealth Ecclesiastical and Civil*. New York: Crowell-Collier.

———. 1994. *Human Nature and De Corpore Politico*. Oxford: Oxford University Press.

Ihde, Don. 1990. *Technology and the Lifeworld: From Garden to Earth*. Bloomington: Indiana University Press.

Jameson, Fredric. 1992. *Postmodernism, or, the Cultural Logic of Late Capitalism*. Durham, N.C.: Duke University Press.

Kern, Stephen. 1983. *The Culture of Time and Space: 1880–1918*. Cambridge: Harvard University Press.

Kimbrell, Andrew. 1993. *The Human Body Shop: The Engineering and Marketing of Life*. New York: HarperCollins.

Latour, Bruno. 1993. *We Have Never Been Modern*. London: Harvester Wheatsleaf.

Lyotard, Jean-François. 1984. *The Postmodern Condition: A Report on Knowledge*. Trans. Geoff Bennington and Brian Massumi. Minneapolis: University of Minnesota Press.

Mill, John Stuart. 1909. *Principles of Political Economy*. London: Longmans, Green and Company.

Mumford, Lewis. 1963. *Technics and Civilization*. New York: Harcourt Brace Jovanovich.

———. 1986. *The Lewis Mumford Reader*. Ed. Donald Miller. New York: Pantheon Books.

Naess, Arne. 1989. *Ecology, Community and Lifestyle: Outline of an Ecosophy*. Trans. and rev. David Rothenberg. Cambridge: Cambridge University Press.

Nordic Track. 1997. (http://www.nordictrack.com).

Nye, David E. 1990. *Electrifying America: Social Meanings of a New Technology*. Cambridge: MIT Press.

———. 1996. *The Technological Sublime*. Cambridge: MIT Press.

Rabinbach, Anson. 1990. *The Human Motor: Energy, Fatigue, and the Origins of Modernity*. New York: Basic Books.

Smith, Adam. 1987. *The Wealth of Nations*. London: Penguin.

Tierney, Thomas F. 1993. *The Value of Convenience: A Genealogy of Technical Culture*. Albany: State University of New York Press.

6

Reinventing the Liberal Self:

Talk Shows as Moral Discourse

In ways that reminisced one of the nineteenth-century campaigns against popular recreations (Malcomson 1973), talk shows have come to the spotlight of public debate and seem to have elicited cultural anxieties about their alleged thirst for sensationalism and shock value. This essay addresses a simple set of questions, obfuscated by the public outrage that is ritually poured over talk shows: What are talk shows *about*? What makes them such a popular cultural form? What segment of the contemporary imagination do they capture? Conversely, what makes talk shows the target for the elite outcry that they cheapen and threaten cultural values? I argue that the cultural appeal of and assault on talk shows may be explained by their cultural *meaning*. In particular, the question that begs to be clarified is why talk shows conflate aspects of the private sphere with the claims and modes of argumentation of the public sphere. Why is the private sphere of such interest to talk shows and why is it telescoped with the codes and modes of argumentation of the public sphere? I argue that talk shows mimic the increasingly contentious character of everyday life and simulate an "ideal speech situation" to cope with the increasingly embattled life-world.

Several studies have examined the meaning of talk shows from the standpoint of the audience's response (Livingstone and Lunt 1994; Raviv,

Raviv, and Yunovitz 1989) or from the standpoint of the people participating in them (Priest and Dominick 1994; Mehl 1996). In this essay, my
intent is to elucidate the social and cultural context on which talk shows
draw and comment, and more specifically to understand the cultural codes
of talk shows in the context of the social transformations that the family
and identity have undergone in recent decades (Giddens 1991; Beck and
Gernsheim-Beck 1995; Beck, Giddens, and Lash 1994; Coontz 1992).
Thus my approach to talk shows is akin to that of the cultural historian
in that I view talk shows as a text that has something to tell us about the
social relations of the contemporary United States. The structure, format,
and conventions of talk shows make sense to their viewers because they
address, in the form of metaphors and morality plays, particular social
conditions from which they derive their meaning and of which they in
turn help make sense. In this respect, when sociologists of contemporary
culture inquire about the cultural, social, and intellectual context from
which symbolic forms emerge, they do not fare much better than historians of the remote past. Like them, sociologists are left with the unnerving
question of trying to explicate symbolic forms from prevailing social conditions and symbolic frameworks (Hunt 1989).

Struggling with that very question, historian Carolyn Marvin (1988)
has persuasively suggested that new media (or media genres) are implicit
discourses about social place and about the distance separating social
groups. As I argue, talk shows displace and twist, symbolically, (some of)
the symbolic boundaries that have been central to the distinction and
distance between the different social spaces (e.g., private–public; home–
work) and groups (e.g., parents–children; men–women; homosexuals–
heterosexuals) that made up the nineteenth-century model of liberalism.
The very format and conventions of talk shows have altered the ways in
which "distance" between various social spheres and social groups was
constructed, and this transformation in turn points to the changing social
order of late modernity. As Paul Willis put it, "TV watching is, at least
in part, about facilitating a dialectic between representation and reality
as a general contribution to symbolic work and creativity" (1990, 36).
To retrieve the meanings of talk shows, I use an eclectic strategy by
bouncing the codes and conventions of talk shows against the backdrop
of contemporary political ideas, recent transformations of the family
(Coontz 1992), the role of psychology in everyday life (Giddens 1991),
and the transformations that modernity has brought to processes of identity formation (Giddens 1990, 1991). To use Gellner's words in his study
of psychoanalysis, my purpose here is to relate the central ideas of talk

shows with (some of) the "major social and intellectual changes of the time" (Gellner 1985, 5).

A Dramaturgic Approach to Talk Shows

My analysis of talk shows derives primarily from a dramaturgic and hermeneutic approach to culture. A dramaturgic approach to culture posits that culture is not simply in the "head" but is lived, embodied, and impersonated through symbols, stories, artifacts, and rituals that organize social reality into meaningful structures and make actors participate in a jointly and ongoingly created social world.[1] Culture, as Clifford Geertz has amply and convincingly suggested, is the intricate network of symbols and rituals through which we make sense of, cope with, and ruminate about the social conditions in which we are thrown. Through the cyclical performance of collective rituals of meaning (e.g., a national holiday, a parade, a sports event, news broadcast, national elections, a talk show), we participate in the social process of making sense of and interpreting our social environment *with* and *for* others. In this perspective, I will not inquire about the question of whether talk shows cripple or expand the scope of the public sphere. Although my interest includes the political metaphors that organize the meaning of talk shows, here I am only peripherally concerned with the role talk shows play in the public sphere and in the formation of a competent citizenry (for an excellent study on these questions, see Livingstone and Lunt 1994). Instead, I approach talk shows as *rituals* of meaning through which particular interpretations of the social world are deployed to explore symbolically the rules, scope, and limits of social relationships. For example, Elihu Katz and Daniel Dayan (1992) have argued that through televised media events, viewers explore the meaning of their loyalty to the social body and reaffirm their allegiance to the institutions of democracy and the authority of political leaders. The referential meaning of the media event (the "funeral," the "peace summit") is less important than the way in which it performs certain meanings, calls on us to reaffirm collective values and symbols, and mobilizes our very participation in the meaning it thereby enacts.

Like traditional folktales or myths, media texts are cultural maps that help actors make sense of and orient themselves in a social order that is historically constituted. To this end, the sociologist may, quite ironically, turn to the ways in which the tools of sociology and anthropology have been used by historians. For example, in a classical analysis of premodern folktales, Robert Darnton (1991) has argued that much of the plots and narrative motifs of premodern folktales can be readily explained by the demography and economy of premodern Europe (e.g., the frequency of stepparents can be readily explained by the high proportion of re-marriages owing to spouses' death; the frequent theme of magic tables filling themselves with delicious foods can be explained by the pervasive-ness of famines, and the prevalence of tricksters by the necessity to skirt feudal regulations). By incorporating into their narrative the actual social conditions in which peasants lived, these folktales *oriented* peasants' under-standing of the economic and social chaos surrounding them. Darnton's approach may seem naive but it offers what cultural sociologists may be in need of, namely, a parsimonious interpretative strategy to understand how texts evolve from and comment on particular historical contexts. By re-maining close to the surface meaning of the text and by inquiring into the ways in which such texts *reflected and reflected upon* social conditions, Darnton is able to find a shortcut from cultural to social structure, without collaps-ing the two together. By making readily visible and available for interpre-tation the harsh conditions of premodern life, these tales functioned like geographical maps, that is, helped orient peasants' interpretations of their social environment.[2] This "realist" approach to cultural texts will guide my symbolic analysis of talk shows. I will argue that talk shows are power-ful texts precisely because they comment on what has become the "hard conditions" of personal life for many in the late-modern era, and provide "moral maps" to orient oneself in such "hard conditions." Broadly, my ar-gument is that talk shows are a symbolic rumination about the "new and normal chaos" of personal relationships in the era of reflexive modernity (Beck and Gersheim-Beck 1995).

Precisely because I remain close to the *surface meaning* of talk shows, to their overt themes and to the relation they bear to social relations, I con-centrate on a theme somewhat neglected by many students of talk shows, namely, that of emotional intimacy and personal relationships. The ques-tion that is tackled by this essay is simply this: Why is the spectacle *of intimacy the dominant and obvious theme of talk shows?* I take emotions, intimacy, and personal relationships to be the central theme and distinctive feature of talk shows. Working from the hypothesis that the meaning of talk shows ought to be explicated *as closely as possible from their overt themes, format, and conventions,* I will argue that the very genre of talk shows is a cultural form through which the nature of selfhood and personal relationships in the late-modern era is discussed. In particular, talk shows articulate two interrogations pertaining to the profound transformations of selfhood and personal relationships in the contemporary era. One is the question of the *norms and principles according to which* we are to settle our conflicts with others. The second concerns the values and narratives that make up a *"good life"* in an era when moral discourse cannot be formulated in collective or foundational terms. In elucidating the way in which talk shows articulate these two cultural interrogations, I will make three arguments: (1) Contrary to the common view that talk shows revel in the bizarre and the deviant, I argue that they stage and dramatize *everyday life itself*, and more especially a self embattled in *everyday life*; (2) I further argue that, far from being sensationalist, the dramatization of emotions characteristic of talk shows stages, obliquely, the difficulty of the self in reconciling *"commitment"* and *individualism* (see Bellah 1985); (3) My final argument is that talk shows are a hybrid cultural construct, at once combining *a procedural model of debate with discussions of the "good life."* My ultimate argument is that such a hybrid construct indicates a transformation of "politics."

The following analysis is based on a sample of one hundred shows watched and taped from December 1994 to April 1995. Because the Oprah Winfrey show dominates the field, it has the largest share in the sample (sixty shows).[3] However, because my analysis aims to reveal broad, rather than specific, patterns of meaning, I will also occasionally refer to other talk shows such as *Montel Williams* and *Rolonda* (no longer being aired). Although each of these shows has its own style and audience segment, they use the same cultural format to address with varying degrees of seriousness the question of selfhood and personal relationships in the late-modern era.

The Moral World of Talk Shows

The demography of talk shows is clear: it is made of a high proportion of women, adolescents, members of ethnic minorities, and members of the working classes, thus making the genre a clearly populist one. Conspicuously underrepresented in talk shows is the highly successful white male—except when he occasionally assumes the position of expert. However, what sets talk shows apart from other such genres is the fact that talk shows twist and mock liberal practice of denunciation of wrongs and faith in rule-governed debates through an aesthetic of the carnivalesque (see Langman in this volume).

A CARNIVALESQUE GENRE

In more than one way, the onslaught on talk shows bears the familiar features of attacks against popular recreations: talk shows are indicted for betraying basic moral codes of truthfulness and moral propriety, for being "voyeuristic," "sensationalist," "sleazy," for encouraging stereotyping, and for debasing standards of debate and political consciousness (see, for example, Heaton and Wilson 1995). Here, as in many other segments of popular culture, the language of cultural value is intertwined with that of morality. To sociologists, such public debates are privileged moments because symbolic struggles make visible what is otherwise left implicit, namely, the boundaries structuring taste and morality (Bourdieu 1979; Ross 1989). In the following analysis, I suggest that talk shows are a particularly strong irritant of middle-class morality because they twist some of the basic tenets of liberalism and recast them into an aesthetic of the carnivalesque. The public staging of private biography through the mediation of the host, and more peripherally of the expert, constitutes the basic format of talk shows, and dubbing this format "sensationalist" leaves unaddressed the question of why the staging of private life in the argumentative format of talk shows is worthy of interest. The question that begs to be elucidated is this: What are the cultural assumptions that implicitly organize people's recriminations, accusations, confessions, justifications, reconciliations, and disputes within the stylized format of talk shows? What does the rule-governed verbal exchange between host, guests, experts, and an anonymous audience *mean*?

Talk shows purport to invert (or make fun of) a number of basic assumptions that are essential to the bourgeois and liberal ethos, and in that respect can be said to display a carnivalesque mockery of the spirit of seriousness of "official" bourgeois culture and an inversion of its dominant symbols (Bakhtin 1968; Zemon-Davies 1975). The first, and perhaps most obvious, tenet that is twisted and parodied by talk shows is the liberal distinction between private and public sphere. The public exposition of "family secrets," intimate relations, and hidden fantasies subverts from within the liberal creed that the public sphere concerns itself with matters of general, rather than particular or biographical, interest and that the domestic sphere must remain inviolably private. For example, the *Montel Williams* show stages the following scene: a couple is introduced to the public as having "problems"; the problem is defined by the woman as the fact that her husband is careless and thoughtless; her husband defends himself; the couple is subsequently taken to a waiting room in which a camera has been hidden; in the meantime, the host, Montel Williams, instructs the man through an electronic device hidden in the man's ear about gentlemanly ways to seek reconciliation with his wife. The viewer is then made the witness of the woman's rebuke of her husband's newfound courtly style.

The main tonality of the scene is not "voyeuristic" but rather comical and bawdy. In the bourgeois sensibility, peering through keyholes is "perverse," but talk shows' gaze is not voyeuristic because we witness people not in their bedroom but mimicking a bedroom scene of reconciliation; that is, we do not witness a refined pledge for reconciliation but a semicomical mockery of gentlemanly ways to court and reconcile with a woman. The bourgeois sanctity of the bedroom is desecrated by the comic spirit of popular culture rather than by a voyeuristic penetration of "hidden family secrets." Like the ritual of charivari, many domestic scenes of talk shows (especially in the *Montel Williams* show) are farcical rather than voyeuristic, because they parody and desecrate known symbols of privacy and exaggerate the pleasure of witnessing profanities, cursing, quarrels between husbands and wives. If, as John Fiske suggests (1987), television contains the spirit of carnival, combining laughter and degradation, then talk shows seem to offer the quintessential spirit of televised carnival, at once degrading and laughing at the holy privacy of the bedroom.

A second moral code infringed upon by this carnivalesque infringement of privacy is that of self-restraint, discipline, rationality, and self-control, especially with regard to the public sphere. The Kantian aesthetic of containment and purification, the bourgeois ethos of discipline, and the liberal imperative to debate rationally all place the public sphere under strict norms of emotional control, sobriety, and understatement. In contradistinction to this moral and aesthetic ethos, talk shows revel in the spectacle of emotional excess, interpersonal chaos, unruliness, and invective. Scholars have noticed the emphasis that talk shows put on emotions and subjectivity (Moehl 1996; Carbraugh 1994), usually interpreting it as an expression of a narcissistic cult of self. I would argue, however, that such excesses point to the popular aesthetic of carnival. Carnival, as has been abundantly remarked, is an event in which social energies are recoded as abundance, comical inversions of social hierarchies, and happy disorder. In carnival, chaos is organized by laughter and by the spectacle of the body. To take one example: in a *Montel Williams* show on "unruly adolescents" (e.g., teenagers who drop out of high school and claim they only like to dance and dress up), the guests come to the studio wearing flamboyant and extravagant clothes that celebrate a style that is an explicit mockery of middle-class accoutrements as signifiers of a self-controlled and productive body.[4] At the same time that it purports to explore and rebuke their unruliness, it clearly plays with a conscious manipulation of their flamboyance and style, thus placing the talk show in the popular genre of the "outrageous" and "bawdy." Talk shows, like carnival, are to be understood against the backdrop of a reigning ideology of productivity and self-control, which they recode into emotional excess and foregrounding of flamboyant bodies. However, in contradistinction to the traditional liminal rituals of carnival (which purport to invert the rules that make up everyday reality), the carnivalesque excess of talk shows is contained within a code of everyday life that seems to be fundamental in organizing selfhood and social relations.

EVERYDAY LIFE: THE PARAMOUNT REALITY OF TALK SHOWS

Television—particularly daytime television—is a notoriously parasocial medium (Horton and Wohl 1956; Livingstone 1990). It invites and solicits viewers in their daily lives and settings, and, if we believe the popularity of soap operas or television series such as *Thirty Something* or *Dallas*, television is particularly successful in inserting itself into the daily lives of viewers. Talk shows represent a deepening of the *parasocial aesthetic* that is the landmark of commercial television because their paramount reality is that of the daily informal conversation. In Northrop Frye's terms (1957), the mythopoetic theme of talk shows, their leading and organizing motive, is language, and more specifically the *daily informal conversation*. Conversations, as ethnomethodologists have pointed out (Garfinkel 1967), are the ways in which routine interactions are sustained and everyday life conducted. Talk shows organize the flow of conversations—natural discourse—within three main categories of discourse: the autobiographical stories of participants; the analytic and prescriptive speech of the expert and occasionally of an "experienced" layperson; and the "interrogative speech" of the host and the studio audience.

Although talk shows primarily stage the natural discourse of people with a civil identity, such a discourse does not use any recognizable pictorial, fictional, or journalistic code of realism. Rather, it is a purely self-referential genre: the talk is about the discursive reality talk shows themselves have created. The talk show is about the talk itself. Talk shows produce the very event they are reporting on, where the "event" is a *linguistic one*: the "confession," the "reconciliation," the "dispute" are speech acts that only point to themselves and not to an order of "truthfulness" or "reality" beyond themselves. The very structure of talk shows has the perlocutionary power of speech acts, which by the mere fact of their being pronounced, produce the reality they are talking about (Austin 1962). Talk shows are performative texts and more specifically perlocutionary speech acts, because they exist solely in virtue of the enunciations they ritually perform and because these acts of enunciation—confessions, reunion, confrontation, dispute—*are* in turn supposed to be the remedy to the very problems they raise. In other words the speech produced in talk shows is always contiguous with the hazy realm of everyday life from which it emerges and which it is supposed in turn to transform. Here is one among many examples of the ways in which talk shows directly lean on everyday life:

> This was a memorable show that we did this past year. I was struck by it because of the honesty of the guest that we had on concerned family members who'd gotten together and confronted the mother of two children. They felt she was allowing her children to continually overeat. The question became: How can you discipline your children about overeating when you have the same problem? *As a result of this show, the children are now on a weight-loss program and they're getting help.* (Oprah, "Fat Family Intervention," August 30, 1997; emphasis added)

Or another example picked almost by chance: "We're always on this show trying to get you to think about yourself and think about ways that you can change yourself if you don't like who you are. *Here's some questions you can ask yourself at home right now to get some insight into your own personality*" (Oprah, "Test Your Personality," June 14, 1994; emphasis added). In these two examples, the performative and therapeutic character of talk shows clearly leans on a more general ethos of self-help enacted in the space of everyday life par excellence, the home. Not only do talk shows address the myriad problems entrenched in the realm of daily life, but they proclaim a performative language that transforms everyday life in the very act of talking about it. In that respect, talk shows are a *therapeutic* genre, in which language has at once a referential (telling us something about the participants) and a therapeutic status (bringing about a change in participants' relations and states of mind.)

This implies that talk shows are not a "moral genre." Although they can and do smuggle in values, stereotypes, and morality plays, they are not committed to any single definition of reality or moral prescription. One show can denounce child abuse, while another will explore and try to understand why people engage in incestuous relations. One show can deal with the inability of men and women to be in "control of their lives," while another will address people who are unable to "just let go" and enjoy life. One show can deplore controlling and authoritative parents, yet another will lament the problem of "rebellious children." If one listens to the voices of talk shows, one hears only a cacophony of moral dilemmas rather than a fixed and predictable set of moral messages. Carbraugh has shown persuasively that beyond the cacophony of these messages, a clear discourse of selfhood on *Donahue* is articulated and that it is imbued with the discourse of rights, self-realization, and tolerance that are the hallmark of modern conceptions of the subject (Carbraugh 1994). Yet, I would argue that the most remarkable and distinctive feature of the ways in which talk shows encode the self is their insistence that the self is embattled in the microscopic struggles of everyday life. Beyond the multiplicity of voices, one meaning is insistently repeated—that *everyday life is of paramount importance to self and identity.*

If at the heart of the modernist imagination lies the image of a solitary entrepreneurial self achieving a great project of "liberation" or alternatively of "success," the core image of the individual of talk shows is an ironic counterpoint to the American dream. More often than not, the individual of talk shows offers a story of failure or pain and, contrary to the mythical figures of Robinson Crusoe or Horatio Alger, is hardly self-reliant or solitary. Talk-show participants are almost always people who struggle with the murky problems of identity, relations with others, abuse, self-control (or lack of it). Mothers, daughters, and their ongoing conflicts; women and their ex-fiancés; divorced couples fighting over child custody; women confronting their past lover who extorted money from them; people who have experienced emotional or sexual abuse; mothers who have been physically injured by their sons; people lacking self-assertion—all these themes have one thing in common: they are about the difficulty of monitoring the self in everyday life and of maintaining relations with others.

If traditional sensationalism is characterized by its publicizing of the shameful secrets of the rich and famous or of the aberrant conduct of ordinary people, talk shows are an exact counterpoint to this traditional form of sensationalism for, like various therapeutic discourses, they purport to address the hidden and tangled problems of *daily life.* In contrast to Freudian archetypal and somewhat grandiose master narratives of family rivalry, talk shows present ordinary conflicts of ordinary people living the myriad problems that make up ordinary lives. The appeal of talk shows resides precisely in the fact that they deal with the ordinary, mundane, and nitty-gritty of the quotidian and, as such, offer temporary and pragmatic truths congruent with the piecemeal and practical logic of everyday life. In contrast to psychoanalysis and therapy, which aim at formulating a "middle-range" narrative to make sense of one's biography, talk shows are organized around the ad hoc sharing of everyday events and the improved management of everyday life through pragmatic solutions to local problems. They address the question of how particular individuals should deal with and solve problems that are not general in scope but relate to ordinary challenges such as "losing weight"; "stopping being stingy"; "learning how to say 'no'"; or "getting out of an abusive relationship." To that extent, they emanate from a profound transformation of selfhood: as philosopher Charles Taylor (1989) and sociologist Anthony Giddens (1990, 1991) have suggested, modernity has shifted the locus of morality and selfhood to the domain of everyday life. Everyday life has become the site within which personal identity is articulated and different conceptions of the good elaborated.

The success of Oprah Winfrey can be explained by the fact that of all talk-show hosts, she has best known how to mix the attributes of a charismatic leader with the codes of the quotation. According to Max Weber, charismatic power, contrary to legal-rational authority, derives from the extraordinary powers of a person, such as endurance, will of strength, or dedication to the welfare of others (Weber 1958b). As he puts it: "Charisma knows only inner determination and inner restraint" (ibid., 246). Like Madonna, Oprah Winfrey has widely publicized her strength of will, hard work, versatile creativeness, and dedication to the causes of women and minorities. However, in contrast to the traditional models of charismatic celebrity, Winfrey has remained famous for having revealed in one of her early shows her own history of sexual abuse, thus turning herself into one of her "confessing subjects." She regularly divulges her difficulties in dieting successfully, her romantic hardships, her psychological anxieties, and the like. Using the confusion between backstage and frontstage that is the hallmark of talk shows, she has occasionally invited her life companion Stedman Graham to the studio and some of her "friends in real life" as participants. In the same way that the show purports to explore the guests' problems of everyday life, it is also continuous with Winfrey's own private life. She frequently begins a show by telling the audience where she spent the weekend, how thrilled she felt about meeting another celebrity, why she wears glasses and not her usual contact lenses, and so on. This in turn suggests that she is not simply another version of the American dream (or an Afro-American "token" of the American dream, as Cloud suggests [1996]), for she self-consciously de-fetishizes her own persona. When Oprah Winfrey tells us how scared she was when she received the Emmy or how difficult it was to lose weight, she is casting stardom and success into entirely new codes: stardom is constructed as being contiguous with rather than extraneous to the murky zone of the ordinary. Her widely publicized struggle against her weight taps into this juncture: her weight loss and physical exercise show her "strength of will," endurance, and sheer ambition; yet, by revealing the painful work to fashion her body, she also de-fetishizes what is otherwise the most revered fetish of media culture: the thin and flawless figure. Quite unlike other women stars such as Madonna, who seems to be a remote plastic image playing with mass-media icons and displaying pristine images of sheer power, Winfrey appears to us as some-one we have come to know intimately in the corners of our kitchen and who addresses us in our daily—rather than ceremonial or fantasy—identity. In cultural terms, she seems to *de-fetishize* the plastic persona and icons of star-dom by casting her exceptional commercial success as a therapeutic victory over the ordinary shortcomings of an ordinary life. Her construction of her self as a star is closely intertwined with the construction of a self em-battled in, but victorious over, the problems of everyday life. What Oprah Winfrey's persona suggests clearly is that it is one's life or biography itself that is self-made. What a "self-made" biography is and why it occupies such a prominent place in talk shows is what I will now examine.

TALK SHOWS AND THE DO-IT-YOURSELF BIOGRAPHY

The centrality of symbols of everyday life takes us far away from the divi-sion between public and private that is at the cornerstone of liberal public philosophy. For philosophers of bourgeois society, most notably Hegel, the public sphere is the realm of the exercise of reason. Family, emotions, and passions are residual categories, not to be reckoned with in the public sphere. Neo-Aristotelian philosopher Hannah Arendt goes as far as to call the domestic sphere a "shadowy realm of the interior" and contrasts it with an "agonistic" public sphere, the only site where debate and contention can legitimately take place. For her, the public sphere is the arena for competi-tion, struggle, and therefore the display of heroic virtues (Arendt 1959).

Undoubtedly, talk shows are an ironic counterpoint to Arendt's char-acterization of the private sphere as the "shadowy realm of the interior." Talk shows shed pomp and light on this shadowy realm, which turns out to be far from "dull" and "quiet"; instead, it is ridden with conflicts, resentment, treasons, and competition. Talk shows are a symbolic pol-lution of the "pure" categories of liberal political philosophy as reason, objectivity, neutrality, for they bring to the public sphere the spectacle of tears, heartbreaking reunions, diseased bodies, broken families, addic-tions, self-destructive behavior, uncontrollable drives, anger, revenge, il-licit lust—that is, categories that simply have no place in the "ideal public sphere" guided by critical reason (Ackerman 1980). And yet, I would like to suggest that we may miss what talk shows are about if we judge them by the standard of a modernist conception of social organization—neatly divided between private and public—with its conception of the subject as struggling for "formal rights" and "emancipation." I explain this through a concrete example.

In the *Rolonda* show, Rolonda (March 28, 1995) invites a middle-aged woman to recount a passionate and lustful affair that lasted three days. When asked to reveal the identity of the man, the woman discloses that he is none other than her son. After the first expression of outrage by the studio audience, the woman proceeds to clarify that up until their sexual affair, she had never met her biological son from whom she had been separated ever since he was born, when she herself was only sixteen years old. The moral judgment passed over the woman becomes even more qualified in the course of the show when an expert comes to the defense of this unlikely couple by claiming that scientific evidence suggests that genetic attraction between siblings is powerful, especially when they have not lived together and have not been able to form attachments in accord with the incest taboo. This psychologist reveals that he himself was an adopted child and further claims that if children placed in foster care sever contact with their biological parents, they run the risk of not developing the incest taboo and may fall prey to their genetic attraction to biological siblings.

This show manages to operate a tour de force of sorts by destabilizing the moral ground for holding the universal and deeply rooted incest taboo. By enabling the moral point of view to shift—from the self-justifications of the guests to the outrage of the audience to the so-called neutrality of the expert—the show destabilizes one's moral point of view and introduces an uncertainty about the meaning of motherhood: "What or who exactly is a mother?" This question is not raised from the standpoint of legal jurisdiction but from the *normative* angle by making the viewer's moral point of view *float*: For which mother—foster or biological—is the incest taboo most relevant? What is the meaning of biological affiliation? What are the ultimate justifications for a taboo when the institutional context (family) that lent its meaning is removed? And this leads to the broader question that is at the cornerstone of the format of talk shows: Who is right—the expert, the mother, or the outraged audience? Which norms should guide our moral opinions and decisions?

What starts as a rather dubious topic proves to be a glaring example of how talk shows raise the problem of the normative grounding of individuals' actions and of the increasing difficulties in defining such norms. Talk shows do not simply invert or subvert boundaries between the moral and the immoral, but rather incessantly engage in a *debate* about the contextual validity of such norms. The desecration of the boundary between "pure" and "impure," silence and talk, moral and immoral is achieved by engaging in a public discussion *about* such boundaries and by conjuring up the *reasons* people have for engaging in "immoral" or "deviant" actions. Even if the host and/or the public often act as the representatives of middle-class morality, the format of talk shows itself ends up *deconstructing* human relationships, in the very sense that Derrida has given to the word *deconstruction*: that is, by showing that their signified—their normative grounding—is empty, shifting, unstable. Talk shows suggest that our actions are now constantly shifting under a multiplicity of signifiers. Thus, in the show just mentioned, the most important meaning of the show is that the referent for the cultural sign "motherhood" is at once *constructed and slipping away from its conventional meaning*. By making it possible for people to raise validity claims about their behavior and to be held accountable through discussion and argumentation, talk shows implicitly endorse the idea that *all norms, classifications, and definitions are negotiable,* and that we can question and discuss their foundations in terms of individuals' reasons for holding such choices. No norm is holy, and no norm can be taken for granted. This is clearly what the cacophony of talk shows seems to say.

The dilemmas that are set up by talk shows point to the fact that it is the normative underpinning of everyday life that is in question. To take one example, in a show on divorce, *Oprah* raises a question that is somewhat at the heart of the sociology of contemporary family: Should people who do not want to remain married stay together for the sake of their children's well-being, or should they pursue their own well-being? ("Should You Stay Together for the Kids?" April 17, 1995). The show presents the results of a major study that indicate, the author claims, that children are better off given up for adoption than living in single-parent families. The issue, as presented by Winfrey, is precisely one of the dilemmas plaguing late modernity. One participant, explaining why she "stayed with her husband for the children," reflects back on her choice:

> MS. SHEA: As I looked out the window when my kids were teenagers and I saw them out there building a car together, I was grateful—so grateful. You know, by the time they were teenagers, he brought something for them that I didn't have in myself.
> WINFREY: Uh, Uh,
> MS. SHEA: A lot of wisdom.
> WINFREY: So you're glad that you had stayed . . .
> MS. SHEA: Very, very grateful. Absolutely.

WINFREY: And sacrificed your own emotional self, your happiness.

MS. SHEA: Very grateful. Absolutely.

WINFREY: For the children?

MS. SHEA: Absolutely.

WINFREY: Now, David [the author of the study], you're saying this is exactly what parents should be doing?

MR. BLAKENHORN: The kind of qualities of character that they showed in this are much denigrated in our society. But I think they deserve a medal.

This show—and so many others—articulates an opposition well known to sociologists: that between "character" and personality; between commitment to roles, traditions, and institutions and a self in search of "authenticity" and self-realization (Bellah 1985; Bell 1976; Riesman 1952). "Should we stay for the children?" "Should we leave an abusive relationship?" "Should we forgive the daughter who has slept with her mother's boyfriend?" All these are questions about the *norms* that ought to guide our action in an era where normative guidance is not readily available. Contemporary democratic cultures have a fragmented and pluralistic normative order, which invites perspective taking and role reversals rather than adhesion to one single set of norms and values. This is what talk shows suggest over and over again.

Far from being "sensationalist," then, the picture of reality provided by talk shows corresponds quite closely to Beck, Giddens, and Lash's account of the contemporary situation as one dominated by *individualization processes*, that is, by the increasing segmentation of each life course by the market and the state. Individualization, Beck writes, "means, first, the disembedding and, second, the re-embedding of the ways of life of industrial society by new ones, in which *the individuals must produce, stage and cobble together their biographies themselves*" (Beck, Giddens, and Lash 1994, 13–14; emphasis added). Because the state and the market increasingly demand that we organize our lives as self-reliant and competitive actors, each individual can only turn to himself or herself. Such transformation can be characterized by the simultaneously constructed and contentious character of the fabric of our most intimate bonds. Actors cannot fall back on known rules and norms to organize their private lives. Instead, they must endlessly improvise and make up the rules according to which they construct their private lives. As Beck and Gernsheim-Beck put it: "it is no longer possible to pronounce in some binding way what family, marriage, parenthood, sexuality or love mean, what they should or could be; rather, these vary in substance, exceptions, norms and morality from individual to individual and from relationship to relationship" (Beck and Gernsheim-Beck 1995, 5). Beck does not suggest that a mild form of anarchism has pervaded social relations. On the contrary, he suggests that with the collapse of traditional normative frameworks biography becomes ever more standardized by the double nexus of the state and the market, and that only within these constraints have individuals become the legislators of their own lives. I submit that it is precisely in the context of such profound transformations of selfhood that talk shows, and their focus on norms and personal relationships, make sense to us. The normative dilemmas staged by talk shows take place in the terrain of what Beck has so aptly dubbed "a do-it-yourself biography," a process of self-fashioning in which we are called upon to choose and fashion our emotional lives (ibid.). Talk shows articulate the fact that autobiography has become a "choice" biography, in which the self must now struggle to find or invent the normative "recipes" to regulate conduct. And Oprah Winfrey, more than any other television star, is the virtuoso par excellence of such a do-it-yourself biography, ensconced between impersonal forces of the global market and a therapeutic ethos of self-creation.

Let me now make a suggestion: as a cultural genre, talk shows stage, symbolically, what is at the core of "reflexive modernization." According to Beck, Giddens and Lash (1994), reflexive modernization—a term they prefer to *postmodern*—means that modernity is faced with the consequences of its own creation. It is forced, so to speak, to face and reflect on the destruction, the losses, and the production of new risks that modernity entails. "Reflexive modernization" is a modernization that looks back on itself and contemplates the destructive consequences of its own creation. Talk shows are the cultural genre of reflexive modernization par excellence. They examine the consequences that modernity has had on personal relationships and endlessly discuss the norms that ought to guide us in our actions and emotions. In that respect, talk shows are a supremely *reflexive cultural institution, discussing and contemplating the losses entailed by modernity in the sphere of interpersonal relationships.* With the disputes, confrontations, and emotional outbursts of talk shows, the highly contested, fluid, and negotiated character of self and relationships is given a cultural form and reflexively examined; that is, talk shows are a symbolic form in and through which audience and participants explore the collapse of "moral foundations," of binding normative frameworks, and the consequent necessity brought about by modernity for the individuals to choose and fashion their own morality, to redefine for themselves social categories such as those of motherhood, to discuss their definition of the good life, or to weigh such values as "equality" against other values such as "marital stability." Talk shows, then, are a cultural form for the staging and expression of the limits and potentialities of processes of individualization, in which all aspects of identity are deconstructed and refashioned. This means that, even though talk shows are not committed to any single definition of morality and even promote a cacophonic multiplicity of moralities, what they do succeed in doing is to discuss competing definitions of moralities.

Although many view the prominent display of deviance in talk shows as a sign of their taste for sensation (Nelson and Robinson 1994), I would suggest that deviants populate the world of talk shows because "chaos" has become the *normal* condition of late modernity: if identity is chosen rather than given, and if all identities are equally protected by constitutional rights, then what really distinguishes a sex-changed transsexual from a born-again Christian? Nothing. This is not because talk shows are frivolous, but because across the sexual and political spectrum, identity has become *constructed*. It is tailored to fit one's definition of the good life, deliberately chosen and deliberately exited. So-called deviance and normality then become equalized because both turn out to be coded in the master code of "choice." As Carbraugh (1994) has persuasively shown, "choice" is one of the central codes of selfhood in talk shows. I would simply add that this code is a great cultural leveler. In the realm of pure choice, any choice is as worthy as any other, and it is this normative equality that, for many, makes talk shows a "tasteless" genre, that is a genre devoid of a priori commitment to the art of making distinctions and hierarchies. Thus, if the world of talk shows is "amoral," this is not because they have forsaken morality but, to the contrary, because they contain *all* moralities yet do not offer any "higher" (foundational) principle to order them. I will now argue that this is also the reason that talk shows stage emotions so profusely. If no public language is available to hierarchize chosen biographies, and if biographies themselves are frequently torn between competing norms ("should we or should we not stay for the children?"), then emotions, the spectacle of suffering, and the solicitation of the viewer's immediate sympathy become the primary ways to gaze at embattled biographies.

THE MORAL WORLD OF TALK SHOWS

According to Steenland (1990), talk shows are a voyeuristic genre because they provide a feeling of intimacy and privilege the display of emotions and tears. But the accusation of voyeurism, like that of sensationalism, says more about its author's moral classifications than about the presumed voyeur. Although I agree that *Oprah*, and talk shows in general, revel in the spectacle and staging of emotions, I would argue that these emotions have a cultural *meaning* that remains to be elucidated. My argument is that emotions are the ways in which the problematic relation between self and commitment to one's social environment is discussed in contemporary American discourse in general and in talk shows in particular. Here again I will proceed with examples.

Titles of *Oprah* read as follows: "Should You Be Ashamed?" (March 15, 1995), "Social Workers: Guilty?" (April 6, 1995), "Can't Get Over Your 'Ex'" (March 28, 1995), "Confrontation between Convict and Victim" (April 1, 1994), "Day of Compassion" (June 21, 1995), "How to Forgive When You Can't Forget" (December 1, 1994). Critics will readily interpret these as lurid titles that catch attention through emotion but, when actually analyzed, the shows reveal that emotions are raised to discuss the difficulties in entering, staying in, and leaving relationships. Let me work through a few examples to explain this.

> WINFREY: One of my favorite Bible verses is "Judge not that you be not judged," because we really—we really—we don't know the whole life circumstances and her pain is her pain. We have no right to tell her what she should do with her pain or how she should be feeling. . . .
> WINFREY [later]: What about—are you hearing her when she says, "You have hurt me," for whatever reason? She feels that you have caused her pain.
> MS. WOLIN: I can't even believe that he [her father] would say that. How can you say I create my own problem? Yes, I'm a victim. I have been a repetitive victim, not once, many times.
> WINFREY: A victim of what? . . .
> MS. WOLIN: Of him not being interested in knowing the feelings of how his actions . . . affected the family.
> WINFREY: Hmmm . . . Hmmm.
> MS. WOLIN: He always told me, "Well, negative emotions, you know, I don't get into that. I don't get into, you know, fears. I don't have any fears. I don't get into fears."
> WINFREY: What is your pain? Just tell us—we want to know, what is the source of your pain here? . . .
> WINFREY: [to Rabbi Klein, author of *How to Forgive When You Can't Forget*]: How do you forgive when you can't forget?
> RABBI KLEIN: Well, I think that this is not so much a question of just forgiveness. This is a question of two people who really need to work on communication skills. . . .

WINFREY: How do you move forward in your life when you can't let the thing go?

RABBI KLEIN: I think that the first thing you do is you say to yourself: my being correct, my being proved right is not as important as my doing whatever I can to get us back together again. That's the first obstacle. No one wants to look as if they were wrong. No one wants to look as if they were at fault.

WINFREY: I'm going to end on that note, because this is what I always say to myself when I get myself stuck in one of those revenge modes: Do I want peace or do I want to be right? (*Oprah*, "How to Forgive When You Can't Forget," December 1, 1994)

This sequence displays many of the traits for which talk shows are usually indicted: abundant focus on emotion, especially on pain and anger; proclivity for "victimization"; staging of conflict; "quick-fix" recipes to resolve tangled problems.

How can we interpret the prominence and staging of conflict and emotions in these shows? In the sequence just quoted, "emotion talk" is quite clearly talk about difficult relations. Whether it is effective or commendable to talk about relations is beside the point. What should interest the sociologist is the fact that in talk shows emotion talk is almost always a way to talk about oneself in the framework of an embattled relation in which the integrity of the self is threatened. However insipid Ms. Wolin's complaint sounds, the deliberate staging of this complaint as pain suggests that pain has become a dominant cultural and political category to discuss selfhood and intimate relations.

The emotion ethic that is cultivated and celebrated by these shows is not simply—as Bell (1976) or Lasch (1984) would have it—narcissistic and consumed with the empty shell of a subjectivity that has only itself as its center. Rather, *emotion talk is talk about social relations*, that is, talk about the simultaneous importance of intimate relations and the elusiveness of the norms that should ground them. The emotions of anger, guilt, and pain—the most frequent emotions on talk shows—are supremely moral; that is, they always point to the problematic relation between self and others. For example, in a show titled "People Who Sold Their Soul to the Devil" (July 14, 1994), Winfrey and her invited expert analyze why people engage in gossip, even passively, and thereby hurt other people's reputations. Encouraged by Winfrey's usual insistence on emotion, the expert identifies fear as a key factor for such morally reprehensible behavior:

DR. RUSK: Why not talk directly with them [rather than gossip about them]? Because you're afraid that you are going to hurt their feelings?
WINFREY: Yeah, Yeah.
DR. RUSK: Or you're afraid that you're going to look bad or you're afraid that if you talk to them about this issue . . .
WINFREY: I think that the key word here is *afraid.*

This show is particularly interesting because its theme is an emotion that can easily be characterized as moral, namely, the shame one feels when one is reluctantly made an accomplice in denigration of others. Indeed, the public discussion of shame is doubly moral, in Émile Durkheim's sense. The emotion of shame that guests discuss hinges on the sociological norm of solidarity and loyalty to friends, kin, and fellow strangers. Thus the revelation of shameful deeds or feelings is also a highly moral act. For example, one participant in the show, recounting how she implicitly endorsed her company's policy of discrimination against people of color, publicly voiced her shame for not living up to standards of morality and solidarity. The public confession of the shameful act also is moral in the further sense that its staging presumably repairs the broken solidarity; that is, such rituals of confession presuppose that by confessing publicly one's faults and pain, one will restore one's membership in the moral group postulated by the show (the group of "emancipated women," of "responsible" parents, or of people who can "speak for themselves").[5]

As a final example, a show titled "I Sent My Son to Jail" (January 31, 1995) explores the emotions and dilemmas faced by people who denounced their son to the police after they discovered that he had committed a serious crime. Again and again, the show revels in the exhibition of emotions (e.g., guilt, pain, feelings of having been betrayed), but only in terms of the social relations and moral dilemmas these emotions raise. Thus, in talk shows, and perhaps in American culture at large, emotions are ways to talk about (broken or longed-for) social solidarity. In this respect, talk shows are a unique cultural forum because they dwell on emotions *as a moral rather than a psychological* component of interactions.

In these ways, talk shows are to sociology what therapy is to psychology, a forum to heal the person *through others.* This is why I call the emotion ethic of talk shows "moral," in the Durkheimian sense that they are oblique ways to discuss the difficulties of being entangled in multiple commitments, and are busy figuring out the best way to live together. I would further argue that the exhibition of emotions and conflict in talk shows is always framed in the context of a moral dilemma about the difficulty of settling disputes. The dispute is the dominant cultural form of talk shows because the dispute is one of the leading social and cultural motives structuring our understanding not only of the polity but also of the relation between self and others. When talk shows stage reunions or confrontations between friends, between boss and employee, or between spouses or parents and children, the meaning of such confrontations is at one and the same time that intimate relations are of paramount importance to the self and that no relation, even that between mother and daughter, or husband and wife, can count on pre-given norms.

Thus, the centrality of emotion and conflict in Winfrey's (and other) talk shows is to be understood in overlapping contexts: the centrality that intimacy has taken in the constitution of modern identity; the deeply embattled structure of everyday life; and the difficulty of using a clear moral language to discuss this embattled self. When social relations cannot be resolved, or even articulated, through pre-given moral prescriptions, then emotions become an alternative cultural code through which these relations can be discussed. Talk shows' obsession with emotions stems from the near impossibility in American culture of discussing moral issues in other than subjectivist and emotional terms, a predicament dubbed "emotivism" by philosopher MacIntyre (MacIntyre 1984). When the normative ground of relations becomes flimsy, the only thing we can rely on with certainty is our emotions. If there is no a priori way to adjudicate between conflicting points of view and moralities, then talk of emotions become a means of reflecting on broken commitments and longing for social solidarity.

Here again, let me put this in a broader sociological framework: the more relationships are chosen—that is, entered and exited in a purposive fashion by individuals—the less stable and secure their normative basis becomes, and the more likely norms are to be up for grabs and the more likely actors are to do battle in the war zone of everyday life. Because individuals, pinioned between the state and the market, have to turn themselves into the center of their own lives, and because no ready-made recipe can guide their actions, actors are left in a peculiar predicament. They are at one and the same time ever more dependent on primary and intimate relations to supply them with an ever more elusive solidarity and identity; and yet, because so much of contemporary identity is geared toward the making of "autonomous" subjects, this leaves actors haggling and bargaining over the norms that should underpin their relations. This implies paradoxically that at the same time that "intimate relations" and "emotions" are of paramount importance to one's identity, actors entering relations for a variety of purposes, interests, needs, and values are likely to argue and argue vehemently about these relationships. As Beck and Gernsheim-Beck (1995) suggest, love, family, and parenthood are under the increasing assault of the market, which makes contradictory demands on people: one is that we make ourselves the center of our own life plan, even at the cost of estrangement from our intimates; another is that, because of the "homelessness" entailed by fading community and tradition, we are in an ever-increasing need of intimacy and personal relations to alleviate the losses in social solidarity. The result is that the same forces that drive people to seek intimate personal relations with an ever growing frenzy are also those that undermine them.

These trends also account for the staging and intense dramatization of emotions in talk shows. Put simply, talk shows perform the ritual claim that personal and intimate relations are of paramount importance to daily life, but also that they are difficult because there is no preestablished normative guideline on which individuals can learn to resolve their disputes. Intimate relations have become central to people's constitution of late modernity, and yet, the impossibility of deciding and knowing in advance how such intimate relations should be conducted leaves actors peculiarly vulnerable to each other. The basic cultural conundrum that talk shows enact and address, then, is how we should talk and argue and decide about ourselves and others when no moral foundation can preside over our discussions. Emotivism is one answer; but equally important is the fact that, continuous with this emotivism, is the linguistic format of talk shows that purports to be the response to this cultural conundrum. The world of talk shows is underlain by the fundamental assumption that language is the paramount reality of personal relationships and that these can and in fact *ought* to be argued over. The accent that talk shows put on confrontation and dispute must be understood as a staging of the fact that social bonds can be discussed, negotiated, and repaired through argumentation and communication.

Showing the Talk

The genre of the talk show is characterized by one essential feature: natural speech ("the conversation") is structured into different genres *that intertwine to tell a story.* Talk shows proceed according to a standard narrative structure: a person or a couple are introduced (exposition); a problem or conflict between them or between the participant and someone absent is raised (complication); the conflict is intensified (by the host's staging of the antagonism or the public's partisan participation); and a quasi resolution (or, more frequently, the promise of a resolution) is reached, usually through the deus ex machina of the intervention of an expert. However, in contrast to classical stories, the internal motion of the narrative does not proceed from characters' actions but from the structured exchange of disputes, arguments, and dialogue. The craft of the talk-show host resides precisely in knowing how to interweave different modes of speech in order to establish a coherent structure in which the interrogative, prescriptive, and autobiographical forms of speech expose, complicate, and resolve the issue at hand. For example, when the audience asks participants vitupera-tive questions, this creates a "complication" in a narrative that, according to the talk-show formula, comes to a resolution not through a change in people's state and actions, but rather through language (the expert's ad-vice, the host's admonition, participants' confessions). The result is that talk shows provide weak narrative closures. Notwithstanding the expert's advice, talk shows have the open-ended, undecidable, and morally am-biguous character of the stories of daily life. If in realist stories the end il-luminates and gives meaning to the whole structure, in talk shows it is the *process* of talking that is of interest, because linguistic exchange *is* the para-mount reality of talk shows. Indeed, the format of talk shows is organized around the question, How do people who disagree with each other talk? *Language, or more exactly an implicit model of "communicative action," is the central motive of talk shows,* which are paradigmatic exemplars of Kenneth Burke's claim that "Language is primarily a species of action . . . rather than an instrument of definition" (Burke 1966; see Gusfield 1989, 53). Talk shows deploy a therapeutic view of language. Their staged confessions, disputes, or reconciliations "liberate" emotions, bring about greater understanding, and generate "communication" and self-understanding, all of which are obtained through the therapeutic belief that the act of talking is "emanci-patory." The format of talk shows—the structured conversation between different parties—is the very answer to the problems they raise. To this extent, talk shows are an almost parodic embodiment of the liberal faith in debate because they apply "debate" to domains that liberalism usually excludes from the realm of debate and argumentation, namely, private life.

The paramount reality of talk shows is language because one of the landmarks of modernity is that social relationships become mediated by and through language (Habermas 1979). As Habermas has suggested, in the modern era, language becomes the crucial site of interaction because normative roles and rules have collapsed, leaving actors to rely on linguis-tic communication to coordinate their actions. Linguistic communication is thus one of the dominant cultural motifs of late modernity because it alone substitutes for a stable and predictable normative order. As I now show, various linguistic formats are instantiated by talk shows. Most prominent among these is that of the support group, of arbitration, and of democratic debate. These linguistic formats in turn correspond to quintessentially modern views of language.

TALK SHOWS AS A VICARIOUS SUPPORT GROUP

Like support groups, talk shows are structured by the triadic relationship between "host" (leader), the individual (telling the story), and the group (whose boundaries are always diffuse because it includes all people participating in the talk show, the studio audience, and TV viewers). At the center of the support group, sociologist Robert Wuthnow (1994) suggests, is the leader who is at once "one of the group" in that she knows intimately the problems discussed by members of the group, and "more than the run-of-the-mill member of the group," because she has charismatic qualities, most notably expressed in her sincere care for others. The leader of the talk show, like that of the support group, displays an "ethic of care" and plays with the boundary between hosting and confessing, leading and being one of "us." Here again, I venture to suggest an explanation for the spectacular popularity of Oprah Winfrey. More than any other nonreligious media figure, she seems to act out an ethic of care. For example, in a show on overweight people, a woman tells how she has not been able to overcome her obesity; at the end of the show, Winfrey hugs her and tells her that "you just remind me of myself," thereby creating an empathic relation based on mutual self-disclosure and an ethic of care. To take another example, the host of *Rolonda*, in a follow-up show on "broken families," declares that since her first show on the topic she has met regularly with one of the "distressed" children to have ice cream and fun, a claim that is confirmed by photos of her having fun with the child.

Support groups, like talk shows, are based on the construction of what Wuthnow calls a sociobiography: a story of one's life that is told in public. This telling differs from the traditional "confession," first because these stories are told *to* a group and second because the aim of such public telling is not to repair a moral fault, but rather to *empower a wounded self.* The public telling thus aims to connect an individual to a transient and voluntarily chosen group—the support group, the talk show—in order to devise pragmatic solutions to problems encountered by the self in daily life. As Wuthnow remarks, support groups do not try to formulate permanent truths, only working modes of living together. Indeed, like support groups, talk shows seem to suggest that they can "round-off the rough edges of our individuality" (Wuthnow 1994, 293).

The support group, like the talk show, is based on the voluntary agreement of each participant. The public sharing of intimate problems as well as the alleged goal of the group—to provide "support"—concur to make the support group a substitute for a benevolent community, only that this community has a transient and purely linguistic existence. Like support groups, talk shows enact the principle of "accountability," for in participating in talk shows people presumably agree to be held accountable for their words and actions. Biography becomes accountable, in the sense that people agree to submit their behavior or thoughts to evaluation (therapeutic or normative). Finally, in talk shows, as in support groups, the relations between members of the transient group are mediated by language. The support group comes into existence through the linguistic exchange of sociobiographies.

According to Wuthnow, the spectacular growth of support groups in American society points to a profound transformation in social relations, to inventive strategies to counter the corrosive effects of individualism and to re-create new forms of community, only that these communities are transient and based on voluntary participation rather than ascription. Quoting one of his interviewees, Wuthnow suggests that small groups might be the place where we could articulate what we agree about, what the goal of democracy should be, and the values on which we are willing to compromise and those that are essential to our definition of the good. The "most distinctive feature of the contemporary small-group movement is its emphasis on support" (ibid., 337), and, I would add, on *linguistically achieved* support.

THERAPY OR ARBITRATION?

Support groups participate in a therapeutic ethos that stipulates that the self can empower itself by *talking* about its predicaments and by exposing one's failings to the nonjudgmental gaze of another. Undoubtedly, talk shows also share and promote the collective belief that voicing problems in front of others can redeem the predicaments of the self. In contrast, in Oprah Winfrey's show this dispassionate gaze is that of the *expert* rather than that of a benevolent group. Talk shows are thus pinioned between sociobiography—the personal story told in front of a group—and the "neutral" discourse of science, which in talk shows claims to be at once informative and therapeutic. As perlocutionary speech acts, talk shows aim to heal, repair, and manage relationships by setting the adequate conditions for speech and communication. In this respect, they share a few common premises with the discourse of therapy. First and most obvious, both deal with emotions, unfulfilled desires, fears, and conflicts. Talk shows, like psychotherapy, are based on the premise that the private part of the self must be restored to "public communication," to use Habermas's expression. But how this is done and why it is done mark a profound difference between the therapeutic genre and talk shows. Talk shows not only blur the boundary between public and private; they also, and perhaps more interestingly, abolish the aura of secrecy that surrounds bourgeois definitions of privacy. Foucault (1978) has suggested that modern sexuality is constructed by networks of psychoanalytic and therapeutic discourse as a secret to be "liberated" by ritualized practices of confession. By contrast, talk shows seem to subvert this confessional mode of producing truth about oneself. In therapy, privacy and secrecy are conditions for the liberation of repressed or hidden desires, which at the same time that they are "liberated" produce the truth about themselves. Therapy articulates and relies on a symbolic topography of the hidden and the covert, of the transgression and the permitted, of the unsaid and the spoken that is entrenched in a modernist view of truth. Such a conception stipulates that at the end of one's effort to "overcome" oneself, one can attain emancipation, rationality, and self-knowledge. By contrast, talk shows contain a distinctly postmodern therapeutic approach to conflicts. By publicizing the shameful family secrets that were the inviolable possessions of the subject of psychoanalysis, they reverse the secrecy and confessional mode that traditionally characterized the therapeutic relationship. Talk shows—and I believe it is one of their essential characteristics—"flatten" the epistemology of "surface" and "depth" that had hitherto characterized the discourse and practice of psychoanalysis; for in talk shows, the public confession becomes discussion. Further, whereas for Freud and Habermas the role of the analyst is that of a "philologist," a translator of the diverse parts of the psyche (Habermas 1972), the talk-show host acts as a *contemporary arbitrator and mediator* between conflicting parties with diverging interests. If the psychoanalyst is like the priest in that they both are the repository of others' secrets and work within the boundary between the forbidden and the permissible through the dynamic of "confession," the talk-show host is an arbitrator of conversation, who makes sure that the rules of conversation are not violated, that each point of view is expressed fairly, with the ultimate goal that each of the parties present comes to a greater understanding of the other's point of view, rather than of himself.

Whereas psychoanalysis promoted self-knowledge and fascination for one's past, talk shows promote skills in role reversal, perspective taking, and communication to resolve conflicts here and now. Aiming to achieve "communication" does not presuppose or entail any prior "truth," but only the pragmatic quest to overcome differences by each one stating his or her needs and listening to the other. Contrary to psychoanalysis, in talk shows there is no unique and unified truth or system or methodology that presides over the presentations and solutions of problems. Instead, each problem invites its own expert, formula, and set of prescriptions. This ad hoc nature of problem solution in turn suggests a paradoxically weak view of the authority of the experts. Because there seem to be as many experts as there are participants and problems, no single voice or message can be clearly deciphered. Because experts proliferate along with their domains of jurisdiction, each expert tends to contradict the others (see Giddens 1991; Brown 2002). This brings me to the ultimate point of this chapter. However cacophonic and ultimately inconsequential expert opinions may be, they nevertheless convey one central idea: that conflicts can be mediated and arbitrated and that the very act of exchanging points of view matters because it implies following certain *procedures of discourse.*

THE COVENANT OF DISCOURSE

We arrive now at the core metaphor of talk shows, which is also at the heart of our political imagination, the metaphor of the "democratic debate." When Oprah Winfrey invites a judge, a social worker, an expert, and contending families to discuss the issue of adoption, she builds a format where "truth" is not known in advance and where it is less important to identify the bearer of the truth than to set up the conditions for the expression of each one's point of view. It is precisely this aspect that makes talk shows the paradigmatic symbols of the "covenant of discourse" that is the hallmark of the liberal faith in debate. The basic motive of talk shows can be characterized as that of a self that overcomes misunderstandings and difficulties of the inner and outer life through debate and through the implementation of rules of debate. In this respect, talk shows do not stage conflict per se, but rather the possibility of *talking* and *arguing* about it. It is the communicative competence, or the ability to argue about the nature and limits of our commitments to each other, that is the topic of talk shows. What talk shows seem to drive home, then, is the message that we "only have language, communication, and debate" and the somewhat uncertain knowledge of experts to come to terms with the difficulties of reconciling the divergent interests and biographies of individuals. We are doomed to a Sisyphean haggling and bargaining over our relationships.

With no foundational values to fall back on, we have only language and procedural rules of debate to come to terms with the difficulties of reconciling competing definitions of what is right and what is good. This is the ultimate lesson of talk shows.

The talk-show format articulates the liberal tenet that the most important objective of a liberal society is to set up rules of debate, or "conversation," that guarantee the exchange of points of view of people who disagree with each other and who agree to talk about their disagreement. Talk shows are predicated on the premise that however vocally the guests might disagree with each other, they have at least agreed to disagree and to debate in public. This follows Bruce Ackerman's (1980) view that liberalism is about setting up "neutral" procedures that enable conversation between people of *different primary groups* who disagree on the definition of the good. Liberalism, according to Ackerman, is a public dialogue, based on certain conversational constraints, the most significant being that of neutrality; that is, liberalism is not based on some foundational or general principle of the moral life, but on a distinctive way of conceiving the problem of public order—how different groups, about whom we only know that they do not share the same conception of the good, can resolve the problem of coexistence through national discourse (Ackerman 1980; Benhabib 1992). That people participating in the debate would not be of the same primary group is, according to Ackerman, one of the guarantees of the public character of that sphere of debate because the public sphere ought to be unobstructed by the private identities of individuals. Talk shows—and this may be why they have so widely captured the imagination of contemporary culture—seem to be hybrid cultural constructs: as rule-governed debates, they are metaphors for *procedural conduct*. Yet at the same time, they address what liberal theory would like to push away from the public sphere, namely, emotions, private life, family, and interpersonal conflict.

Central to classical liberal theory is the belief, institutionalized in law, that the private sphere must be free of any interference from the norms and constraints of the public sphere. Furthermore, because liberal theory refuses to pronounce itself on the nature of the good life, it is concerned with setting up institutions and modes of discourse that guarantee each one fair access to his or her own definition of the good life, as well as institutions and modes of arbitration that are ethically neutral. This in turn suggests that liberal theory puts the accent on the procedures by which each one can enter and participate in the public sphere and its modes of neutral arbitration, and leaves the private sphere entirely to individuals' choice. In that way, liberal polities become notoriously plagued by a highly formalistic and procedural view of the public sphere, leaving little room to substantive rationality (Weber 1958; Sandel 1980). The interesting feature of talk shows, by contrast, is that they function like informal and popular "courtrooms," at once using procedures of debate and discussing the grounds for "substantive" rationality.

Let's take one example among many: A show titled "Hugging Our Children" begins with an episode filmed in the "candid-camera" style, showing a child crying and screaming "Mummy, Mummy, I am scared. Where are you?" Passersby look at the children but continue on their way and do not try to comfort or help the distressed child. In contrast to the levity of the candid-camera style, however, the show proceeds to probe and explore the meaning of the fact that these children were not helped and comforted by the passersby. The show explores in a quasi-anthropological fashion the ways in which the very boundary between permissible and nonpermissible physical contact has increasingly shifted and has become the subject of legal battles and moral crusades. In the same show, a school cafeteria worker recounts that she quit her job because children's parents and the school administration had deemed the way she hugged children "inappropriate." The interesting thing about the show is that it chooses to address the problem not as a confrontation between private parties, but rather as an issue concerning the social fabric, as a conflict that tells us something about changing definitions of social solidarity and about the intense legalistic contentiousness of social bonds. Even more interesting, these questions are not approached as legal, but rather as *moral*, issues; that is, they are treated as issues that cannot be settled by reference to the rule of the law, but rather by mobilizing public discussion on the normative content of our relations. The show sets up a normative dilemma between solidarity (at the cost of leaving undefined the boundary defining appropriate physical contact) and a tightening and closer enforcement of norms that regulate physical contact (at the cost of estrangement). What is the cost of regulating and scrutinizing our behavior toward children? What is lost when we make physical contact with children yet another issue of legal scrutiny? These are the quasi-sociological and moral questions addressed by the show.

I am not saying that talks shows are actual political forums. Nor do I suggest that they raise political consciousness. My point is that they *activate*—without crossing—the point of contact between the private and public spheres and that they make sense to us because they point to the fact that virtually *any* issue can become a part of the public sphere and thus subject to public debate. This is congruent with Seyla Benhabib's critique of Ackerman's interpretation of the liberal tradition. As she puts it: "The public sphere comes into existence whenever and wherever all affected by general social and political norms of action engage in a practical discourse, evaluating their validity. In effect, there might be as many publics as there are controversial general debates about the validity of norms. Democratization in contemporary societies can be viewed as the increase and growth of autonomous public spheres among participants" (Benhabib 1992, 105). Benhabib has argued that the public sphere must enable unconstrained debate between conflicting moral points of view and that citizens must feel free to introduce *any* moral argument into the conversational field. "All struggles against oppression in the modern world begin by redefining what had previously been considered 'private', non-public and non-political issues as matters of public concern, as issues of justice, as sites of power which need discursive legitimation" (ibid., 100). Benhabib thus suggests that the range of topics that can make up the public sphere must not be restricted, precisely because of the shifting definitions of what constitutes a political struggle.

Talk shows activate that uncertain zone between the "micropolitics" of everyday life and the public sphere in which universal norms and procedures of justice are discussed and performed. The staging of interpersonal conflict by talk shows deploys ordinary forms of argumentation that stipulate that we can hold each other accountable for breaking agreed-upon norms of fairness, loyalty, trust, and equity. It is noteworthy that many talk-show topics concern conflicts that have been, or are about to be, *settled in courts*. The purpose of talk shows then becomes to judge the judges or to retry the case, but this time not by using the formal letter of the law, but rather by using and discussing the grounds for Max Weber's substantive (as opposed to formal) law and rationality. Norms, morality, and taboos are discussed by bouncing them against the decision of tribunals, which are in turn denounced for applying laws in ways that violate moral common sense. For example, in a show where victims confront their aggressors, the show reveals that a man who killed a guest's husband was freed after sixteen months of incarceration, whereas a man who had stolen another guest's car stayed in prison for thirty-two months, a fact duly noticed and derided by Oprah Winfrey. Or, to take another example, one of Winfrey's shows presented four middle-aged women whose money was stolen by the same man, who had been, at different points, a lover of each of the women. After each woman tells her story, the man appears on the screen, talking to the women from his prison cell. The show, like many others, takes place *after* the case has been settled in court and after the offender has been convicted and condemned. The point is precisely the fact that the legal punishment is less interesting than the human and moral distress implied by the case. What does a man who has abused the trust of his lovers tell them? What does it feel like to have one's money stolen by a professional crook? Another show, about the "little Richard" who was taken from his foster parents in order to be brought back to his biological parents, is brought up on talk-show television precisely because the legal and administrative decision touches upon norms of justice that do not match the procedural norms of the legal system. A final example, the show "I Sent My Son to Jail," explores the moral dilemmas that parents of criminals confront when they realize that their children are authors of widely publicized crimes (in this case, arson). The very questions that do not interest the tribunal and formal justice are precisely those that are addressed by talk shows. In other words, although many of the issues addressed by *Oprah* have been digested and adjudicated by the institutional apparatus of procedural justice and the state, they are brought up in the talk show to be discussed in terms of the lived emotions and moral assessments of the actors who experienced them.

Here again, this can be illuminated by Beck, Giddens and Lash's characterization of reflexive modernization as enabling an opening out of the political toward the emergence of "subpolitics" or "life politics." "Subpolitics," says Beck (1994, 24), "is distinguished from politics first, in that agents outside the political or corporatist system are allowed to appear on the stage of social design, and second in that not only social and collective agents but individuals as well compete with the latter and each other for shaping the emerging power of the political." Subpolitics means "shaping society from below" and putting every part of social life into question, making the best of living in an era of uncertainties. In the final section, I examine more closely what characterizes the "sub-" or "micropolitics" of talk shows.

Concluding Remarks: Biography as Commodity

A hermeneutic analysis of culture of the sort I have worked through so far seems hardly compatible with a critical interrogation of cultural material in terms of its politics. Indeed, most analysts who have been concerned with understanding the meanings and pleasures of popular culture usually denounce critical theorists as elitists who hide their distate for (and misunderstanding of) popular culture under a patronizing discourse of emancipation (Ross 1989). However, the indictment of a critical evaluation of popular culture as elitist is theoretically and politically disempowering, as it does not enable us to discuss and distinguish between what is regressive or emancipatory (see Radway 1991 or Kellner 1995 for examples of a dual hermeneutic and critical approach to popular culture). I would like therefore to submit that a hermeneutic of popular culture should not disempower us from evaluating those cultural forms in the broader context of a politics of emancipation. I suggest that a critical evaluation of popular culture can properly take place only after we have elucidated the meanings it has for those who participate in it.

Talk shows are contained in the larger economic order of commercial TV. Yet, it is important to notice that they differ from the rest of commercial television because it is the participants' own life stories and biographies that are transformed into commodities and circulated in global markets. The commercialization of biographies is different from other processes of commodification by the media. A comparison with a writer invited to Phil Donahue's show clarifies the difference. After an appearance on the show such a writer will sell between ten and fifty thousand more books (see Supplee 1982). In this case, the media function as amplifiers of the market mechanism and benefit everyone, so to speak: Donahue, the writer, and the industry. But talk shows in which ordinary people expose their life stories are different in that they do not publicize or advertise a commodity already circulating in the market. Instead, they create commodities—TV time sold to advertisers—from the raw material of their stories of pain, deprivation, and conflict.

In this respect, talk shows represent the ultimate penetration of global capitalism into the innermost fabric of our lives. Not only are the ordinary stories of ordinary people turned into commodities, but these commodities are unpaid and represent a pure surplus value.[6] Talk shows thus would seem to point to a new face of global capitalism: it is not the "flesh, bones, and blood" of people that are mobilized for the engine of capitalist profit, but their life stories and family secrets that supply the invisible commodities of techno-capitalism. Talk shows seem to be characterized by "person" and not "commodity" fetishism. In talk shows, it is not commodities that seem divorced from the people that produced them, but people and life stories that seem divorced from the commodity logic through which they are marketed. Thus talk shows are morally and politically dubious not because, as several journalists have vehemently argued, they distort a given standard of truth and of moral propriety, but rather because they manipulate the conflicts and pain of those who are already dominated, *for the profit of media entrepreneurs.* If famous people invited to talk shows only enhance their commodity value by a media appearance, talk shows inviting ordinary actors twist the rationality of classical economic exchange and even the postmodern rationality of an image-based economics. Here, life stories are traded for the ephemeral appearance in the public sphere of talk shows, only that this appearance, contrary to that of stars, has no economic returns or symbolic surplus value. Instead, the psychological and status rewards soon return to the shadowy and nonremunerated realm of the interior. In that respect, talk shows are at the vanguard of the same economic system that has made biographies so embattled, and life and relationships so much a struggle, in the late-modern era.

However, as many critics of popular culture have pointed out (Willis 1990; Fiske 1987; Kellner 1995), media texts are supremely amphibious creatures. They help expand the scope of techno-capitalism and at the same time are popular by virtue of the fact that they address popular frustrations and hopes. Media texts are moved by the commodity logic of techno-capitalism and yet are forced to resonate with the concrete social conditions in which people live. As anthropologist James Scott has suggested (1990), conventional politics and tactics are always preceded by an invisible realm of cultural practices, that of *infrapolitics*. Infrapolitics is the nonpolitical and nonvisible realm of culture in which the experience of dominated groups is expressed and their opposition to oppression articulated, albeit in a veiled form. Infrapolitics is not resistance as such, but rather what precedes and makes resistance possible in the first place. Talk shows are such a form of infrapolitics because the very category of autobiography that they mobilize and exploit is at the interface between the apparatus of capitalist organization and everyday life and articulates discussions about new forms of social pains that have not been codified in the traditional liberal discourse.

What are these new forms of social pain? If classical liberalism was set to identify a finite and well-known repertoire of victims (e.g., the "working class," "women," "minorities"), talk shows propose, quite literally, a carnival of victims. Anyone and everyone is invited to join the parade of suffering people. But participants are never presented in the terms of socioeconomic exclusion with which sociology has made us familiar. Indeed, as many detractors have pointed out, talk shows cast their guests as "victims" in ways that extravagantly enlarge the concept of victimhood. If my analysis is correct, such a wide spectrum of types of "victims" is intelligible in light of the fact that it is now the very moral fabric of our societies that is under scrutiny. Indeed, as moral and personal life has become deeply embattled in the United States, political discourse has tilted from questions of distributive justice to such questions as "What kind of *persons* are we able to be in a given social arrangement?" (see Giddens 1990, 1991; Rustin 1991; Brown in this volume). How should we live our lives in an era where no one can reasonably legislate unshaking definitions and contents of the good life? What are the criteria by which people should be held accountable when individuals are deemed sovereign in choosing and making their own definition of the good life? Confronted by these basic, and today basically irresolvable, questions, most people can be construed as "victims." Undoubtedly, talk shows address these questions by searching for titillation. But titillation does not imply meaninglessness, for however lurid talk shows may be, their appeal is to be clarified and explicated in terms of the social and cultural processes that make them appealing in the first place.

Seyla Benhabib (1992) has argued that the struggle to make something public is characteristic of the modern public sphere and is the struggle for justice itself. According to Benhabib, in a nonhomogeneous society in which no agenda can be predefined, putting something on the public agenda *is* at the center of the public sphere and of the struggle for justice. In this, talk shows accomplish something that is foreign to liberal politics: they put on the agenda of discussion the wounds and pain of ordinary private actors. In contradistinction with the great narratives of oppression (or liberation), talk shows voice a multiplicity of local pains. Why does one suffer and how shall we be happier? This seems to be the question that haunts talk shows, and the contemporary imagination at large. Talk shows thus seem to be a sort of popular and populist discourse of theodicy, a discourse trying to explain, rationalize, and come to terms with forms of pain that seem increasingly difficult to legitimize and account for.

Some might argue that one cannot advance the thesis that talk shows talk seriously about such an important topic as pain. Yet, I would suggest that critique and efforts at rational understanding are not the sole prerogative of social scientists, and that participants in talk shows, however muffled or manipulated their voices, do engage in a kind of "infrasocial" criticism. In *The Company of Critics*, political philosopher Michael Walzer compares the task of the critic—academic or public intellectual—to Hamlet's gesture to his mother when he gives her the glass to see herself as she really is in the innermost corners of her heart. The task of the critic, Walzer suggests, is no different, for the glass he or she raises appeals to values and ideals that all of us spontaneously agree with and that we ourselves invoke to make other people accountable for their actions. Talk shows are very much like Hamlet's glass because they demand that we gaze, with a mixture of cynicism and compassion, at the ever-growing fragility of our commitments and our difficulties in finding and invoking norms that we all implicitly recognize as our own. There is no doubt that the language and format of talk shows leave much to be desired, and that they never quite make the political connections that academics would like them to make. But they do offer something else, namely, powerful metaphors to discuss the content of everyday life and reconcile the contradictions that saturate liberal polities. In this way, they represent a popular, informal forum to discuss the microscopic ills and battles of daily life as they are reflected in the collapse of normative foundations. And if talk shows suggest any sustained message, it is that in a complex and pluralistic society, no one can issue any definitive statement. We can only use language, and rules about how to use language, if not to resolve, at least to cope with the breaches that are opened by late modernity.

Notes

1 The meaning of *dramaturgic* here differs from Goffman's or Habermas's meaning of action that is oriented to the presentation of self. *Dramaturgic* refers to the idea that meanings are embodied in scenarios that are collectively rehearsed.

2 I do not think that all texts can be equally highlighted by the strategy I follow here, that is, by prevailing social conditions. Religious icons, poetry, or cartoons may contain a more euphemized, and therefore indirect, picture of the social conditions in which they take place.

3 Responding to the mounting middle-class castigation of talk shows and using a strategy of "distinction" that has maintained her upper hand in the field, Oprah Winfrey proclaimed that she was moving to an upgraded format of her show. Distancing herself from the rank and file of the "cheap" and "sleazy," *Oprah* regained middle-class respectability and the leadership of the field. However, beyond the self-proclaimed distinctions that actors in the field are eager to draw, talk shows can be approached as a cultural genre that has something to tell us about contemporary culture and social relationships in the United States.

4 One might suggest a historical continuity between the flamboyant style of working-class women at the turn of the last century and the cult for flamboyance that is (probably) manipulated and re-created for the show (see Peiss 1986). "Style," as Paul Willis (1990) has suggested in his study of the contemporary working class, is quite central to working class identity and is the very cultural material through which identity, opposition, and subcultural meanings are fabricated.

5 See Moehl (1996) and Priest and Dominick (1994) for a fuller account of the effect of exposure.

6 Or rather, if they are paid, it is under the form of "barter," where people's participation is remunerated by limousine pickups and suites in luxurious hotels. It is not incidental that Oprah Winfrey is one of the richest people—and certainly the richest woman—in the media world.

References

Abt, V., and Seesholtz. 1994. "The Shameless World of Phill, Sally and Oprah: Television Talk Shows and the Deconstructing of Society." *Journal of Popular Culture* 28.1: 171–91.

Ackerman, Bruce. 1980. *Social Justice in the Liberal State.* New Haven: Yale University Press.

Arendt, Hannah. 1959. *The Human Condition.* Garden City, N.Y.: Anchor Books.

Austin, J. 1962. *How to Do Things with Words.* New York: Oxford University Press.

Bakhtin, Michael. 1968. *Rabelais and His World.* Cambridge: MIT Press.

Baudrillard, Jean. 1988. "The Masses: The Implosion of the Social in the Media." In *Jean Baudrillard: Selected Writings,* ed. Mark Poster. Cambridge: Polity Press. 208–19.

Beck, Ulrich. 1992 [1986]. *Risk Society: Toward a New Modernity.* London: Sage.

Beck, Ulrich, Anthony Giddens, and Scott Lash. 1994. *Reflexive Modernization: Politics, Tradition and Aesthetic in the Modern Social Order.* Cambridge: Polity Press.

Beck, Ulrich, and E. Gernsheim-Beck. 1995. *The Normal Chaos of Love.* Cambridge: Polity Press.

Bell, Daniel. 1976. *The Cultural Contradictions of Capitalism.* New York: Basic Books.

Bellah, Robert. 1985. *Habits of the Heart: Individualism and Commitment in American Life.* Berkeley: University of California Press.

Benhabib, Seyla. 1992. *Situating the Self: Gender, Community and Postmodernism in Contemporary Ethics.* Cambridge: Polity Press.

Beniger, J. 1987. "Personalization of Mass Media and the Growth of Pseudo-Community." *Communication Research* 14.3: 352–71.

Bourdieu, Pierre. 1979. *Distinction: Critique sociale du jugement.* Paris: Minuit.

Brown, Richard Harvey. 2002. *America in Transit: Culture, Capitalism, and Democracy in the United States.* New Haven: Yale University Press.

Carbraugh, D. 1994. *Talking American: Cultural Discourses on Donahue.* Norwood, N.J.: Ablex.

Cerulo C., J. Ruane, and M. Chayko. 1992. "Technological Ties That Bind." *Communication Research* 19.1: 109–29.

Coleman, J. 1991. "Constructed Social Organization." In *Social Theory for a Changing Society,* ed. Pierre Bourdieu and James Samuel Coleman. New York: Russel Sage Foundation.

Coontz, Stephanie. 1992. *The Way We Never Were: American Families and the Nostalgia Trap.* New York: Basic Books.

Darnton, Robert. 1991 [1984]. "Peasants Tell Tales." In *The Great Cat Massacre.* London: Penguin. 17–78.

Dobos, J. 1992. "Gratification Models of Satisfaction and Choice of Communication Channels." *Organizations* 19.1: 29–51.

Durkheim, Emile. 1965 [1915]. *The Elementary Forms of Religious Life.* Trans. Joseph Ward Swain. New York: Free Press.

Fiske, John. 1987. *Television Culture.* London: Routledge.

Foucault, Michel. 1978. *History of Sexuality,* vol. 1, *An Introduction.* Trans. Robert Hurley. New York: Random House.

Frye, Northrop. 1957. *Anatomy of Criticism: Four Essays.* Princeton, N.J.: Princeton University Press.

Garfinkel, Harold. 1967. *Studies in Ethnomethodology.* Cambridge: Polity Press.

Geertz, Clifford. 1973. *The Interpretation of Cultures*. New York: Basic Books.

Gellner, E. 1985. *The Psychoanalytic Movement*. London: Paladin.

Giddens, Anthony. 1990. *The Consequences of Modernity*. Stanford, Calif.: Stanford University Press.

———. 1991. *Modernity and Self-Identity*. Stanford, Calif.: Stanford University Press.

Gusfield, Joseph. 1989. *Burke: On Symbols and Society*. Chicago: University of Chicago Press.

Habermas, Jürgen. *Knowledge and Human Interests*. Trans. Jeremy Shapiro. London: Heinemann.

———. 1979. *Communication and the Evolution of Society*. Trans. Thomas McCarthy. Boston: Beacon Press.

Heaton, Jeanne Albronda, and Nona Leigh Wilson. 1995. *Tuning in Trouble: Talk TV's Destructive Impact on Mental Health*. San Francisco: Jossey-Bass.

Hunt, L. 1989. *The New Cultural History*. Berkeley: University of California Press.

Katz, Elihu, and Daniel Dayan. 1992. *Media Events*. Cambridge: Harvard University Press.

Kellner, Douglas. 1995. *Media Culture: Cultural Studies, Identity and Politics between the Modern and the Postmodern*. London: Routledge.

Krause A. J., and Elizabeth M. Goering. 1995. "Local Talk in the Global Village: An Intercultural Comparison of American and German Talk Shows." *Journal of Popular Culture* 29.2: 189–207.

Lasch, Christopher. 1984. *The Minimal Self: Psychic Survival in Troubled Times*. New York: Norton.

Levy, D. 1989. "Social Support and the Media: Analysis of Responses by Radio Psychology Talk Show Hosts." *Professional Psychology: Research and Practice* 20.2: 73–78.

Livingstone, S. 1990. *Making Sense of Television*. New York: Pergamon Press.

Livingstone, S., and P. Lunt. 1992. "Expert and Lay Participation in Television Debates: An Analysis of Audience Discussion Programmes." *European Journal of Communication* 7.1: 9–35.

———. 1994. *Talk on Television: Audience Participation and Public Debate*. London: Routledge.

MacIntyre, Alisdair C. 1984. *After Virtue: A Study in Moral Theory*. Notre Dame, Ind.: University of Notre Dame Press.

Malcomson, R. 1973. *Popular Recreations in English Society 1700–1850*. Cambridge: Cambridge University Press.

Marvin, Carolyn. 1988. *When Old Technologies Were New: Thinking about Electric Communication in the Late Nineteenth Century*. New York: Oxford University Press.

Mehl, D. 1996. *La Télévision de l'intimité*. Paris: Seuil.

Munson, W. 1993. *All Talk: The Talkshow in Media Culture*. Philadelphia: Temple University Press.

Nelson, E. D., and B. W. Robinson. 1994. "'Reality Talk' or 'Telling Tales'?" *Journal of Contemporary Ethnography* 23.1: 51–78.

Priest, P. J., and J. R. Dominick. 1994. "Pulp Pulpits: Self-Disclosure on Donahue." *Journal of Communication* 44.4: 74–94.

Radway, J. 1991. *Reading the Romance: Women, Patriarchy and Popular Literature*. Chapel Hill: University of North Carolina Press.

Raviv A., Alona Raviv, and Ronith Yunovitz. 1989. "Radio Psychology and Psychotherapy: Comparison of Clients Attitudes and Expectations." *Professional Psychology: Research and Practice* 20.2: 67–72.

Riesman, David. 1952. *The Lonely Crowd: A Study of the Changing American Character.* New Haven: Yale University Press.

Ross, A. 1989. *No Respect: Intellectuals and Popular Culture.* New York: Routledge.

Rustin, M. 1991. *The Good Society and the Inner World: Psychoanalysis, Politics and Culture.* London: Verso.

Sandel, M. 1980. *Liberalism and Its Discontent.* Cambridge: Harvard University Press.

Scott, James. 1990. *Domination and the Arts of Resistance.* New Haven: Yale University Press.

Steenland, S. 1990. "Those Daytime Talkshows." *Television Quarterly* 24.4: 5–12.

Supplee, C. 1982. "Selling the Write Show." *Washington Post*, April 28, B13.

Taylor, Charles. 1989. *Sources of the Self: The Making of Modern Identity.* Cambridge: Harvard University Press.

Turner, Victor. 1974. *Dramas, Fields, Metaphors: Symbolic Action in Human Society.* Ithaca, N.Y.: Cornell University Press.

————. 1986. *The Anthropology of Performance.* New York: PAJ Publications.

Walzer, Michael. 1983. *Spheres of Justice.* New York: Basic Books.

————. 1989. *The Company of Critics: Social Criticism and Political Commitment in the Twentieth Century.* London: Peter Halban.

Weber, Max. 1958. "The Sociology of Charismatic Authority." In *From Max Weber: Essays in Sociology*, ed. Hans H. Gerth and C. Wright Mills. Oxford: Oxford University Press. 246–52.

Whiting, G. "Empathy: A Cognitive Skill for Decoding the Modernization Import of the Mass Media." *Public Opinion Quarterly* 35.2: 211–19.

Willis, Paul. 1990. *Common Culture: Symbolic Work at Play in the Everyday Cultures of the Young.* Philadelphia: Open University Press.

Wuthnow, Robert. 1994. *Sharing the Journey.* Chicago: University of Chicago Press.

Zemon-Davies, Natalie. 1975. "The Rites of Violence." In *Society and Culture in Early Modern France.* Stanford, Calif.: Stanford University Press. 153–82.

Reflections in an Unblinking Eye:

Negotiating the Representation of Identities

in the Production of a Documentary

For documentary filmmakers to collect footage they must "gaze" (Nichols 1991, 79–89) at their subjects through the apertures of visual recording devices. The "camera consciousness" that is stimulated by the gaze of visual recording devices can often encourage individuals to "mug" or to create "stylized performances" that have been invented largely for the benefit of the gazing cameras (Heider 1976, 50–55). However, scholars (Becker 1986, 255–58; Denzin 1989b, 217–18) have suggested that reactions to the visual researcher's gaze can be offset and minimized, and that the gaze of motion-picture cameras, in fact, produces reactive effects that are of no greater significance than those precipitated by other observational techniques (Smith, McPhail, and Pickens 1975). Furthermore, the postmodernist critique of modernist science has recast the discussion of whether or not the activities of researchers should even be considered "contaminations" (Brown 1989; Richardson 1991, 1994) of the social environments that they study. Nevertheless, postmodern and feminist critiques have also stimulated concerns about the voyeur's "license to gaze" (Denzin 1995, 201).

Denzin argues that we now live in a postmodern society "that has been radically transformed by the invention of film and television into a visual, video culture" (1994b, 184). This transformation has had significant impacts on the processes and experiences through which contemporary "selves" are defined (Denzin 1995, 200): "Along with flux and mobility, the screen and its refraction are fundamental determinants of everyday events" (Baudrillard 1988, 55). In addition, it has been suggested that "the human sciences and public discourse can no longer conceive of themselves outside the domain of mass media" (Clough 1996, 165). Thus, the postmodern social transformation has had important implications for the techniques of social documentation that need to be employed in order to examine the identities of individuals in a "cinematic, dramaturgical society" (Denzin 1992, 138; see Archer 1997, 82; Lincoln and Denzin 1994, 583).

In this essay, I describe a research project that I conducted during a cross-country trip on the Green Tortoise, an adventure travel bus company. In the context of this adventure trip, I had the opportunity to observe and participate in the shooting of a documentary film titled *Songs of the Open Road*. This journey across the United States provided an opportunity to investigate the nature and power of "simulations" in a manner that departs from Baudrillard's (1988) exploration of the American landscape. In addition, this journey afforded unanticipated opportunities to reflect on my own scientific gaze and to reevaluate the justifications for my "self-serving voyeuristic project" (Denzin 1995, 214).

A New Twist on a Familiar Adventure

In July of 1994, I took an eleven-day, New York City to San Francisco adventure trip on the Green Tortoise, as part of a research project. The Green Tortoise is not only a bus but also a travel company, based in San Francisco, that emerged from the rebellious youth countercultures of the 1960s and 1970s. The philosophy of the Green Tortoise (e.g., "Arrive inspired, not dog tired") is to transform traveling from a misery into an adventure. This goal is achieved in part by converting bus interiors into an unrestricted lounging space filled with cushioned benches, tables, and platforms. Also, whereas conventional travel may often be characterized as "being alone in a crowd" (Riesman 1950), the open arrangement of the Tortoise's interior space practically compels one to associate with others as one travels. Last but not least, the Tortoise also carries its own food and kitchen. Thus, although its amenities are simple, the Green Tortoise attends assiduously to a wide variety of creature comforts.

Shortly after I had made travel arrangements for an adventure trip on the Green Tortoise I received a letter from a film producer named Debra who was in charge of Diem Productions, a New York-based, independent film company. Debra explained that she had made arrangements to shoot a documentary on the July 1994 westbound Green Tortoise cross-country trip. She acknowledged that although she intended for her documentary to capture the "natural" events on the Tortoise trip, she was also aware that she and her crew were going to be an unusual intrusion. Nevertheless, she believed that her filming of the documentary could actually enhance the spirit of adventure on this Green Tortoise journey, as her introductory letter stated: "I would like to say at the outset that we are not going to be invasive and if you do not want to participate, we will not force you. . . . We hope that our filming of this trip will make it an experience above and beyond what you expected when you first signed up."

I felt confident that Debra's optimistic forecast would prove to be prophetic. I could imagine that the presence of the documentary team would precipitate an interesting range of "reactive" effects (Becker 1986; Denzin 1989b; Smith, McPhail, and Pickens 1975) in the passengers. I also sensed that my interactions with the camera crew would produce a fascinating reflexive puzzle: in the course of my own "voyeuristic" (Denzin 1995) observation project, I would be observing "voyeuristically" the ac-tivities of other voyeurs as they were engaged in the process of observing the people whom I was observing—and, of course, numbering among the "observed" would be *myself*. Thus, much as one's visible reflections are multiplied by positioning mirrors closely together, the presence of the camera crew's "gaze" would augment substantially the number of reflective "angles" through which the events of our adventure trip might be ana-lyzed. Therefore, while I resolved to remain acutely aware of the reactive effects that the camera crew's gaze had on the westbound adventure, I was also determined to monitor closely the impact of the camera's gaze on my own thoughts and actions.

My cross-country trip on the Green Tortoise began in New York City on Sunday, July 17, 1994. I was accompanied by my wife, Susan; she was embarking on her first Green Tortoise trip, I on my second. We rendez-voused with the bus in upper Manhattan next to the George Washington Street bus station. The Green Tortoise and its passengers appeared out of place in the dense, urban environment: in the glowing haze at the end of a hot summer day, a disorganized crowd of people—with camera operators in their midst—lingered on the sidewalk next to a travel-weary, green bus.

A small, white van was parked behind the Tortoise—the film crew needed to bring along too much equipment (cameras, sound recorders, film, etc.) to carry on the bus. In total, there were five members of the film crew: Debra and her coproducer, Amy, two camera operators named

Ken and James, and one camera operator/van driver named Chuck. As we were being filmed by squinting men with portable cameras on their shoulders, I almost forgot the routine of getting loaded onto the bus. One of the drivers, the "lead" driver named Jeff, was preoccupied with the task of getting off the streets of New York. Thus, before Susan and I had even paid for our tickets, Jeff asked us to board the bus to speed our escape from the city. When he had driven about ten miles south, Jeff stopped at a roadside pullout and finally calmed down. As we sat in the grass eating freshly baked Italian cookies, Jeff explained his philosophy as a Tortoise driver.

Jeff's attitude toward running the bus was different from that of other drivers. First of all, he did not allow drinking on the bus when he was driving—that is not the usual policy on Tortoise adventure trips. Jeff also enumerated a number of policies that appeared to be geared toward making his passengers' transition to life on the Tortoise relatively gentle (e.g., he would stop for restroom breaks anytime and, incredibly, he would try to maintain an itinerary). Jeff acknowledged that some of his policies were different from the norm for Tortoise drivers. Thus, he added that he would need the film crew—who were filming at the time—to edit some of the things that he had said in order to protect his job. I thought this was a curious "problem" for Jeff to have. Whereas it was against the law for people to drink alcohol on the bus, the documentary could provide the kind of evidence that might land Jeff in trouble with his employer for having overly "uptight" policies. At the same time, another thought entered my mind. Although Jeff did not appear out of place on the Tortoise, I could imagine that his law-abiding policies and his accommodating attitude might project the kind of image that would minimize negative publicity for the Tortoise.

After our orientation, we got back on the bus. Jeff wanted to drive farther that evening before performing "the miracle." "The miracle" is the process through which Tortoise buses are transformed into sleeper coaches. There is nothing especially miraculous about these transformations, but they do require an immense amount of reorganization to create enough interior space to stretch out thirty-five sleeping bags. Jeff stopped the bus to perform the miracle at a truck stop on I-80 in Pennsylvania. He threw himself into this labor with vigor and accomplished the entire task practically by himself. When the transformation was completed, we packed into the bus like sardines and then jostled through the night in a haze of semisleep.

The morning dawned bright and early. It is difficult to sleep late on the Tortoise because the breaking sunlight sears relentlessly through the bus's many windows. Soon after crossing into Indiana, Jeff exited the freeway and found a state park where we could make breakfast. Jeff set to work immediately on the production of breakfast, while almost everyone else went for a swim in a nearby lake. It was a cool morning, so most of the swimmers were out of the water quickly. For me, the worst part of swimming in cold water is the initial shock, so once I was in I decided to linger. My extended swim provided an opportunity to become acquainted with the other two remaining swimmers, Daniel and Mark. Mark was a vacationing arts columnist and Daniel was in the midst of a "pause" in his life during which he was traveling to California to find out where *he* was. I was puzzled to find that neither Mark nor Daniel registered any alarm when I told them that I was engaged in a research project.

On previous Green Tortoise trips, when I had explained to other passengers that I was conducting a research project, they generally responded with wide-eyed amazement and said things like "You mean you're doing research *right now*? On *this*? On *us*? On *me*?!" Thus, I had anticipated that Daniel and Mark would be startled when I exposed the "voyeuristic" nature of my presence on the Tortoise. Although I was caught off guard by their unruffled acknowledgment of my project, it was clear that Daniel and Mark's "unusual" response had much to do with the presence of the camera crew. The passengers on this trip had been prepared in advance to be observed by the documentary team. Thus, even though I was not working with the camera crew, I numbered as simply one more of the already many "voyeurs" on this journey. In addition, the documentary team's use of cameras made their observational activities comparatively more noticeable and intrusive than mine. Thus, my more low-key observational techniques were relatively less distressing to the passengers.

Still, although my observational and recording techniques were different than those of the documentary team, I had to admit that they were not necessarily any "better." Despite the fact that I routinely informed other passengers that I was engaged in a field-research project, the people I observed were often less aware of my "scientific gaze" than that of the camera crew (Denzin 1995). Although "modernist" researchers might consider this to be a strength of my observational strategy, this form of "uncontaminated" observation tends to obscure, rather than eliminate, the influences of the observer on the observed (Denzin 1994a; Harman 1996;

Schwandt 1994). Thus, the documentary team's form of observation was a bit more "honest" than mine because the presence of cameras alerted their subjects without ambiguity to the fact that they were being observed. Consequently, by utilizing overt observational techniques the camera crew created more "honest" or explicit opportunities for the passengers to exercise some control over the way that their "selves" were documented. However, simply because the overt use of cameras might be a somewhat more "honest" documentary technique does not imply that such techniques necessarily capture the "real" or "true" essence of their subjects. The presentation of the passengers' selves was indeed problematized by the cameras. The "collaboration" in self-presentation that was facilitated by the cameras could also generate "simulated" departures from subjects' "normal" self-presentations.

Reactivity and Negotiating the Representation of Self

After breakfast, Jeff announced that he had a full slate of activities planned for the rest of the day. We were going to drive directly across the state to Indiana Dunes State Park. There we would have a swim in Lake Michigan and then make supper next to the beach. As we drove across Indiana in the muggy midday heat, Jerry, one of the youngest male passengers, got out a pair of drumsticks and started clattering them on a variety of surfaces (e.g., the inner wall of the bus, wood paneling, plastic water bottles) to produce an interesting combination of sounds. He quickly drew the attention of a circle of nearby passengers as well as that of James, one of the film-crew members.

It occurred to me as I observed this scene that the point of making a documentary on the Green Tortoise—or conducting a field-research project, for that matter—was that it was an unusual or "weird," and therefore intriguing, setting. Thus, the interest that the documentary had for its potential viewers lay in capturing that "weirdness" on film; for the crew to make a film that would be interesting to people who were curious about the "weird" travel experience that the Green Tortoise offers, the film crew would have to make an effort to capture all of the unusual activities that developed during the course of our trip. However, the instantaneous and conspicuous attention of a camera had an effect that modified events. In a sense, because of the simultaneity of the action and the recording of it, the cameras could not help but convert the events they were filming into "performances." By gazing upon the activities of particular individuals, the cameras had a tendency to create a "center of attention." As the camera gazed at Jerry, his drumming became the focus of interest for a widening circle of people, who then related to Jerry's drumming much as an audience would to a performer (cheering, clapping, etc.). Thus, the cameras had the effect of creating "performer–audience" relationships between the subjects of their gaze and those people who directed their gaze toward the "center" that had been created by the camera.

As the "performance-making" power of the cameras had a propensity to restructure the activities on which they gazed, this process also had the result of heightening the interest and enthusiasm that the passengers had for those activities; that is, the gaze of the cameras had a doubly stimulating effect on the passengers: the gaze of cameras not only created performances—and, thus, sources of entertainment—but also conferred significance on those performances (i.e., the gaze of the cameras implied that activities were "important enough" to warrant documentation). Visual media have a great deal of power insofar as this technology can confer significance on people, objects, or events merely by gazing upon them; that is, mundane objects and events can achieve an elevation in their perceived significance simply by becoming "objects of attention." This phenomenon is similar in nature to Baudrillard's distinction between seduction and meaning: "I believe that, by also describing the sites of fascination, where meaning is supposed to implode with great flourish, you bestow beauty on that void and give meaning to what shouldn't have any" (1996, 35). More than merely contributing to the structure of identity in the postmodern social experience, visual media technology also defines the boundary between the "real" world of the ordinary and the simulated sphere of the "extraordinary." Baudrillard argues that in the contemporary world of visual media imagery, the relationship between simulations and the phenomena that have been simulated becomes resynthesized:

> The cinema has absorbed everything—Indians, mesas, canyons, skies. And yet it is the most striking spectacle in the world. Should we prefer "authentic" deserts and deep oases? For us moderns, and ultramoderns, as for Baudelaire, who knew that the secret of true modernity was to be found in artifice, the only natural spectacle that is really gripping is the one which offers both the most moving profundity *and at the same time the total simulacrum of that profundity.* (Baudrillard 1988, 69–70; emphasis in original)

Thus, in a postmodern, visual age, what is "real" is accessible with the greatest profundity through images. "Video, everywhere, serves only this end: it is a screen of ecstatic refraction" (ibid., 37). In producing "simulated" images of individuals, objects, and events, visual media technology transforms the status of these phenomena with respect to the sphere of "meaningful" cultural constructs. Via their simulations, the individuals, objects, and events that have been simulated are inducted into the world wherein media representations are preserved for possible re-presentation: "Everything can have a second birth, the eternal birth of the simulacrum . . . which is, as we know, a repeat performance of the first, but its repetition *as something more real*" (ibid., 41; emphasis in original). Whereas unsimulated events wallow in eternal obscurity, in becoming simulated recorded images become "larger than life." Simulations exist in a state of preservation wherein they may be distributed to, and consumed by, potentially unlimited numbers of people who, in turn, may each exult in the confused significance of the otherwise mundane phenomena that have been aggrandized in their simulation. Consequently, not only did the cameras generate a source of entertainment for the passengers, but the cameras elevated the degree to which the passengers tended to be stimulated by the profusion of simulacra that were created by the cameras' gaze. The cameras made a "spectacle" of the events that drew their gaze and thereby stimulated passengers to indulge and glory in the "weirdness" that was associated with our Tortoise adventure.

Indeed, it was impossible to avoid sensing the palpable energy and enthusiasm that emanated from Jerry's drumming performance. However, even as real and potent as that enthusiasm happened to be, I found myself disgruntled by the fact that the performance was a "simulation." Much as Jerry's drumming may have been a spontaneous product of the unique environment that inhered within our Tortoise adventure, it nevertheless had not been "real." In other words, the drumming "spectacle" had been driven and structured by the presence of the cameras. Without the gaze of the cameras, the centrality of focus, the structure of the performance, and thus the significance and the intensity of energy surrounding the event would not have existed. Although I had seen or heard of an abundance of wacky happenings on other Green Tortoise trips, none of these had ever taken on the structure of the drumming performance, nor had they exhibited such a self-indulgent celebration of "weirdness." As such, owing to its departure from "reality," I felt more repulsed by Jerry's performance than drawn to it. Still, "simulated" as the drumming spectacle had been, it had been a very "real" and compelling event for many of the passengers on the bus; whether I liked it or not, the simulating presence of the cameras made such performances an integral and "real" component of the "simulated" journey in which we were taking part.

While the filming offered a unique source of entertainment for the passengers, they continued to struggle to manage their self-presentations under the watchful gaze of the cameras. After having supper in Indiana, we awoke the next morning in Wisconsin to find Jeff searching for a breakfast site along the banks of the Mississippi River. Following breakfast and a swim in the river, we loaded onto the bus and settled in for another long day of driving. Over the next twenty-four hours, Jeff was hoping to traverse much of the Midwest in order to arrive at Badlands National Park, on the west side of South Dakota, in time for a predawn hike.

This long day of driving provided the film crew with an opportunity to conduct brief interviews with each of the people on the bus, a process that created a stir because of its novelty for many of the passengers. The camera crew conducted their interviews by having Ken train his camera on one interviewee after another, while Amy handled a boom microphone and Debra kept an eye on the audio recording levels. The brief interviews were composed of questions about the interviewees' names, occupations, and their reasons for being on the Tortoise. Slowly, Ken worked his way over to Greg, a friendly German man, who was sitting next to me. Greg got a bit flustered under the glare of the camera. While the crew was taking a break after his interview, Greg explained that he had not been able to understand Ken's questions clearly and thus had been forced to fumble for answers. I tried to reassure Greg that he had done a good job in his interview. I also gave him some offhand advice about responding in German whenever he could not understand an interviewer's English. Greg laughed a bit uncertainly at my advice, and I soon understood why. In the midst of my chat with him I found that Ken was training his camera on me.

It is a very strange feeling to be on camera. There are various ways of dealing with the stress-related energy one may encounter while being "gazed" upon. Whenever Flaherty (1976) began filming "Nanook," he became overcome with laughter (Massot and Regnier 1994). Also, in several instances, Inuit children who were being filmed by Massot and Regnier (1994) ran for hiding places when they came under the gaze of cameras. No matter how one compensates for the nervous energy that being on camera can produce (e.g., laughing, running away, acting like a nervous wreck, or creating a "performance"), in each case the camera affects one's behavior.

The process of being interviewed added a radical twist to my voyeuristic project. Whereas in gazing upon the interactions between the film crew and passengers, I had been fascinated by the effects that I had perceived the film crew to be having on the other passengers; in being interviewed my outward gaze suddenly was reflected back inwards; that is, beyond feeling as though my voyeuristic activities had become "exposed" (Denzin 1995, 49), my scientific gaze was suddenly reversed and synthesized with the gaze of the camera into an intense gaze of "double scrutiny." In being doubly scrutinized (i.e., gazing upon myself self-consciously and scientifically as an "object" of the filmmakers' gaze), I became preoccupied excessively with my presentation of self. Having been identified as "the resident sociologist" (quotation from the narration in *Songs of the Open Road*), I felt as though I needed to maintain face on a number of different levels. As a "professional sociologist," I felt responsible for creating the impression that I could analyze the challenges of identity construction in an age of "simulations" (Baudrillard 1988; Denzin 1995) without simultaneously suffering from those difficulties even while my own self-image was undergoing simulation. In addition, I felt responsible for offering samples of the kind of penetrating sociological insights that "could only come from someone with an advanced academic degree." And I wanted to do all of this while I avoided creating the impression that, owing to my awareness of the various responsibilities under which I needed to bear up, my performance was not actually "a performance." Consequently, in this brief interview, I had a powerful introduction to the difficulties involved in sustaining a carefully crafted presentation of self before the unblinking stare of the camera.

In my on-camera interview, I became better able to empathize with the subjects of the voyeur's gaze. I learned that, under the searching gaze of voyeurs, the enactment of even the most routine activities can become a struggle. In addition, in being gazed upon by other voyeurs, I obtained a sense for the distortion of reality that can precipitate from encounters with voyeurs. This might have been news to me, but the documentary team understood all too well what corrupting effects their cameras' gaze might have on the "truths" they wished to capture. Consequently, as part of the process of capturing the "real" experiences of Green Tortoise passengers, the documentary team also adopted measures to restructure their "documentary gaze" and, thereby, assisted passengers in the deconstruction of their "documentary selves."

Restructuring the Voyeur's Gaze

After our long day of driving across Minnesota, we stopped in a small city park to make dinner. Throughout the course of our meal teenagers from the town cruised through the park and gaped at our bus. While we ate dinner, Jeff gave us a preview of the next major stop on our trip, Badlands National Park. One reason that Jeff was excited about getting to the Badlands was that we would be having our first overnight campout in the park. This, for Jeff, would be a rare night of uninterrupted sleep. Another noteworthy element of our stop in the Badlands was that we were going to rendezvous with another Tortoise bus.

The Green Tortoise often operates two cross-country buses concurrently, one eastbound, the other westbound. Thus, the two buses sometimes are able to coordinate meetings in the middle of the country. Rendezvousing with the other bus sounded like it could make for an entertaining evening. Jeff explained that it was not unusual for big parties to result from encounters with other Tortoise buses. Further, I thought that it would be interesting to compare the progress of our trip with another group of travelers who had not been exposed to the gaze of a documentary team's cameras.

It was well after dawn when we arrived at Badlands National Park—Jeff seemed to have a knack for making "gross miscalculations of time and distance" (quote from an interview with a male passenger named Dennis). We began our day by hiking along the Castle Rock trailhead that traced a line between the grassy plains of the Dakotas and the eroded contours of the Badlands. After our hike we took a bus tour of the park—including stops at the visitor center and the company town of Scenic. From Scenic we drove to a remote spot where we could go swimming.

When he had parked the bus, Jeff explained that we had arrived at the first place where it would be okay to swim nude and do "mud yoga." He also explained that the camera crew was going to be hanging around. Thus, he thought it would be natural for some people to feel uncomfortable about skinny-dipping and, therefore, he insisted that anyone who felt the least bit uncomfortable about swimming in the nude should not be pressured to do so. "If you don't want to be caught in the nude, then wear a suit. If you don't care, you don't care." However, he also added, "I, personally, am looking forward to being nude and on film" (dialogue transcription from *Songs of the Open Road*). Good to his word, Jeff was one of the first people to have his clothes off and to plunge into the mud on the bank of a nearby stream. Despite the presence of the cameras, quite a few of the passengers cast aside their clothing and inhibitions, and joined Jeff in the mud. However, I was particularly surprised to observe that some of the most enthusiastic mud-bathers were the members of the documentary team. Amy shot footage of people rolling around in the mud for a while, but then she turned the camera over to Loni, a passenger from the

Netherlands. Loni then reversed her relationship to the camera's gaze by filming the documentary team, who had suddenly become the subjects of their own documentary.

The simple act of transferring their equipment into the hands of passengers profoundly modified the structure of the documentary team's voyeuristic project. By ceding control over the camera equipment, the film crew enabled the passengers to participate more fully in the construction of the documentary. With the cameras in the hands of the passengers, the subjects of the documentary were able to shoot footage that contributed to the construction of the tale of their own experiences (Issari and Paul 1979; Mamber 1974; Stoller 1992). Moreover, the camera crew's enthusiastic participation made it possible for their project to become more deeply embedded in the events that they were filming. As the film crew themselves became active participants in the "weirdness" of the Tortoise adventure, the documentation of events fell increasingly under the influence of "real" participants on the trip. Passengers who had taken an interest in shooting footage became part of the "crew," and members of the camera crew who had become absorbed into the Tortoise's experience became "passengers." Nevertheless, the presence of the documentary team and their equipment could not help but continue to influence the trip as a performance. The principal source of this influence was rooted in the cameras' proclivity to generate their own source of excitement. Captivating as the attention of the cameras may have been for some, not everyone shared an equal passion for the excitement, "significance," or "reality" of events as they unfolded on our adventure trip.

An Instructive Encounter

When it became too cool and breezy to swim or slosh in the mud any longer, we sat on the dusty grass around the bus and bathed in the sun. Jeff wanted to proceed to the restaurant where he had arranged to meet the other bus, but he was voted down by all of the people who wanted to drink beer and listen to music. Happy hour carried on until Jeff spotted the other Tortoise bus. As familiar as our own bus had become, it was still odd to see another big, green bus rolling along the hillside on the opposite side of the river. Rather than dawdling by the river any longer, Jeff got everyone loaded onto the bus and we set off for our rendezvous.

We were going to meet the eastbound bus at a nearby restaurant that was run by Native Americans. Shortly after we arrived at the restaurant, the other bus appeared. The documentary team immediately set to work filming and collecting release forms from their new subjects. The restaurant was little more than a hut with a small counter and a few tables. Three women, who were behind the counter, were serving "Indian tacos": fried bread with beans, salad, free-range beef, and a selection of hot sauces. We remained at the restaurant while Jeff went on reconnaissance with the restaurant's owner to search for a suitable campsite. As night was beginning to fall, Jeff returned with the news that he had found a great campsite. We loaded into our respective buses and then drove a few miles from the restaurant to a dirt trail. Jeff turned onto the trail and then crept into the midst of an open field. Following a bit of indecisiveness, he parked next to a sunken pit that was about forty feet across and ten feet deep. The pit served admirably as a meeting place and fire circle.

Soon after a crackling bonfire had been set ablaze in the center of the pit, a loud call was raised for Jerry to play the drums. As Jerry began playing drums it became evident that the activities of the passengers on our bus were being influenced by the film crew's overt recording technique. The bonfire had transformed the pit into a blazing orange arena. The drummers, the firelight, and the boisterous members of our bus created the kind of fantastic spectacle that made for great documentary footage. As the cameras gazed attentively on the drummers, the activities in the fire pit took on the structure of a staged performance. Jerry and several other people who had joined him in the drumming had become the center of attention. They were "the performers" and as such were distinguishable from the other people in the pit by being the focus of attention—both of the documentary team and of the audience of passengers who cheered and responded with encouragement to their efforts.

The avid attention of the documentary team added to the excitement of this particular spectacle; that is, because the camera crew was so attentive to the performance in the fire pit, the "significance" of the event became elevated correspondingly. As the drummers and their audience began to feel that they were indeed involved in a "spectacular" event, their enthusiasm increased and so did the value of the spectacle for the documentary team. Indeed, these dynamics combined to generate a truly spontaneous and spectacular event. However, not everyone who was present was equally impressed by the fireside performance.

We did not hit it off very well with the people from the other bus. As the performance in the pit advanced, the people from the other bus slowly disappeared. As the people from our bus became more involved in the performance by the fire, the people from the other bus lost interest. Daniel told me that a few people from the other bus went so far as to suggest that the passengers on our bus were "a bunch of posers. . . . You know, [like] we're just putting this on as an act" (interview transcription). It was easy to understand how the performance in the fire pit could appear to be a "simulation"—because it certainly was. The fireside drumming performance was a consequence of the evolving integration of the documentary simulation into our Tortoise trip. However, the people from the eastbound Tortoise witnessed the fireside performance merely as the "artificial" conduct of blowhards doing their best to get their faces on camera. Because the people on the other Tortoise bus had not been exposed extensively to the cameras, they did not share the same motivation or appreciation for "celebrations of weirdness" as we did.

Later in the evening, while the drumming in the pit was still going strong, Susan and I stumbled across a small group of people who were almost undetectable outside the noise and the bright firelight in the pit. They were people from the eastbound bus who were trying to enjoy the fire, but who were also trying to avoid the drumming spectacle. I was struck by the contrast between the activities of the people inside versus those outside the fire pit: the people from the other bus were sitting a short distance from the rim of the pit, talking quietly, sipping beer, and paying vague attention to someone in their midst who was strumming a guitar. Because their activities were not influenced by the focus of cameras, they were not stimulated to create a spectacle or to structure their entertainment. I could not help feeling a little envious of their calmer, more dignified composure. Early the next morning the eastbound Tortoise bus packed up and left without ceremony. Our meeting provided ample evidence that we were indeed proceeding in much different directions.

Transforming the Adventure

As we drove away from Badlands National Park the next afternoon, Beth borrowed the camera crew's walkie-talkie and sent goofy messages to James, who was driving the van. The camera crew had become very permissive of passengers who wished to use their equipment. In fact, Daniel had begun working so closely with the documentary team that he achieved the honorary status of "sixth member of the camera crew." On one occasion Daniel drove the camera crew's van through the night because Chuck had become so starved for sleep that he had begun hallucinating as he was driving.

Over the next couple of days we drove through many national parks and scenic wonders of Wyoming, Colorado, and Utah. Jeff arranged for our second campout of the trip to be in Moab, Utah. Our day in Moab began with a raft trip on the Green River. After the raft trip, we returned to Moab, got some supplies, and then drove to a riverside campsite that was set amid giant slabs of red rocks. During dinner that evening Debra announced that she wanted to share a case of champagne she had purchased as a way of thanking everyone for being so cooperative with her documentary. The champagne celebration was, in fact, only the beginning of the entertainment for the evening. As we sipped champagne, a number of people began beating on plastic buckets that they had taken into a large culvert running beneath a set of nearby train tracks. The tunnel added extra reverberation to the drumbeats and provided an environment in which the most spectacular group event of the trip could take place.

Spectacular group events are common to Tortoise trips and this one was similar in many ways to others that I have witnessed (McGettigan 1997, 1998); that is, the unconventional atmosphere on the Tortoise (e.g., tight living quarters, a lack of privacy, communal sleeping and eating arrangements) can cause its passengers to cling firmly to their conventional inhibitions. Generally, the tension between the passengers and the unconventional environment on the Tortoise builds until group events evolve that serve to "explode"—or "deconstruct" (Denzin 1989a, 1994b)—the influences of conventional social constraints over the passengers' thoughts and behaviors. These are usually very energetic events owing to the fact that they are fueled by the sudden release of tension that has been building up for days or even weeks. As a result of these "deconstructive," tension-relieving events, passengers often feel more comfortable about flouting conventional social constraints for the balance of their journey. On this trip, because of the influences of the documentary team, such tension-relieving events tended to be organized around visual spectacles. This night's visual spectacle was even more fantastic than the drumming performance in the Badlands. The dancers added to the booming resonance of the drumming by waving their flashlights as they wriggled in their makeshift discotheque. The people in the culvert danced and drummed for a couple of hours until they emerged as a worn-out, sweaty mass, and then took a skinny-dip in the nearby river.

As much as such visual spectacles may have been perceived by "critics" (e.g., the passengers on the eastbound bus and myself) to have been an "artificial" contrivance, in a discussion related to this topic, Daniel suggested that the presence of the cameras had enabled him and others to "reflect" upon their identities in ways that would not have been possible otherwise. His initial reaction to the cameras had been to create an "epic" representation of himself, but this impulse had faded as he developed a more insightful analysis of his "real self": "I will admit that at first I thought, 'Wow, you know, I really would like them to get pictures of me, you know, climbing a mountain.' You know, the 'epic,' forever me. Immortal on film. But then I realized, you know, that's basically the uh . . . video version of making a face at a camera" (interview transcription).

Thus the documentary team captured images of passengers whose level of enthusiasm about participating in this Tortoise adventure had been intensified—much as Debra had predicted. At the same time, however, the "indexicality" (Nichols 1991) of the documentary simulation was not utterly compromised as a result. Although long-term exposure to the gaze of cameras had a tendency to stimulate and structure "performances," being gazed upon for an extended period of time also enabled some passengers to progress toward a fuller reflectiveness and more "verisimilar" (Lincoln and Denzin 1994) presentation of their identities.

The Self-Perpetuating Significance of the Simulacrum

During the next day we traveled from Bryce Canyon to Zion National Park. After a very late dinner in Zion, we settled in for the last stage of the trip. Jeff was planning to drive throughout the night so that we could spend the final evening of our journey on the California coast. In the middle of the night—from 2:00 to 3:00 A.M.—we made a brief, nightmarish stop in Las Vegas. The lights of Las Vegas exploded out of the desert in such a shimmering conflagration that, combined with the stifling desert heat, it was not hard to imagine that we had arrived in Hell.

When dawn broke we had almost emerged from the Nevada desert. Upon arriving in California, Jeff piloted the bus toward Bakersfield in order to drop off Andie, the first passenger to depart from our adventure trip. Andie had made arrangements to meet a friend at the Greyhound station in Bakersfield. Because our arrival in Bakersfield coincided roughly with the lunch hour, Jeff announced that we should make use of this stop to find refreshments. Most of the bus's complement ate their noon meal at a deli near the Greyhound station. After devouring a quick sandwich in the frigid deli, Susan and I returned to the fiery air of the afternoon and then joined the crowd on the shady sidewalk next to the bus. While we were waiting to get back on the road, a reporter from a local TV station arrived with the intention of shooting footage of the Green Tortoise for the evening news. The presence of the reporter activated the documentary team, who, in a flash, had their cameras rolling as well.

The ensuing scene characterized many of the unique aspects of the medium of motion-picture documentation, while it also displayed how "significant" components of postmodern reality become caught up in endless cycles of visual simulation. As much as motion-picture cameras can be the *seekers* of spectacle, they can also be the *sources* of it; that is, the TV news reporter was interested in documenting a story about the Green Tortoise, but he became even more interested in the Tortoise when he discovered the presence of the documentary team. Thus, an important element of the reporter's "story" was that there was a film crew at work on the Tortoise. As a result, we were treated to a somewhat surreal spectacle of documentation. The local TV reporter had come to film the people on the Tortoise, but then he had found another film crew filming us; thus, he filmed the crew that was in the process of filming us, and he did this while the film crew that was filming us filmed him as he filmed them. To complicate matters further, as the camera crews filmed each other, the Tortoise passengers—whose experience the camera operators were intent upon documenting—gazed upon the spectacle created by the camera operators' simulation of each other, and wondered. In the end, it was difficult to decide where the simulation of our Tortoise adventure began and ended—or, as Baudrillard (1988, 1994) points out, if in fact reality was in any final way distinguishable from its simulation.

After this orgy of documentation we got on the bus and headed for the coast. We spent much of the day making a long, hot drive across California. Although Jeff had hoped to travel as far as Big Sur, we made it no farther north than San Simeon State Park—still a strikingly beautiful beachfront location. While we cooked and ate dinner, anticipation grew for the last drumming party that was being organized on the beach. The sparsely populated coast offered an ideal location to build another roaring bonfire. As Jerry and a woman named Mannie drummed on plastic buckets, a few passersby accompanied them on driftwood logs. The passersby remained in the shadows outside the firelight and, when they were encouraged to join in the "performance," they shrugged off the opportunity. It remained the case that kindred spirits still chose to remain outside the glow of the firelight and well beyond the gaze of the cameras. Ours had been a unique adventure that, while following a course that was similar to that of other Tortoise trips, had blurred the boundary between simulation and reality in the postmodern world.

Conclusion

The conception of self in contemporary culture has come to be increasingly influenced and defined through various forms of visual media and simulations. But this interaction of cultures, selves, and media is not yet well examined. Americans "are themselves simulation in its most developed state, but they have no language in which to describe it, since they themselves are the model" (Baudrillard 1988, 28–29). Despite being influenced extensively by the world of visual simulations, being gazed upon by motion-picture cameras remains for most people an unusual, exciting, and even anxiety-provoking experience. Yet, it was through the novelty of being exposed to the process of motion-picture documentation that Green Tortoise passengers were able to deconstruct the power that visual media exercise over their definition of self. In other words, the gaze of the cameras made it possible for myself and the other subjects of the documentary "to visualize not only theory and culture as products of a complex visual cinematic apparatus, but to show how that apparatus entangles itself within the very tellings we tell" (Denzin 1995, 200; see Denzin 1989a, 1994b).

In generating a "simulated" experience for the passengers on the Tortoise, the documentary team collaborated in the production of the transformative cultural critique that is the "real" substance of the Green Tortoise travel experience—and which, as it turns out, also happens to be the crucial subject matter that it was the goal of the documentary team to capture. In the end, the documentary team captured the "journey" into the identities of the passengers that they set out to record. In exposing themselves to the gaze of their cameras, the documentary team emphasized the fact that "truth" is not to be found merely in gazing upon others. Although it may not be possible to gaze upon truth no matter where one's camera is focused, it is through the unblinking eye of the camera that "a new form of self-awareness is produced, an understanding that moves to the core of the other's self" (Denzin 1995, 218). The filming techniques of the camera crew emphasized that the virtue of gazing upon others—either in visceral or in simulated form—is not to locate truth, but rather to employ a "reflexive mechanism" through which we can come to be more aware of the contemporary "cinematic" influences that structure our own voyeuristic gazes.

References

Archer, Dane. 1997. "Unspoken Diversity: Cultural Differences in Gestures." *Qualitative Sociology* 20.1 (spring): 79–105.
Baudrillard, Jean. 1988. *America*. Trans. Chris Turner. New York: Verso.
———. 1994. *Simulacra and Simulation*. Ann Arbor: University of Michigan Press.
———. 1996. *Cool Memories II: 1987–1990*. Trans. Chris Turner. Durham, N.C.: Duke University Press.

Becker, Howard. 1986. *Doing Things Together: Selected Papers*. Evanston, Ill.: Northwestern University Press.

Brown, Richard Harvey. 1989. *A Poetic for Sociology: Toward a Logic of Discovery for the Human Sciences*. Chicago: University of Chicago Press.

Clough, Patricia Ticincto. 1996. "The Cinematic Society: The Voyeur's Case." *Symbolic Interaction* 19.2: 163–65.

Denzin, Norman K. 1989a. *Interpretive Interactionism*. Newbury Park, Calif.: Sage.

———. 1989b. *The Research Act: A Theoretical Introduction to Sociological Research Methods*. 3d ed. Englewood Cliffs, N.J.: Prentice Hall.

———. 1992. "The Conversation." *Symbolic Interaction* 15.2: 135–50.

———. 1994a. "The Art and Politics of Interpretation." In *Handbook of Qualitative Research*, ed. Norman K. Denzin and Yvonna S. Lincoln. Thousand Oaks, Calif.: Sage. 500–515.

———. 1994b. "Postmodernism and Deconstructionism." In *Postmodernism and Social Inquiry*, ed. David R. Dickens and Andrea Fontana. New York: Guilford Press. 182–202.

———. 1995. *The Cinematic Society: The Voyeur's Gaze*. London: Sage.

Flaherty, Robert Joseph. 1976. *Nanook of the North*. International Film Seminars. Home Vision.

Goffman, Erving. 1959. *The Presentation of Self in Everyday Life*. Garden City, N.Y.: Doubleday.

———. 1967. *Interaction Ritual: Essays in Face-to-Face Behavior*. Garden City, N.Y.: Anchor Books.

Harman, Willis W. 1996. "The Shortcomings of Western Science." *Qualitative Inquiry* 2.1: 30–38.

Heider, Karl G. 1976. *Ethnographic Film*. Austin: University of Texas Press.

Issari, M. Ali, and Doris A. Paul. 1979. *What Is Cinema Verité?* London: Scarecrow.

Lincoln, Yvonna S., and Norman K. Denzin. 1994. "The Fifth Moment." In *Handbook of Qualitative Research*, ed. Norman K. Denzin and Yvonna S. Lincoln. Thousand Oaks, Calif.: Sage. 575–86.

Mamber, Stephen. 1974. *Cinema Verité in America: Studies in Uncontrolled Documentary*. Cambridge: MIT Press.

Massot, Claude, and Sebastien Regnier. 1994. *Nanook Revisited*. Princeton, N.J.: Films for the Humanities.

McGettigan, Timothy. 1997. "Uncorrected Insight: Metaphor and Transcendence 'after Truth' in Qualitative Inquiry." *Qualitative Inquiry* 3.3: 366–83.

———. 1998. Utopia on Wheels: Blundering Down the Road to Reality. Manuscript.

Nichols, Bill. 1991. *Representing Reality: Issues and Concepts in Documentary*. Bloomington: Indiana University Press.

Richardson, Laurel. 1991. "Value Constituting Practices, Rhetoric, and Metaphor in Sociology: A Reflexive Analysis." *Current Perspectives in Social Theory* 11: 1–15.

———. 1994. "Writing: A Method of Inquiry." In *Handbook of Qualitative Research*, ed. Norman K. Denzin and Yvonna S. Lincoln. Thousand Oaks, Calif.: Sage.

Riesman, David. 1950. *The Lonely Crowd: A Study of the Changing American Character*. New Haven: Yale University Press.

Rothschild-Whitt, Joyce. 1979. "The Collectivist Organization: An Alternative to Rational-Bureaucratic Models." *American Sociological Review* 44 (August): 509–27.

Schwandt, Thomas A. 1994. "Constructivist, Interpretivist Approaches to Human Inquiry." In *Handbook of Qualitative Research*, ed. Norman K. Denzin and Yvonna S. Lincoln. Thousand Oaks, Calif.: Sage. 118–37.

Smith, Richard L., Clark McPhail, and Robert G. Pickens. 1975. "Reactivity to Systematic Observation with Film: A Field Experiment." *Sociometry* 38.4: 536–50.

Stoller, Paul. 1992. *The Cinematic Griot: The Ethnography of Jean Rouch.* Chicago: University of Chicago Press.

Lauren Langman

From Subject to Citizen to Consumer:

Embodiment and the Mediation of Hegemony

In the advanced horticultural societies of antiquity that produced agricultural surpluses, certain groups gained disproportionate control over
power, property, and prestige. But how could small minorities, then and
now, maintain and reproduce their class privileges when gross inequalities
might foster envy, resentment, and even resistance and rebellion? As Max
Weber (1946) noted, force is insufficient to maintain power. Ruling classes
require popular acceptance of their claims to authority; they need to con-
vince themselves and others that their power and wealth are deserved.
Over several millennia, theodicies of good and evil, of fate, and of natural
or divine inheritance have justified systems of domination.

In the modern period, as Karl Marx argued, bourgeois ideology, with
its promises of *liberté, égalité,* and *fraternité,* served to mystify the domination
of new elites who, unlike earlier aristocrats, were seen as representing the
"people." The critical analysis of ideology, as, for example, in the work
of Antonio Gramsci or the Frankfurt School, developed Marx's insights
to explain how the control of culture and consciousness sustained dominant classes. For Gramsci, certain "historic blocs" maintained their power
through hegemony—the cloaked ideological control of culture—and
through this hegemony they in turn controlled consciousness and action.
Meanings and understandings produced by intellectuals allied to the ruling

classes disguised ruling-class interests as the "general good." Hegemony naturalized historically arbitrary social arrangements and made domination seem "divinely ordained," "necessary," or "commonsense."

Following the emergence of market societies, the bourgeoisie became carriers of Enlightenment ideas that would challenge traditional legitimations. The bourgeoisie not only contested dynastic rule as contrary to inalienable human rights, but in the process created the "people" whose freedom it would defend. Indeed, the bourgeoisie and its spokesmen became the advocates of popular sovereignty and republicanism that fostered the modern nation-state, aroused popular nationalism, and created a new form of political self-determination (Gellner 1983). In this, however, the bourgeoisie provided justifications and legitimations for its own claims to authority. Intellectuals such as Fichte, Herder, and Renan conceived of "peoples" with traditions, legacies, and common languages, often invented from many dialects and idioms. Each such people had a distinct spirit, history, and identity, and a golden age that had been repressed by kings, conquerors, or colonizers (Hobsbawm 1991). Bourgeois nationalist leaders contested this domination and advocated the "self-determination" of their peoples in order to realize the unique culture of their golden past in a glorious future. Nationalism became the justification for new classes of leadership to challenge dynastic rule and claim power in the name of popular sovereignty. Thus nationalism and citizenship obscured class rule and the extent to which popular will was in fact directed by the will of new elites. The republican sympathies of the bourgeoisie were melded into broader notions of nationalism in which identities and loyalties based on citizenship glorified the state and masked class differences and exploitation.

With the current restructuring of industrial capitalism into a digitally organized, electronically integrated, computerized global political economy, in which information and signs are the primary commodities, the relative power of the nation-state has waned and, with this, the power of nationalism to legitimate class rule also has declined. The hegemony of global capital and the power of its transnational classes are now sustained by consumerism and promises of the good life.

In each of these ideological shifts—from divine right of kings to popular sovereignty and from nationalism to consumerism—the body has played a central role. Every society regulates ways for people to find bodily pleasures, alleviate pain, and assuage fears of death. The body is thus a primary point of intersection between political economy, culture, and selves. As such, bodies are the target of historically variable, hegemonic ideologies. Thus, although specific forms of hegemony tend to dominate in distinct historical periods, the general question remains: Why do the majority of people so often assent to the conditions of their subjugation and actively reproduce class relationships? Indeed, why do they so often give their lives for the sake of elites and elite interests? To answer these questions more fully for the contemporary period, Gramsci's analysis of ideology needs to be supplemented by a depth analysis of character and desire. In such an analysis, ideology becomes the means by which society colonizes individual desire and subjectivity in order to foster "willing assent" at the level of consciousness and the reproduction of the habitus in the actions of everyday life. But how is ideology insinuated within the person deeply enough to colonize consciousness and foster intense passions?

Whereas the psychoanalytic model clarifies processes of mediation between parent and child and the internalization of ideology as an aspect of character development, Frankfurt School writers go beyond Freud to argue that socialization is always historically specific, and that parents as role models and socializers are located in systems of class relations. In the contemporary period, however, with the decline of the authority of the father, schools and especially the mass media play an ever greater role in socialization. Indeed, they present alluring role models and standards of desirable behavior and of desire itself. Although the Frankfurt School's analyses provided trenchant insights into the psychological appeal of mass-mediated images and messages of political or consumer propaganda, we also need to consider how the very organization and form of media in itself shapes consciousness. Those who control the means of production also control the means of communication; that is, not only are ruling ideas of a society shaped by its ruling classes, but so too do ruling classes control the *means* through which ideas are communicated and recorded. The influence of the political economy on the production of ideology has been well charted. But, as will be argued, the mediation of ideology through conversations and speeches, public readings of sacred texts or private readings of printed words, or, today, through viewing electronically transmitted media has *independent* consequences. More specifically, communication not only transmits information, but *the media through which that information is transmitted impact the body in ways that dispose the acceptance or rejection of what is transmitted.*

In all societies, the economy, ideology, and media impact group life, collective values, and in turn bodily practices and images, as they thereby construct and valorize embodiedness within larger narratives of body standards (aesthetic, erotic, health, etc.) that may include body type and shape, musculature, facial features, complexion, posture, and the like.

The economy, ideology, and media also interact to regulate and discipline the body, to colonize bodily desire, and thereby to socialize the person and impel "appropriate" attitudes and behavior (Turner 1983; Shilling 1993), including predispositions toward certain ideological orientations.

Modes of Communication and the Shaping of Body, Desire, and Consciousness

Media theory has been little noted by other disciplines or critical perspectives. Yet a long tradition of scholarship by people such as Harold Innis, William Ong, Marshall McLuhan, and Jack Goody have traced the impact of media on consciousness to show how the very form of media shapes the nature of society and consciousness. Thus, whether a culture is oral-, scribal-, print-, or now electronically mediated has significant consequences for the rest of social life, including political life, because each medium has distinct consequences for the body politic and the politicized body. Scribal literacy made possible the administration of empires; mass literacy (or print capitalism, as Benedict Anderson calls it) enabled the rise of nation-states; and electronic media from phones to the Internet enable contemporary globalization. But further, each form of media impacts the body in such ways that the "schooling" of the person involves the insinuation of ideology and colonization of desire to shape consciousness, experience, and actions and hence to reproduce the political economy. In other words, people learn the skills needed to work and live in that society and, at the same time, they internalize values that sustain the social arrangements and patterns of hierarchy that result from that work. Otherwise said, following Pierre Bourdieu, the mediation of ideology as embedded practices and understandings (the habitus) depends on the schooling of bodies by media. The very media of communication, in colonizing and shaping the body, are just as important as the contents of the ideology that is conveyed in securing the hegemony of ruling groups. As will be seen as we examine oral, scribal, and print media cultures, the medium of schooling contains in itself a predisposition for certain ideologies and feelings.

Many social theorists, in the spirit of Michel Foucault and Erving Goffman, have seen the body as the site where social texts and discourses inscribe subjectivities or self-presentations that typically help to sustain power arrangements. In such a perspective, socialization into a group is not just acquisition of language, norms, and values, or even of identities on the cognitive and reflexive level. In addition, and perhaps more significantly, the body, with its inherent capacities for pain and pleasure, and its symbolic abilities to define what are appropriate and inappropriate pains and pleasures—this body is the site in which socialization instills various practices, dispositions, tastes, olfactory sensibilities, and physical abilities that undergird the mind, self, and society as well as reflexivity about them (Bourdieu 1984; Shilling 1993). Thus, I will suggest that the means of production and the means of communication interact to dispose certain forms of embodiedness. In turn, these forms of embodiedness enable the values, skills, and actions required in the economy, shape the motives and desires to impel appropriate behaviors, and foster the modes of consciousness and subjectivity that sustain and reproduce hierarchies of domination even in the face of resentment or resistance.

Although reflexive selfhood is overlaid upon archaic bodily affects, the person as agent can choose to achieve or avoid certain emotions and feelings, which is not to say that he or she chooses well. This view of the social transformation of affects into emotions and feelings suggests a theory of desire that discards Freud's dubious notion of drives that *impel* the person to act. Moving from a theory of need or drive to one of socially shaped feelings helps us to understand how people find certain gratifications in subjugation. Thus, in contrast to Louis Althusser's concept of "interpellation" in which subjects are constituted by the cultural apparatuses, and the notion of agency is a humanist fiction, I would prefer the concept of affective "impellation," which suggests that people, qua agents, actively seek certain affective states, or seek to avoid others, and thus while socially constructed values and goals of action may be undergirded by feelings and emotions, agents have choices and resistance is possible. Thus, structures of social control, mediated through the colonization of affects and emotions, insinuate themselves within the person so that, in the articulations of socially constructed identities, the person embodies certain understandings of the world that lead him or her to enact the routines of the quotidian or formulate plans and strategies. The typifications of everyday life thus provide or avoid emotional states and feelings that motivate the activities that reproduce the system and its structures of power.

In sum, ideology is more than a systematic production by an intelligentsia allied to ruling classes; it also is sustained by a variety of nonverbal emotional and bodily resources. At this point the basis of hegemony becomes clear, not only as a product of the forces and relations of production, but also as constructed in communities of meaning and identity that in turn provide the empirical subject with a variety of emotional goals and satisfactions. Otherwise said, feudal society, modern nation-states, and the amusement society of globalized capital not only foster claims for the authority of their elites, but also socialize the bodies and emotions of the majorities to embrace these claims and identities. They thereby are granted inclusion into a community, a sense of recognition, realms of agency, and amelioration of anxiety. Hegemony, in sum, is supported by desires so powerful that domination is not only little questioned but often strongly embraced.

The Scribal Culture of Early Empires and Kingdoms

For most of human (pre)history, people lived in oral cultures, small, face-to-face communities in which most information, legacies, traditions, and cultural understandings were transmitted in conversations told and retold from generation to generation. These typically were small lineage societies such as hunter-gatherers, pastoralists, or horticulturalists, people who lived together in more or less permanent groups and worked with limited technologies. Such societies tended to conform closely to traditions interpreted by male elders, and in turn maintained a high degree of continuity and cohesion. The primary means of social control was direct surveillance and possible exclusion insofar as most people were known to and dependent on each other. There was no privacy; indeed, the very idea of privacy had not emerged.

A key element of oral cultures is the value of emotional participation and narration. For example, the storyteller dramatizes his or her telling and retelling of the history and lore of the group. The storyteller uses emotion and passion in telling the myths of origins and destiny, the adventures of heroes, and the fate of villains. Thus the ability to express and evoke powerful emotions is an important aspect of oral cultures. It was in such cultures that, according to Émile Durkheim, religious rituals evoked an efflorescence of passions.

Scribal cultures emerged as metal tools increased the productivity of agriculture and metal weapons and armor gave warriors a military advantage. With settled agriculture and the production of more food than needed by the producers, full-time specialists emerged such as rulers, warriors, priests, merchants, and artisans. Such societies were marked by extreme inequality. How and why would the majority of the people living in scribal cultures assent to such disparities of wealth, status, and power? Briefly, three factors were involved. First, literate groups monopolized written communication, which often had a sacred or hiereophantic quality. They crafted and recorded religious doctrines and ideologies that served the hegemonic purpose of sacralizing rulers. The massive temples, plus the ceremonial and theological expertise of religious specialists that was articulated in spectacular public ceremonials, dramatized sacrosanct doctrines and fostered identities that naturalized the historical. Second, scribal elites commanded esoteric knowledge of mathematics, astronomy, engineering, and often medicine that gave them specialized functional competences and ideological power over the uneducated. Third, the leadership cadres controlled the military classes. When societies gained the technological and organizational sophistication to build civilizations and empires, they sustained their legitimacy by disciplining the male body, turning him into either a military leader or soldier or a restrained priest or acolyte. The same doctrines that legitimated rulership typically valorized the warrior and scribal priestly classes and celebrated the appropriate values.

As agricultural productivity increased and populations grew, so too did the wealth and power of ruling elites, including the priestly classes, who established and monopolized systems of writing that helped men to organize large-scale waterworks, cadastral surveys, and agricultural production, and also linked them to the cosmos through the sacred king or emperor. Thus the ability to keep records and transmit information had enormous political and economic consequences. The enhanced capacity to govern (to "bias space" in Innis's terms), enabled the state to field large armies and extend its administration over wide areas. This was central in the rise of the ancient empires and civilizations of Sumer, Egypt, the Indus Valley, and China. Writing became an instrument of domination and social control in these early civilizations, as well as the means by which the elites crafted legitimating ideologies with theological justifications for domination. Pharaohs, kings, and emperors were now thought to be either gods or selected by gods, or to have gained power through divine inspiration.

But the use of writing by a scribal class itself has had consequences that have varied in space and time. For example, "media which are durable but make transportation difficult, will tend to be controlled by religious groups. Media which are easily transportable but less durable, will emphasize a bias of space and will tend to be controlled by political and class groups. Thus, different communication technologies encourage different structures of 'monopolies of knowledge'" (Jhally 1993, 4). Time-binding media such as manuscripts "favored relatively close communities, metaphysical speculation, and traditional authority" (Carey 1992, 134). The development of papyrus and phonetic alphabets enabled the expansion of rule over far larger areas—consider Alexander's brief empire and, later, that of Rome. Paper served a similar function in China, allowing a mandarin class to create and maintain a high universalistic culture and administer

a vast empire. Space-binding media such as print and electronic media encourage expansion and control. According to Carey, space-binding media
"favored the establishment of commercialism, empire and eventually tech-
nocracy" (ibid.). As Innis (1972) notes, with easily portable information
the range of control increases, but, at the same time, the society becomes
less stable. Scribal cultures, in which literacy was monopolized by few and
edicts were carved in stone, produced rigid hierarchies of power and more
or less passive subjects disposed to accept written codes of law and the
authority of the literate elites to interpret or enforce them.

It is important to remember that in scribal cultures, most people remain
illiterate. There was much local solidarity and often highly local dialects,
and communities often were physically isolated from each other. As in
oral cultures, illiterate people tend to be emotionally labile and more affective. Thus, in traditional scribal societies, part and parcel of socializing
the population into docility was the use of physical controls and bodily
punishments. Most early codes of morality included constraints upon the
body—for example, over diet and sexuality. Dietary restrictions stand as
affirmations of the power of the social; these include dietary laws of Jewish
kosher, Islamic halal, or the rules of Hindu (and especially Brahmin) meals.
Power operated upon the body through diet, lifestyle, housing, and population sizes and pressures. Restrictions on sexuality were a primary means
by which authoritarian states secured the docility and compliance of their
subjects (Kroker 1984).

Further, as Foucault would suggest, punishment, often extremely cruel
and painful, was typically conducted as a public ceremony, including torture, dismemberment, stoning, blinding, and beheading. It is important
to notice this was an expression not merely of the sadism of rulers or
executioners, but rather a dramatization of the power of the state and the
sanctity of its religious or legal codes. Said another way, power in scribal
societies was celebrated in spectacular public rituals of bodily punishment
that advertised the power of the state—as, for example, the codes of
Hammurabi or the Hebrew Old Testament. Although life was oppressive
in many ways, such societies provided a high degree of cohesion and solidarity, status and honor, and a variety of meanings to assuage distress.

Print Culture and the Rise of the Nation-State

The fall of Rome left a legacy of fragmented kingdoms with unique features
that would eventually foster modern industrial nation-states. Whereas
feudal trade had been largely confined to local villages, a growing class of

itinerant merchants organized trade across local jurisdictions. The rise of a market society eventually transformed feudal Christendom as widespread commerce with abstract markets fostered forms of organization radically different from the manorial system. Buyers, sellers, and shippers who had never met before needed to cooperate on a routinized basis to enable money transactions and credit transfers between autonomous individuals, firms, and nascent banks. This form of commerce depended on abstract values, rational procedures, consistent weights and measures, standard terms of value (money), pricing, bookkeeping, and accounting. Promissory notes, letters of credit, contracts, laws, and lawyers emerged to regulate commerce between anonymous traders.

Slowly the patchwork of largely self-sufficient manors and local guilds gave way to extensive networks of trading cities from the Hanseatic League in the North to the Italian city-states in the South. Small towns and ports along water or trade routes became large cities, the division of labor proceeded, and eventually the merchant classes gained power to contest political arrangements or to inspire dynastic rulers to embrace nationalism. Although the Middle Ages are often seen as stagnant, there were important technological changes during this period, including the greater use of windmills and waterwheels, new techniques of construction, gun powder, and movable type. The magnetic compass that had come from China enabled long-range naval navigation, which expanded sea routes for trading regimes and the growing merchant classes. Political and business elites used these innovations to promote national wealth and to sustain or legitimate their own power.

As the economy grew and became increasingly rationalized, so also was there consolidation of smaller administrative units—princedoms, bishoprics, free towns, and fiefdoms—into larger states. Governance become more centralized and rationalized. The state began to play a major role in the enforcement and adjudication of contracts, and in form and personnel it moved toward bureaucratic organizations of administrative specialists rather than familistic networks of notables and kin. The administration of states came to depend on officials, soldiers, retainers, and judges whose incomes were not based on land (fiefdoms) or ownership of offices (prebends and benefices), but on salaries from the state. Hence they were loyal to the crown and not the nobility, whose power began to wane. State administrations became more rationalized and eventually wielded more actual power than the monarchs whom they served.

With these innovations came the demise of feudal armies. Then a new question emerged: If feudal armies fought for God and honor, and for land or booty, what might inspire service in the large mass armies of guns, regiments, and machines? Although the formation of mass armies emerged along with its enabling technology, it soon became clear that their motivation to fight depended on political ideology and systematic indoctrination. Eventually, men in huge conscripted armies fought each other out of devotion to their nations. Warrior nobles had fought for land and honor, but to motivate ordinary soldiers they first had to be transformed from isolated peasants into citizen soldiers.

Such contradictions between dynastic particularism and the universalism of growing bureaucracies, national administrations, markets, and armies eventually led to the demise of feudalism. Whereas the Italian bourgeoisie were members of the ruling classes, as with the Borgia's popes and princes, eventually the bourgeoisie would become a class "for itself," with the economic power and subjective dispositions to create its own leadership cadres that would contest and finally overthrow dynastic rule. This would require new cultural understandings and frameworks of legitimacy apart from the church and its conceptions of the divine right of rulers. The self-governance by autonomous Protestant congregations of internally disciplined believers likewise established a foundation for self-government in general. Little by little, feudal serfs became subjects of thrones and then national bodies of citizens—members of abstract communities, loyal to their Nation, and willingly assenting to the interests of the new elites. The self-restraint required by literacy, together with the diffusion of manners and the disciplines of a market society, disposed a modern subjectivity that was individualized, enterprising, and oriented toward the future.

With the emergence of new technologies to transmit information, such as printed books, journals, pamphlets, and, later, mass media, there was a diffusion of new ideas, cultural understandings, and critiques that found a growing audience in the literate bourgeoisie. This enabled the rise of a public sphere situated in cafés, salons, and restaurants where the literate classes could join together in camaraderie to discuss the events of the day, exchange news from afar, or debate the various ideas of John Locke or the philosophes of the Enlightenment (Habermas 1968; Sennett 1974; Tester 1992). "Civil society" as a realm of discourse apart from the state, economy, or private life allowed the emergence of a "civilized" political culture distinct from, if not opposed to, dynastic regimes (Habermas 1968; Calhoun 1997). The English Civil War might be considered the first major challenge to the aristocracy. Notwithstanding the restoration of Charles II, a parliamentary system was strengthened and a significant political constituency developed to challenge arbitrary rule.

One of the most salient contradictions of early modern society was that between the more rational legal conduct of governance and trade, on the one hand, and the need for inclusive communities of meaning and identity on the other. Enlightenment republican political theorists from Locke to Rousseau to Fichte created rhetorics of freedom and fulfillment through popular sovereignty variously defined. They valorized democracy and proclaimed the universal rights of man. Political and intellectual leaders increasingly claimed that these rights could be realized only in the nation-state. They then invented traditions and collective memories, histories, and mythologies replete with symbols and rituals, to create "nations" as distinct peoples who were members of long-standing communities with unique cultures and identities. At this point the bourgeoisie's claim to authority coincided with widespread crises of community, identity, and meaning that the emergent social imaginary of the Nation served to reconcile. More specifically, the Nation reconciled the new rational order with a romantic image of a traditional society lost but soon to reappear. The Nation was a socially constructed "imaginary community" with powerful ties of solidarity, frameworks of meaning, and newly valorized collective identities. Peasants and workers also now moved from the margins of society to become members of national polities. Henceforth, their individual identities were linked to the fate of their Nations.

The civilized, print-oriented, disciplined body became incorporated into various national political bodies. Nations required large numbers of young male bodies to serve in the industrial armies that mass-produced death upon bodies of national Others. Personal bodies and identities came to articulate the Nation's "general will," to reproduce her children, to soldier in the national army, and to work in the factories and mines (Synott 1993). When Napoleon established legal obligations of male citizens to serve in conscripted armies to fight for France, this soon became the model for all nations for nearly two centuries, until the volunteer armies of today.

Following the American Revolution—a harbinger of nineteenth- and twentieth-century struggles against kings, shoguns, emperors, czars, and colonial powers—nationalists of various stripes gained political power and control of the state. As this happened, national governments embraced mass education and established or expanded schools to teach histories, traditions, and legacies in order to cultivate identities based on distinct conceptions of national culture and citizenship. Various sites became sacralized historical places, the birthdays or deaths of various leaders became ceremonial occasions. Certain dates became "historical" when marked by annual rituals of patriotism that affirmed the bonds of a national community unified within a common patriotic identity as citizens. So too did literate mass media and even religion help to ensure a seamless "national" worldview. The public sources of information such as journalism, expert opinion, and, ultimately, "common sense" secured the stability of the new social order.

Print Culture and the Creation of Civic Bodies

By the eighteenth century, the spread of Enlightenment thought, mediated through the same literacy that disposed a "civilized" body, enabled the growth of a bourgeois public sphere. Writing, through print capitalism and more general literacy, supported the construction of symbolic or abstract communities. The rising bourgeoisie created "peoples" as allies in their challenge to dynastic rule, peoples who also would be legally individual citizens in the new nation-states as well as legally individual workers in the emerging industrial factories. Widely circulated texts that were critical of dynastic rule supported new forms of inclusive symbolic communities based on "popular sovereignty" or "the will of the people" that had first existed only in the imagination. As republicans and bourgeois elites created unified peoples of disparate groups and promised to guarantee their freedom from "tyranny," these emerging republican sensibilities, dependent on disciplined bodies, became a basis on which nationalism would rise.

Print and electronic media bind space and foster expansion of control. Space-binding media favored the establishment of commercialism, empire, and the heightened influence of expertise. Indeed, one could say that modern Western history began with temporal organization and ended with spatial organization. Thus, the evaporation of an oral and manuscript tradition also meant the decline of concern for local community, tradition, and metaphysics, and their replacement by print and electronics that were biased toward space (Carey 1992, 134, 160).

First in the West and then almost everywhere, print cultures fostered the decline of tribe and lineage societies and the rise of the nation-states. However, long before the Reformation, the Enlightenment, republicanism, and the "proto-nationalism" of elites that would give rise to nationalism proper, there were transformations that disposed subjectivity to embrace the ideas and promises of nationhood. One of these was religious individualism, which emerged in monastic orders of the eleventh century and was linked to the ascetic work ethic and bodily restraints.

This encouraged transformations of subjectivity that would lead to individualized subjects who viewed themselves as agents, as later expressed in the Protestant ethic (Baumeister 1986; see Brown, in this volume). The movement to print-based literacy also impacted the body to foster a new form of agenic subjectivity. Indeed, the repression of sensuality in the monastery and later in Protestantism created a scarcity of fulfillment that the person might try to alleviate in work and reflection. Self-disciplining Protestant subjects held a rational, methodical work ethic devoted to accumulation above and beyond immediate needs (Collins 1986). The rise of the merchant economy created spaces for a secular realization of this ascetic work ethic founded on bodily control. In sum, two radical transformations fostered each other. On the one hand, the new form of subjectivity dislodged persons from enclaves of clan and estate and disposed them toward more individualized identities as workers or citizens. On the other hand, the emerging capitalist nation-states used various institutions, mediated through print literacy, to foster a national self.

The new political economy also brought about a separation of public and private realms. Peasants became proletarians, work was removed from the home, and the grand houses of the affluent bourgeoisie created a domestic sphere where family life was spatially and psychologically separated from the public realms of business and politics (Zaretsky 1976; Duby and Ariès 1987). The spatial separation between children and adults paralleled the recognition of childhood as a distinct stage in the life cycle with its own places, clothes, games, and formal schooling that would prepare children for the requirements of adulthood (Ariès 1962). This private realm provided a context for childhood socialization that fostered reflexivity and the view of the self as agent. An ascetic orientation to inner bodily desires, combined with a proactive orientation to the outside world, shaped a character type well suited for the rise and spread of capitalism (Fromm 1947). Whereas the emergence of a more individuated agenic self initially was "accidental," in part simply a result of Protestantism, commerce and contract law made such forms of subjectivity more "successful," and child-rearing practices became a more systematic process in which caretakers attempted to intentionally foster an internally disciplined child.

After the invention of movable type in the West in 1431, the development of the printing press, wide-scale distribution of the Bible, and the expansion of literacy together enabled people to read the sacred texts in the vernacular without benefit of clergy. The rise of bourgeois commerce was itself increasingly dependent on literacy and written records and this, along with the spread of new cultural understandings fostered by the Renaissance, also encouraged the flourishing of printing and literacy. Within a century, more than a million books had been printed. The process of learning to read itself disciplined the body, but at the same time, reading empowered people to criticize authority. The first printed book was the Bible, and it was assumed that the spread of literacy would make society more religious; but insofar as the reader was empowered, and insofar as alternative authorities could be read, the spread of literacy ultimately eroded the scribal monopolies of an earlier period. By fostering agency on the part of literate believers, and presenting competing sources of information and belief, reading had revolutionary consequences—not the least of which was the cultivation of alternative social imaginaries and challenges to the feudal and clerical elites.

In the world of ideas, Copernican challenges to the Ptolemaic worldview, the spread of humanism, and the rise of Protestantism ultimately eroded the theological legitimation of dynastic rule. Moreover, by encouraging individualism and agency, Protestantism made people appear weak if they submitted uncritically to authority. Print cultures foster and presuppose a disciplined body in which bodily impulses are regulated through internalized controls, thereby yielding individualism (reading alone) and a democracy of individualized readers. Further, in focusing on the individual spirit, Protestantism tended to desacralize the world and the body, making the body more easily the object of discipline and instrumental control, including the control of sensual impulses, physical lassitude, and sexuality. In all this, Protestantism shifted the locus of control from the church to individual believers, and thereby took the social discipline of the monastery into the personal body of everyone in the world.

The civilizing process also created a civilized body, in which the gradual acquisition of manners and politeness came with the repression or control of desire. For Norbert Elias, this process began as warrior chieftains and their councils were transformed into princes of courts, and diplomacy became more and more important for the administration of states and interstate relations. In courtly society, manners and social graces replaced threats and fights. The mannered practices of the aristocratic elites spread to other classes, especially as these "civilized" behaviors and manners were conducive to the rationalization of commerce in an ever-expanding marketplace of strangers. But it should be noted that the rapid spread of "civilized" behavior flourished *only after* the invention of printing and the spread of literacy. This was not a coincidence, because learning to read required the early discipline of the body and bodily desires—concentrating, not speaking or fidgeting, and the like. Thus, the socialization of children became a microcosm of the larger, long-term civilizing processes that were condensed into the few years of childhood. Childhood as a distinct stage of the life cycle emerged as a new social invention (Ariès 1962). But that said, this new period in the life cycle, as the moment in which literacy is best acquired, was also the time and site to instill the manners and politeness that would lead to control of bodily desires. Through reading, the manners and bodily discipline of the court spread "downward" both socially and developmentally—from the court to the bourgeoisie and from adults to children.

Reading requires the disciplining of the body—sitting still and giving focused attention. Learning how to read also is a kind of deferred gratification, because pleasure in reading comes only after one has struggled to learn to read, that is, once the process of reading has become transparent. To learn to read at an early age, the best (perhaps the only) way to become truly proficient, requires some mastery of bodily impulses, including tendencies for the mind to wander. For young children, the control over impulsivity is not "natural," yet early book learning has profound effects even at the level of neurological development. The very nature of arbitrary visual shapes indicating sounds and words that themselves represent something other than themselves fosters capacities for abstraction. Thus there was a close relationship between the disciplining of bodies and the rise of literacy, schools, and learning to read. A child learning to read also has learned to control his or her body, beginning with toilet training and extending to control over sexuality.

The first manuals of child rearing appeared in the sixteenth century, as the rise of childhood was becoming highly intertwined with a larger civilizing process that began in the courts and was embraced and deepened by the merchants. For the children of the merchant classes, by the seventeenth century childhood had become a time and site for formal training in literacy and mathematics that in turn required and instilled a sense of self-control and *shame* based on fear of losing honor in front of one's classmates (Postman 1986). The first panopticons were not Bentham's prisons, but bourgeois classrooms. Thus, schooling served to produce particular forms of bodily control and expression that disposed persons to feel and act in ways the mind alone could not otherwise direct (Shilling 1993, 22).

At the same time, schooling provided an active engagement with the rediscovered and newly invented cultural and scientific symbols, and new vernacular literatures fostering the active use of the imaginary (Postman 1982). Literacy, along with changing social-structural relations, encouraged a growing sense of empowerment of an expanding middle class.

With changing spatial practices, urban life, and early education, bourgeois children slowly acquired a more autonomous, agenic selfhood disciplined by a sense of shame and personal guilt. In Freudian terms, historical forms of ego and superego gained greater control over the id as manners and self-discipline came to suppress impulsivity. Eventually, as Elias has noted, nation-states and citizenship would depend on these internal controls.

In sum, in print-based cultures large numbers of the population learn literacy as children and acquire a sense of control and empowerment. The self-control of bodily desires enables reading, and mastery of literacy expands knowledge. This in turn gives readers access to alternative authority. Building on earlier cultural transformations, reading expanded and accelerated the emergence of persons as agents. Later, mass literacy would contribute to the democratization of society as the distinction of elite or scribal literacy and mass illiteracy waned, and new publics emerged that had access to information and means of communication beyond their immediate clans or neighbors. The discipline of the mannered courtier, and then of the general reader, predisposed the emergence not only of the self-disciplined citizens required by nations, but also of the soldiers of empire and the workers of industry.

Electronic Culture, Global Capitalism, Consumer Society

Two significant developments occurred in the early twentieth century. Nationalism became the dominant political trope, leaving untold death and destruction wrought in the name of national interest and realpolitik. And, with the spread of department stores, arcades, amusement parks, and the like, a culture of consumerism emerged. With movies and records, and then television and now the Internet, electronic communication came to have as much influence as did the spread of print literacy. Merchants and advertising agents began to employ mass-mediated images of selfhood, desires to be realized, and adversities to be overcome through the purchase of their products (Ewen 1976). With the commercialization of the airwaves and the flourishing of photojournalism, advertising and commercials began to encourage a good life through consumption.

Little anticipated at its inception, consumerism is leading to the erosion of the Nation as the dominant source of bodies, identities, and meanings. By the latter part of the twentieth century, with its electronically mediated system of transnational finance and production, and a globalized mass culture, capitalist nations were transformed from industrial societies based on the mass production of things into information societies based on the mass consumption of signs (Brown 2002). The key unit for under-standing bodies and identities today is thus the global consumer society with its myriad subcultures of hedonistic consumption.

At the same time, we are seeing the emergence of a new transnational class of capitalist elites and, in this incarnation of capital, the nation-state becomes less central, nationalism becomes anachronistic, and the new form of hegemony becomes consumerism (Sklair 2000). But to understand this transition, we must again note the importance of the media in and on the body. The print-based national body that paved the way for citizenship is being refigured electronically to become the consumer self. The new desiring self no longer supports self-sacrifice, even to the point of giving one's life for the sake of an imagined Nation. Consumer society encourages self-indulgence more than self-discipline—the pursuit of one's personal pleasures in the realization of a self defined through consumption.

Insofar as the new global economy produces both vast wealth and ob-scene inequalities, its elites have sought to secure their social positions in the face of new forms of resistance and critique. We suggest that consumer-ism has become the dominant hegemony of this new world. Innis recog-nized that the speed and distance of electronic communication greatly enhanced the possibilities of centralization and imperialism in matters of culture and politics. Whereas globalized capitalism has become more de-centralized and decoupled from nation-states, transnational corporations actually have more autonomy and influence. Indeed, through their regu-latory agencies such as the World Trade Organization, the International Monetary Fund, and the World Bank, major transnational corporations have more power than most countries. At the same time, through mergers, consolidations, and eliminations, there are now fewer languages as well as sources of media culture. For example, more than 80 percent of the world's films, television programs, books, music, theme parks, and the like are produced by some twenty major corporations.

Slowly, almost imperceptibly, there has been a growth of consumer-based identities, shopping-mall selfhoods, fandoms, taste cultures, and lifestyle enclaves, especially in the wealthier countries. One of the most important aspects of modern marketing has been the fostering of plural-ized life-worlds of consumption. That is to say, people of distinct age, education, occupational, or regional groups constitute markets for par-ticular products, whether cookies or clothes, Kentucky Fried Chicken or the Kirov Ballet. If the Nation brought diverse groups together under the fiction that they were a "people," consumer society fostered the splinter-ing of society and pluralization of life-worlds. This transformation has been occurring at the same time that national boundaries are ceasing to be barriers to the growth of transnational capital. Moreover, given the nature of mass media and the Internet, groups are no longer dependent on face-to-face interaction to share immediate experience; instead, they exist in realms somewhere between fantasy and virtual reality (Langman 1993). These expressions of self now sustain the social order not so much through "willing assent" in Gramsci's sense, but as an indifference to the political born of the migration of subjectivity from the public worlds of work, politics, or religion, to various private and personal realms. This process began when consumption first shifted from buying products for use, to marketing images that promised the fulfillment of repressed or stimulated desires. But in order for consumerism to become hegemonic, its dominant media would need to dispose the body to consumption as a major source of identity.

The creation of consumer bodies began more than a century ago with the beginning of advertising and the opening of department stores—the new palaces for purchasing by the popular classes. These processes have accelerated and become electronic in recent decades. Most people born in the West after 1950 have had television in their homes since infancy. This has eroded childhood as a stage in the life cycle separated from, but devoted to preparing for, an adulthood based on literacy (Postman 1986). The illusion of immediacy of visual media—that "it" is happening here and now—compresses both time and space and fosters the erosion of internalized discipline and restraints, and undermines the value of deferred gratification. Otherwise said, a major consequence of electronic media is a *decivilizing* process. Instead of impulse control and deferred gratification, television is preparing people for consumerism in an amusement society orienting them to gratification in the present. Indeed, it is important for late-capitalist, consumer societies to rid themselves of constraints and frugalities. The aural and visual media are impacting the body to transform subjectivity and identity in this direction. For example, viewing television requires no extended training period; most children can operate a television set before they can walk or talk. Changing channels brings an immediacy of visual gratification as colors and images change. The rapidly changing images, not to speak of the resolution of plots or crises, foster a compression of lived time. Stories unfold in twenty-four- or forty-nine-minute shows or in thirty-second spots. In other words, the self-indulgence required by consumerism is first instilled by privileging the visual and affective and thereby relaxing former constraints of childhood that were part of print-based nationalism.

As Postman (1986) suggests, literacy as a dominant sensual orientation requires shame that once guarded a private realm in the control of desire. As visual media foster hedonism and immediacy, however, its *content*, especially the revealing of what had previously been hidden from children, namely, adult sexuality, is no longer a matter of shame. Thus, television has made the backstage the front stage (Meyorwitz 1985). Although few would like to go back to the hypocrisy or repression of earlier eras, a number of cultural forces, not least of which are the visual media, have eroded the barrier of public and private and thus made hypocrisy itself less possible. From the highly erotic themes of regular programming to the self-aggrandizing tell-all talk shows, Internet porn, and even detailed descriptions of President Bill Clinton's oral outings, we have seen the erosion of shame as a social control.

In these ways, electronic cultures are much like feudal culture before "civilization" emerged in the form of manners, privacy, and shame. Indeed, today in "advanced" societies the trend is the opposite—a great deal of what we had come to assume was "private" is now public, overt, and shameless. In addition to the wide availability of pornography, for example, another innovation of the Internet is the twenty-four-hour-a-day Webcam monitoring of people's lives at home, including their most intimate activities. What previously was considered the "private sphere" now is where the subscriber (typically for about thirty dollars a month) can join women at "home" in images that include tooth flossing, toilet functions, sexual activities, and the like. Other sites offer scenes of "gynecologists," tanning beds, and leather fetishes. The television and Internet culture not only caters to voyeurism, but also encourages the exhibitionism and willingness of people to expose both the parts of their lives that are private and their private parts. The immediacy of the visual, and the opening up of what used to be backstage private and personal areas of life, is now eroding the culturally based shame and bodily disciplines on which literate-based national cultures have depended.

Conclusion: Culture, Media, and the Body

We can now suggest that in every complex society, elite intellectuals, whether they be philosophers, theologians, or literati, have produced an ideology of cloaked ideas, beliefs, and values that inhabit an invisible habitus. Yet the control of culture and the colonization of consciousness depend on the shaping of preconscious dispositions and receptivities to certain ideas. Just as Durkheim argued that society depended on its "precontractual" solidarity, hegemony depends on preconscious receptivity. Whether or not an individual or group is receptive to certain ideas depends, of course, on the extent to which these beliefs and understandings have an elective affinity with the conditions of everyday life that people face and the categories through which they understand them. As Weber and more recently Bourdieu have noted, status locations dispose beliefs and practices that both mask domination and ensure social reproduction. But this is too rational and logical. One must also note psychocultural dynamics that dispose ideological stances, especially those that foster assent to domination. Perhaps this was most clear in the work of Erich Fromm, who argued that acceptance or rejection of ideas depends as much on underlying character structure as class location. Certain ideas, whether the great chain of being, the Enlightenment, fascism, democracy, or consumerism, have been accepted or rejected on the basis of their appeal to an underlying "social character." Thus, as Fromm argued, medieval peasants saw a stable social hierarchy of land ownership as ordained by God in a society in which the nonexistence of God was, literally, unthinkable. Petit bourgeois merchants embraced Luther and Calvin, and the German lower middle classes in the 1920s and 1930s expressed their class-based character when they rallied behind Hitler. As suggested earlier, hegemony in Gramsci's sense of ideological control over culture was based on fundamental conflict between the current historic bloc, the subordinated classes, and those who would rule. But to Gramsci's understanding add the fact that in order for the dominant or would-be dominant class to rule, it must offer ideas and agendas with appeal to social and bodily character.

Thus, the Marxian understanding of ideas as imposed by elites must be amended to note that such ideas must have a more visceral appeal to that with which people are prepared to identify. It is at this point that social structures and media practices impact the body to predispose motives and beliefs that, while securing the interests of ruling classes, do so by providing various gratifications or, at least, alleviation of fears, anxieties, and malaise. Scribal cultures in which access to written knowledge created a vast gap nevertheless typically fostered cohesive societies in which the authorities provided people with solidarity, dignity, and a stable worldview. Such cultures often provided encapsulated sites for the expression of agency and free expression outside the realms of predominant power and authority. Print cultures depended on "civilized bodies" with disciplined subjectivities that found solidarity through mediated ties to abstract communities, and honor based on achievement. These disciplined subjectivities eventually became characterologically disposed to abstract ideologies, meritocractic entrepreneurship, and rational administration. In much the same way, as capitalist nation-states have entered more deeply into a globalized economic system that depends on consumerism for profits and legitimacy, electronically mediated visual culture is eroding the basis of nationalism and creating a space for consumerism as the hegemonic ideology of our age.

Hegemony as the control of culture enables the construction of meaning systems and identities that sustain power arrangements though assent. But that depends on the prior receptivity of those who are to be subjugated. Thus different kinds of media shape differing forms of subjectivity and the bodies and identities that find emotional gratifications from the ideologies that constitute them. Scribal cultures fostered subjects of the throne, print cultures fostered citizens of the state, and electronically mediated amusement cultures foster consumers at the mall and audiences to the spectacles of globalized capital. The power to define the subject and to dispose his or her body to certain ideologies serves to reproduce relationships of power.

References

Anderson, Benedict. 1991. *Imagined Communities: Reflections on the Origins and Spread of Nationalism.* New York: Verso.

Ariès, Phillipe. 1962. *Centuries of Childhood: A Social History of Family Life.* New York: Vintage Books.

Aronowitz, Stanley. 1992. *The Politics of Identity: Class, Culture and Social Movements.* New York: Routledge.

Baudrillard, Jean. 1974. *The Mirror of Production.* St. Louis: Telos Press.

Baumeister, Roy. 1986. *Identity: Cultural Change and the Struggle for Self.* New York: Oxford University Press.

Becker, Ernst. 1973. *The Denial of Death.* New York: Free Press.

Bourdieu, Pierre. 1984. *Distinction: A Social Critique of the Judgement of Taste.* Cambridge: Harvard University Press.

Brown, Richard Harvey. 2002. *America in Transit: Culture, Capitalism, and Democracy in the United States.* New Haven: Yale University Press.

Calhoun, Craig. 1997. *Nationalism.* Minneapolis: University of Minnesota Press.

Carey, James W. 1992. *Communication as Culture: Essays on Media and Society.* New York: Routledge.

Collins, Randall. 1986. *Weberian Sociological Theory.* New York: Cambridge University Press.

Duby, Georges, and Phillipe Ariès, eds. 1987. *A History of Private Life.* Cambridge: Belknap Press of Harvard University Press.

Ekman, Paul, with Klaus R. Scherer, eds. 1983. *Approaches to Emotion.* Hillsdale, N.J.: Lawrence Erlbaum.

Elias, Norbert. 1982. *Power and Civility.* New York: Pantheon Books.

Ewen, Stuart. 1976. *Captains of Consciousness: Advertising and the Social Roots of Consumer Culture*. New York: McGraw-Hill.

Freud, Sigmund. 1961. *Beyond the Pleasure Principle*. New York: Norton.

Fromm, Erich. 1941. *Escape from Freedom*. New York: Farrar and Rinehart.

———. 1947. *Man for Himself: An Inquiry into the Ethics of Psychology*. New York: Farrar and Rinehart.

Gellner, Ernst. 1983. *Nations and Nationalism*. Ithaca, N.Y.: Cornell University Press.

Gramsci, Antonio. 1972. *Letters from Prison*. New York: Harper and Row.

Habermas, Jürgen. 1968. *Knowledge and Human Interests*. Boston: Beacon Press.

———. 1982. *Legitimation Crisis*. Boston: Beacon Press.

Harstock, Nancy. 1998. *The Feminist Standpoint Revisited*. Boulder, Colo.: Westview Press.

Hobsbawm, Eric. 1991. *Nations and Nationalism since 1780: Programme, Myth, Reality*. New York: Cambridge University Press.

Hochschild, Arlie. 1983. *The Managed Heart: Commercialization of Human Feeling*. Berkeley: University of California Press.

Innis, Harold Adams. 1972. *Empire and Communications*. Toronto: University of Toronto Press.

Langman, Lauren. 1993. "Neon Cages: Shopping for Subjectivity." In *Lifestyle Shopping*, ed. Rob Shields. London: Sage.

———. 1998a. The Agenic Body. Unpublished manuscript.

———. 1998b. "Identity and Social Reproduction." In *Current Perspectives in Social Theory*, ed. Jennifer Lehmann. Hartford, Conn.: JAI Press.

Kroker, Arthur. 1984. *Technology and the Canadian Mind: Innis/McLuhan/Grant*. Montreal: New World Perspectives.

Mann, Michael. 1986. *The Sources of Social Power*. New York: Cambridge University Press.

Marcuse, Herbert. 1964. *One-Dimensional Man*. Boston: Beacon Press.

Meyorwitz, Joshua. 1985. *No Sense of Place: The Impact of Electronic Media on Social Behavior*. New York: Oxford University Press.

Postman, Neil. 1982. *The Disappearance of Childhood*. New York: Delacorte.

———. 1986. *Amusing Ourselves to Death: Public Discourse in the Age of Show Business*. New York: Viking Press.

Sennett, Richard. 1974. *The Fall of Public Man*. New York: Alfred A. Knopf.

Shilling, Chris. 1993. *The Body and Social Theory*. London: Sage.

Sklair, Leslie. 2000. *The Trans-National Class*. London: Macmillan.

Slater, Don. 1997. *Consumer Culture and Modernity*. Cambridge: Polity Press.

Synott, 1993. *The Body Social*. London: Routledge.

Tester, Keith. 1992. *Civil Society*. New York: Routledge.

Tompkins, Silvan. 1962–92. *Affect, Imagery, Consciousness*. 4 vols. New York: Springer Publishing Company.

Turner, Bryan. 1983. *Body and Society: Explorations in Social Theory*. New York: Blackwell.

Weber, Max. 1946. *From Max Weber: Essays in Sociology*. New York: Oxford University Press.

Zaretsky, Irving. 1976. *Capitalism, the Family, and Personal Life*. New York: Harper and Row.

9

Narration and Postmodern Mediations

of Western Selfhood

Modern Western philosophies, social sciences, and popular psychologies posit a radical distinction between individual and society in which wants, desires, and cognitive states are thought of as "internal" to the person. In René Descartes's (1960 [1637]) writings, for example, the self is a castle of consciousness, a kind of mental Robinson Crusoe separated from all external society or sensation, like an anchorite in the desert. Descartes and other thinkers such as John Locke and David Hume were concerned primarily with self-certainty and mastery. Their focus on the individual was, in effect, a revolt against earlier forms of government based on hierarchy and lineage yet they still sought cognitive certainty akin to that of God or revelation. Obligation and accountability began to shift, from courts of bishops and kings to the inner sanctum of the self. Will, including political will, increasingly was vested in the properly mastered sovereign self (Seligman 1992; Schochet 1975; Fox-Genevese 1991).

By the seventeenth century, when God left the throne from which he had ordered the universe, given a name to each thing, and told good from evil, the world was thrown into moral and epistemological crisis. The one unified divine truth began to issue into a myriad of particular human truths, each contending for faith and each representing an alternative form of life. Descartes attempted to restore certitude by finding a foundation for knowledge in doubt. By contrast, Cervantes accepted the multiplicity of partial perspectives and embodied this diversity in his imaginary characters. Thus was born the novel, and with it a principal vehicle for the articulation of modern consciousness.

Little by little the unbounded universe that Don Quixote had set out to explore became smaller. In the eighteenth century, Diderot's *Jacques le fataliste* is also on a journey in an unbounded space, but in the nineteenth century this openness is filled by civil society, by law, business, politics, and other social institutions. Time, too, becomes constricted. In Balzac, for example, time "no longer ambles along as it did for Cervantes and Diderot; it now races along the rails of History. Later still, the horizon closes in yet further for Emma Bovary, and comes to seem like a cage. . . . Dreams and daydreams surge into the monotony of the quotidian. The lost infinitude of the outside world is replaced by the infinite expansion of the soul" (Kundera 1984, 15). In other works, such as Hugo's *Last Day of a Condemned Man* or Dostoyevsky's *Notes from the Underground*, most of the action is interior to the person. The moral typography also shifts, from the exteriorized ethical universe depicted by Dante to the radically interiorized moral world of Albert Camus. This interiorization of psychological space is a counterpart to the expansion of physical space, as seen in the emergence of travel literature as a genre, and with tales such as *The Swiss Family Robinson* or *Robinson Crusoe* combining psychological isolation (and survival) within the vastness of a globalized world.

This movement toward inner-worldly individualism also had a grain of pathology, as implied in Cervantes's *Don Quixote* and developed in Diderot's *Le Neveu de Rameau*, but the comedic theme of these works turned to pathos with Melville's *Bartleby* and was brought to despair with Céline's Bardamu of *Journey to the End of the Night* (1932). Balzac, Dickens, and other writers of the realistic novel of the nineteenth century celebrate individualism and still find society a proper field for personal praxis. Their novels are filled with orphans, bastards, foundlings, and parvenus—all self-naming heroes and heroines who literally make themselves (Ermarth 1984). But contemporary protagonists do not realize their destinies through the system, which was still possible for Balzac's Eugène de Rastignac or Stendhal's Julien Sorel. Instead, they are averse to society, alienated, and "psychotic."

The penchant for self-created heroes is seen still in popular narratives, from *Horatio Alger* novels to *Rocky* films to the biographies of presidential candidates. Yet such stories have become fraudulent, masking more than revealing contemporary social structure and experience. Optimism in society and in literature is replaced by skepticism. Serious writing has shifted from representing the best hopes of society to revealing the worst fears of the individual. Yet this anguish is at the same time a humanism, for it implies in its radical and self-destructive will to truth that society should be a place for authentic human life.

The radical distinction between individual and society also has consequences for ethics: it encourages a polarization between egoism and altruism, in which altruism becomes a sort of nonutilitarian (irrational) sacrificial motive to "do good" for others even against one's own rational interests or desires. With these bifurcations, morality can only mean the sacrifice of one's wishes in favor of other, external persons and their interests. In this perspective, the interests of ego and the interests of alter approach a zero-sum game. Moreover, reason is defined narrowly as calculation, and body intelligence, emotional intuition, aesthetic sensibility, and moral judgment are relegated to the realm of subjective unreason.

This radical segregation of mind from body and of self from society is still taken uncritically as a foundation of analysis, even in the social sciences, where society is often viewed as an aggregate of atomized, utilitarian individuals whose relationships consist of rationally calculated exchanges. This view is useful for certain purposes, but it is blind to the transgenerational world of public goods and civic values. Indeed, to speak of such a public world, the individual–society distinction must be modified by a more sophisticated view of personal identity, one that stresses the dialectical continuities between body, psyche, and world and the ways in which public persona, ends, norms, ideals, other persons, and even objects are present within the selfhood of each person, that is, within the structure of subjective desire.

Philosophers, novelists, and social scientists advanced the project of modernity by discovering the individual, but because their search often was either wholly inward, or wholly social, the individual that they found was abstract and disembodied, exterior and prior to society or a mere product of social forces, a self only to itself. Either by omitting subjective actors, or by accounting for personal identity solely in terms of inner psychological states or interests, many thinkers ignored the body and its social and historical contexts that are the sources of selfhood. By contrast, these contexts are provided by the more inclusive concept of narrative and of the unity of characters and plot that a good story requires (Brown 1987, chapter 7; MacIntyre 1989, 202). This narrative view of the self brings bodies, identities, and societies together.

Narrative is an iconic social representation of moral action, an expression and preparation, therefore, for the most inclusive social representation—the democratic political community. By contrast, in the contemporary moral order, behavior is judged largely in terms of adjustment to the dominant technological system. Yet, as Habermas pointed out, "even a civilization that has been rendered scientific is not granted dispensation from practical [moral] questions; therefore a peculiar danger arises when the process of scientification transgresses the limit of technical questions. . . . For then no attempt at all is made to attain a rational consensus on the part of citizens concerning the practical [moral] control of their destiny" (1973, 255). The attempt to ethically master one's destiny is, of course, the stuff of which narratives are made.

I deploy and elaborate this perspective in this essay, first by advancing the metaphor of narrative as a way of understanding bodies/selves as they are shaped socially and historically. I then tell a story of Western identity, beginning with the early Protestant body/self as it emerged from medieval Catholicism and evolved into modern individualism. I then examine the emergence of a postmodern body/self, especially in the contemporary West, and how mass media are central in its formation. Finally, I compare postmodern and narrativist views of the body/self to suggest a discourse that is adequate for critical theoretical analysis as well as moral and political counsel.

Narration and the Body/Self

Identities, consciousness, and desires are shaped by and realized through the roles, institutions, and histories in which they are implicated. Yet, for the contemporary individual, who possesses capacities for both self-consciousness and social mobility, the body/self is never exhausted by any particular set of roles or situations. We always could have been or could become someone else, and usually we know this. Because of this very awareness and mobility, however, contemporary self-identity is all the more fragile. Dignity and meaningfulness in the life-world depend on one's ability to endorse the way of life one actually lives. But contemporary persons increasingly can or need to alter their biographies and write their own scripts and, in doing so, they relativize the value and legitimacy of any identity or life course that is chosen or imposed. Here, for example, is the "Icon Woman" celebrated by management guru Tom Peters (Time, May 22, 2000, 70). "She is an adventurer! She is the CEO of her life! . . . She submits her résumé on the Web and keeps it active there. . . . She creates and conducts scintillating projects . . . via a far-flung stable of teammates (most of whom she's never met)."

Yet most people do not choose changes of their roles, institutions, or biographies. Instead, we *suffer* them. This is especially true in poorer classes and countries that are peripheral in the world economy, and that are usually the objects rather than the agents of modernization. Thus, the labile and often coerced relationship between personal identity and institutional practice complicates the question of legitimacy, for to be so uprooted or transplanted from what one regularly does also is to become disaffected from the self that one has been or has become. This condition can lead to self-contempt because now one appears to be either unfree (acting only under duress) or deceitful (only pretending to endorse one's roles), or it may cause a hollowing out of identity as the self becomes more and more virtual and disconnected from shared embodied experiences. Because one does not dwell long in any role set or identity, one feels estranged from *one*self, anxious and ambivalent (Schutz 1964, 227).

This condition, of course, represents a democratization of reflective selfhood insofar as "the principles of natural subordination," as Edmund Burke (1958, 271) called them, have given way to an egalitarian conception of life chances and choices. The alternatives of *The Red and the Black* that confronted Stendhal's hero Julien Sorel give way to the red and the black, and the green, the pink, and the black and blue. In this context, traditional fatalistic conceptions of identity appear limited and even self-defeating, whereas atomized, utilitarian views seem narrow because the person and his or her interests are neither unitary nor fixed. Yet it is hard to go beyond such conceptions of self and legitimacy so long as the moral education of desire begins with the question "What do I want?" where all "I's" and "wants" are treated as already given empirical data. Instead, a more properly sociological moral education begins with the question, "Toward what aspects of the social-symbolic world in which I dwell (and which dwells in me) are my desires and my actions oriented?" "Which aspects of it do I, in being what I am, help reproduce?" These questions direct reflective attention to the layers of identity that mediate world and desire. Such reflection becomes in itself a kind of moral education because what seems to be the purely evaluative question "What should I want and do?" becomes in part the empirical question "Who really am I?" A sophisticated response to this question leads us to ask, "Do I want to be who I am, or someone else?" Such a framework of interrogation turns every specific problem of action into an instance of the general question "What is it rational for me to want and do if I desire to be the person I am (or wish to become)?" (Stanley 1978). Such an inquiry is also the beginning of the narrative creation of an autonomous and socially responsible self.

To the extent that the adult can take over and be responsible for his or her own biography, to really become the CEO of one's life, he can "come back to himself in the narratively preserved traces of his own interactions. Only one who takes over his own life history can see in it the realization of his self. Responsibility to take over one's own biography means to get clear about *who one wants to be,* and from this horizon to view the traces of one's own interactions as *if* they were deposited by the actions of a responsible author, of a subject that acted on the basis of a reflective relation to self" (Habermas 1987a, 98–99). For example, when someone complains that life is meaningless, as the suicidal often do, he or she is perhaps characteristically complaining that the narrative of his or her life has become unintelligible, that it lacks any point, any movement toward a fulfillment or telos. Hence the point of doing any one thing rather than another at crucial junctures seems to have been lost, and the question "Why bother to go on living?" becomes both pressing and difficult to answer.

The perspective of narrative thus is a method not only of psychosocial understanding but also of moral analysis, because the subjects of narratives make themselves accountable for the actions and experiences that compose their lives; that is, to have a narratable life is to open oneself to be challenged to account for what one did or witnessed or suffered at any past or present time. For example, to say of someone under one description (Superman) that he is the same person as someone characterized quite differently (Clark Kent) is precisely to say that he should be able to bring these apparently discrete identities, times, and places together within an intelligible narrative account (MacIntyre 1989, 202). To be responsible for one's life involves the capacity to tell such stories even if, as in the case of Superman/Clark Kent, one chooses to be silent. Indeed, character or integrity *is* that we have become the character/author of the autobiography through which we tell ourselves.

Narratives are never invented out of experience only. They also are provided as standardized genres into which happenings are organized into meaningful experience and memory and, indeed, through which we build the very lives we live and tell. As Jean-Paul Sartre observed in his autobiography, "a man is always a teller of stories, he lives surrounded by his own stories and those of other people, he sees everything that happens to him *in terms of* these stories and he tries to live his life as if he were recounting it" (cited in Bruner 1987, 21). Narratives exist in a community composed of those who both tell their own lives and listen to those of others, and shape their accounts accordingly. Such persons share certain ideal metaplots about "life," or certain forms of life, that make their respective particular stories good or instructive or at least intelligible. Without some shared rules of life-telling, tellers and listeners would regularly fail to grasp what the other is saying or hearing.

Such failure of understanding occurs cross-culturally, and increasingly between contemporaries, as the division of labor, rapid change, and post-modern fragmentation increase. For example, when clients in therapy or members of Alcoholics Anonymous seek to "take charge of their lives," they try to recount them as stories with a telos, as movements from the "was" of drunk to the "is" or "ought to be" of sober; or conversely, their stories/lives appear to be "flawed" or "unresolved" for lack of a cogent beginning, middle, and end. One also hears such narrative devices among psychiatric patients, transsexuals, enchanted persons, and others who wish to construct their current distress as merely temporary. As soon as I get out of the hospital, as soon as I am eighteen and can leave home, as soon as I get tenure, or the operation, or divorced—all are narrative devices for bringing order, cohesion, or hope to life (Frank 1981, 49).

Such strategies also can be effective for whole peoples or nations—especially in "dark times," as Hannah Arendt put it, when even our finest theories are not compelling and "ever-recurrent narration" becomes our best way to understand and master what has happened. "It is rather as though the colorless light of historical time were forced through and refracted by the prism of a great character so that in the resulting spectrum a complete unity of life and world is achieved" (Arendt 1968, 33; see Luban 1983).

In these ways, the intelligibility of moral and political life depends on narrative discourse. This is because the sense and meaning of individual acts are necessarily construed through attributions of motive and intention, and these depend on temporal contexts and on the larger moral traditions of which these contexts are a part. Although they might be cast in terms of psychological science, attributions of motive presuppose a narrative logic that gives moral meaning to particular acts and unity and continuity to particular lives. Narrative thereby links personal conduct with the possible impersonal good of the community by showing that past actions are causes of the present and that the future is a potential extension of present conduct (Frentz 1985, 5).

Yet, for many people today, any possible public narrative discourse must be characterized by an awareness of its own impossibility. More and more people today believe that there is no telos outside of human experience around which human conduct might be organized in narrative form. This indeed is a prime symptom of secularization. But perhaps we may say that the quest for such a telos *is* the moral telos of contemporary humanity. Such a master metaphor or central image, even though posited *as if*, enables persons or peoples to organize their lives into a drama that provides a purpose or a "reason to go on living." Then present "alienation" can be changed into expected "liberation," or the "suicide bomber" can become a "martyr." The master metaphor facilitates this by providing a central image and plot that persons can enact over and over again until it becomes what they really are—be it breadwinners, scholars, good mothers, warriors, or sober since 1992. Thus the grammars of "therapy" and "recovery," or "martyrdom" and "liberation," help to strengthen social bonds and identities in the ritual telling of stories by which persons try to live their lives, stories from which aspirations can be shaped and models or pathways sighted.

Standardized cultural texts, like tribal myths of origin, thus serve as templates from which identities are constructed (Langman 1992, 19). For example, heroes are the exemplars who face and overcome adversity, thereby realizing the qualities that a culture values. There also are particular identities based on social locations such as age, class, ethnicity, or gender. Other identities may be systematically produced by specialized institutions, such as a religious identity that is inscribed by the church, or a national identity that is instilled through schools and patriotic rites and celebrations. Other identities may be chosen from those available on the countertops of cultural consumption, from Madonna fan to mountain biker. This was adumbrated in *The Education of Henry Adams* (1980). Adams conceived of his subject—himself—as "broken into separate pieces" (ibid., 209) and "halves" (ibid., 294), and he generates various figurative identities for himself such as an eighteenth-century boy, a historian, a begonia, and a statesman (Staude 1990, 33). And finally, Adams's book is the story of his writing his story, which cannot contain his multiplicities in a conventional narrative form (Brown 1985). His narrative is thus a *quest* for narrative form.

Such multiplicity has expanded since Henry Adams wrote. It has moved "downward" to the popular classes in wealthy societies, and "outward" to include privileged or simply mobile groups in poorer countries. The "choices" of identities also are more labile and comprehensive. Lifestyles from yuppie, to Sloan Ranger, to BSBG (*bons sens, bons gens*), to Shicki-Micki provide identities. So does being an aficionado of power tools or power boats. Other identities may simply emerge through the enactment of everyday routines, such as women at the village well, or data clerks at the office. Some identities may be created or embraced by the actors themselves, such as muscle heads or heavy metal freaks, whereas others may be prompted by political events such as the antiwar movement of the 1960s and 1970s, the pro-life movement of the 1980s, or the survivors of September 11, 2001. Still other identities are imposed, such as Kaffir, kike, or faggot. Many of the social movements understood as identity politics can be seen as efforts to negotiate, redefine, and finally reject or embrace such identities. They are efforts, in effect, to create a better collective auto-biography (Langman and Scatamburla n.d., 18).

In sum, the narrative approach is a method both of research and of practice for understanding how selves are constructed, and for actually constructing them, in specific social-historical contexts.

Western Bodies/Selves from Early Protestantism to Modernism

One story of the modern body/self and of self-reflexivity starts with the Catholic confessional practices of twelfth-century Europe, which issued into diaries and manuals of spiritual development, piety, and Protestantism, and to the Counter-Reformation and Baroque elaboration of these themes, and then to psychoanalytic self-revelation, and the therapeutic "sharing" and talk shows of today. In this story, language is a common thread, the medium through which selves are cleansed, purified, normalized, made or made whole. Another theme is the progressive secularization and democratization of self-articulation or self-realization. In increasing sectors of contemporary societies, for example, "the possibility of the body/self as a project is now open to a mass audience, being no longer the goal or ideal of an elite court group or high bourgeois culture. Dieting, jogging, the work-out, mass sport, and physical education all have brought the idea of the perfect body to a mass audience" (Turner 1994, viii). In late or postmodern societies, the ideal body/self is pursued largely through consumption, as in the expensive gear, personal trainers, classes, or memberships that now for many are a prerequisite to working out.

Max Weber's (1991 [1904–5]) studies of the role of Protestantism in the shaping of modern societies contain insights into the creation of early modern bodies. Lutheran and Calvinist doctrine and practice, especially, separated the body from both sacral and superstitious belief and instead emphasized the ability and importance of the mind (in this case, to receive the word of God) (Mellor and Shilling 1997, 10–11). Thus the Protestant Reformation advanced modernity by secularizing the body, and with that, physical nature generally. Mind was separated from body, and reason from the world, which was now disenchanted as an object for rational inspection or calculation. As spirit became more inward, bodies, sociality, and nature became more "outward" and increasingly desacralized. This shift of the category "body" from sacred toward secular encouraged the movement toward a scientific inspection and commercial calculation of a now disenchanted, purely material world, and it also protected (or impoverished) modernity against the sensuality, magic, and superstition of the Middle Ages.

In its emphasis on individual consciousness and its desacralization of the body, the Protestant Reformation also fostered more individualistic and diffuse social groupings. Group orientation and bodily presence became less important as community and clan became less significant in relation to more broadly based and inclusive associations. The re-formation of the body was thus part of a movement in modes of interaction from *Gemeinschaft* to *Gesellschaft*, from relations of bodily proximity, as in extended lineage households or group sleeping, toward more abstract and impersonal relations at a distance, as in commodity purchases or labor contracts. Similarly, associations of faith, based on shared commitment to Protestant *beliefs* drawn from personal engagement with the Bible, began to replace communities of bodily interaction that had depended on carnivals, processions, or ritual eating. The sacred now became radically transcendent, whereas the worldly present became thoroughly profane, thereby facilitating greater instrumental social interaction with strangers, governance by abstract laws, and punishments aimed more at reforming the spirit than torturing the flesh (Mellor and Shilling 1997, 16; see Foucault 1979a).

The sensual became less significant as a way of being and knowing, and also was diminished as a mode of relationship. Touching, smelling, burping, nose blowing, farting, and other sensual expressions generally became private, even shameful, activities, not integral to broader social bonds, not so embedded in lived communal activities (Elias 1982). Bedrooms ceased to be communal, sex became private. Likewise, the *word* of God was distinguished from the *body* of Christ or the *embrace* of the church. The existing community of medieval commensals who ate together was replaced by associations of like-*minded* believers who prayed alone. Incense, icons, glowing gold leaf, and effervescent sociality gave way to a more somber interiorized and transcendental relationship with God. As affective expressions and bodily functions became more private, and as a public sphere emerged above the kin and communal, there was a parallel shift in the priority of the senses. The senses of proximity (touch, taste, smell, and feel) became relatively less important compared to the senses of distance (hearing and especially seeing). Reading, Bible study, commercial reports, and what

Anderson (1991) called print capitalism all became more important and literacy more widespread.

In emphasizing the individual's direct spiritual relationship to God, Protestantism undermined the sacredness of community and, indeed, of the social and material world in general. The ties that bound people together and linked their subjectivities into a more communally experienced identity were weakened. Further, the economies that were encouraged by the Protestant ethic eventually produced a profane consumer culture that came to undermine the very spirit of Protestant capitalism itself. Eventually the sacred itself was marginalized and a banal culture emerged that eschewed transcendence and encouraged the pursuit of ever more extreme intensities to stimulate desire, ward off boredom, and encourage consumption. Living collectively around an ideal gave way to living individually and instrumentally or indifferently toward others. The body and emotions (one's *own* body and emotions) became at once more important and more in need of attention, not as an obstacle (or vehicle) to transcendence, but now as a direct source of (potential) attractiveness and pleasure.

As interaction with kin and clan declined, the body became more armored and sovereign as it dealt increasingly with strangers. This also was encouraged by growing commerce, urbanization, social mobility, and formal rules and laws. Strangerhoods encroached on neighborhoods. Georg Simmel (1971) noted the centrality of bodily sovereignty and the priority of visual sensing in the urban way of life. Simmel shows how the individualization of urban life and the spatial structure of the city emphasize sight over the other senses, especially in street life, where one's *outward* appearance and one's *first glance* are very important.

A further transformation of the Western body/self begins at the opening of the twentieth century, when a streamlined, lighter, dynamic, and more mobile body emerges, defined now in dance, diet, posture-release regimes like the Alexander technique, and film, which render the body as fitness on display. "Advertising, from the patent medicines of the late nineteenth century to the body-care products of the 1920s and 1930s, links bodies and consumption; while in a reverse cycle bodies sell products as images of erotic attainment. Fetishized and abstracted, the body takes on the burden of modernity itself, of the circulation of image, desire, and ultimately of capital" (Armstrong 1996, 11). The body is now instrumentalized to express the individual self. Bodily movement, gesture, tone, and appearance become a silent speech as selves are offered for consumption.

The sign system of the body, including clothes, gestures, and illnesses, becomes more labile and shifting, no longer a set of static and direct markers of one's social status, and no longer regulated by law. Instead, in a society of "free" subjects moving in and out of various social positions, where bodies are in principle equal, the body and other markers of status become more achieved than ascribed, something to strive for and acquire. "Whereas formerly status preceded the sign, . . . the sign now takes precedence over status: by assuming certain signs a man achieves the status they signify" (Falk 1994, 54–55; see Bourdieu 1984; Baudrillard 1981).

Yet amid this surfeit of semiotic resources, it has become difficult to establish one's image and self because the meanings of social markers themselves are always changing, and because they must be arranged and displayed for so many changing publics, some of which are indifferent or unfriendly. The pervasiveness of surveillance deepens and extends this condition. Like guards seated in front of myriad monitors, urban dwellers also participate and assist in rituals of electronic voyeurism on their own and other people's activities. Persons are seen, and often see themselves, on surveillance cameras that register people entering buildings, riding on elevators, in front of bank tellers, or strolling the mall. Such technological images increasingly become mirrors in which to look for a body identity—in the checkout line, on the weight scale, in the mirror at the gym. Such identities are as discardable as they are malleable—indeed, disposable *because* malleable. The do-it-yourself biography, however, is always at risk, a corporal narrative in perpetual danger of dismemberment.

This lability of the body/self is created in part by the multiplicity of audiences and positions from which it can be viewed (and on which it can draw). These positions are discourse standpoints as well as social placings that include, for example, the legal discourse of prohibitions and offenses; the increasingly fluid discourse of sexuality and gender; the critical yet formalizing discourse of social science; the Internet discourse of cyberbodies that erases boundaries between people and machines and articulates bodiless selves and selfless bodies; the medical discourse of pathology and disease; and the death-baiting discourse of extreme sports (Armstrong 1996, 6). Indeed, the multiplicity of such discourses, and our fascination with the body as image and topic, suggest how tightly entwined bodily experience, visual pleasure, and social discourse have become.

Media as Socialization into Selfhood

Representation is crucial in the social construction of bodies and identities. Conversely, that representations be taken as real is a social accomplishment. Such realism necessarily requires exclusion. Thus, the representative institutions of politics, like the body that represents the self, are predicated on the silences and lies that are part of every discourse; that is, representations depend on necessarily exclusionary but presumptively comprehensive symbolic codes and communicative actions for their accomplishment *as* experienced. Thus, the presentness of all people and things in human experience—their establishment as real—also requires that much be *absent* or *un*real.

As such, representation depends on metaphor—the taking of one thing for another, the present leader for the absent voter, the present flowers for the absent lover, the visible body for the evanescent self, the present flawed material for the absent immaterial ideal, the present bread for the absent flesh of Christ. Insofar as the representation of change must involve what can be represented as real, or at least intelligible, representation secures continuity. In this sense, processes of change take place in and through semiotic structures that shift more slowly than events. From this semiotic *durée*, things commonly regarded as opposites—such as presence and absence, self and other, mind and body, individual and collective, change and continuity—appear as interdependent dyads whose opposition is not negation so much as mutual constitution. Thus, the representation of bodies and identities generally, and the representation of citizens in democratic polities, is always a simultaneous presence and absence, a constitution of that which is from that which is not (Norton 1988, 7).

Images have become central in the competition for recognition of bodies, identities, and brand names. Competition through mutually defining and negating images also becomes a vital aspect of the competitive quest for respectability, quality, prestige, reliability, or innovation that is associated with business firms. Corporate investment in image building, such as sponsoring art exhibitions, television productions, and new buildings, as well as direct marketing, becomes as important as investment in new plant and machinery (Harvey 1989, 289). The image serves to establish an identity in the market not only for products but also for status or sociability. The acquisition of an image, say, by signing with a Mont Blanc pen or dressing in Doc Marten boots, may be helpful in the presentation of self for job interviews or first dates. Then particular representations become central in the quests for individual self-realization, brand recognition, or political campaigning.

A major new agency of socialization into selfhood is electronic media that have radically escalated flows of images and information. These have grown extraordinarily in scope and power in recent decades, and have shifted the dominant mode of perception and expression, of presence and representation, from abstract verbal codes to more impressionistic and fragmented aural-visual images. Ease of communication with strangers combined with packaged media information enables people to know more about other members of society, but usually more superficially as stereotypic members of categories rather than as distinct persons experienced through diffuse copresence. Moreover, the proliferation and content of media information are generally more centrally controlled (except for the Internet), even while people have more easy and widespread access to it. The public arena is defined by broadcast media in advanced societies, but usually in ways that render citizens into passive consumers (Calhoun 1987, 24). This not only sells goods, it also sells capitalism itself *as* good, and makes other forms of political-economic organization less imaginable. Media are no longer simply means of transmitting information, but also of colonizing bodies, desires, and identities to secure consumption (Ewen 1988).

The viewing of public spectacles on TV in the privacy of one's home also serves as a kind of electronic ritual that can generate collective sentiments without requiring reasoned consensus or even copresence, particularly in heterogeneous societies, as Langman notes in his discussion of the American Super Bowl in this volume. Such rituals provide communion and social identification through common public imagery. One example of this is the commodification of "personality," which capitalist marketing strategists create to sell products or which they sell as a product in itself. Thus celebrity gurus offer personalized mantras to their celebrity acolytes, such as the Maharaji and the Beatles, and ordinary salespersons offer suits to ordinary customers that are "made for you." Likewise, as personality becomes part of the market, there is less difference between Jay Leno, George W. Bush, Oprah Winfrey, and Bill Clinton. Indeed, political figures get more face time with Leno or David Letterman than that available to them on "news" TV, presumably because the (scripted) banter reveals more of their true character than the (scripted) sound bites of newspeak. Of course, the commodified charisma of the media depends for its effectiveness on historically and politically shaped desires. But insofar as the media present themselves as objective, informal, or amusing, their manipulation of deep-seated sources of identity remains beyond scrutiny or even awareness. Increasingly in media-saturated societies, we become what we view, not as we do.

Even resistance to this commodification of self and reality, as in the search for authenticity, can be subverted by marketeers—as in the self-mocking of some advertising, or stores that sell "neat imitation bush hats" or "authentic reproduction bomber jackets." In an earlier time, the quest for authenticity was about putting mind, heart, and body back together again; but today it has become the project of correctly accessorizing one's persona in the fashion mart of selves, of assembling the right brand-name goods and looks (Allen 1995, 35; Lears 1994).

In using words to manipulate, today's advertisers use an ignoble rhetoric in Aristotle's sense. It is a colloquial language of verbal flicks and sound bites, with their casual inflations and enticing vagaries and lack of reasoned judgment. Wow! Really! Cool! Indeed, today advertising is less a promoter of materialism than a dissolver of people's connections with the material world. The imagery of media ads undermines the world of practical human activity and instead advances a world of images and dreams, of signs without referents. Contemporary selfhood becomes less connected to either work or personal relations and instead is more invested in the idea of unlimited personal consumption of goods, signs, experiences, relations.

In these and other ways, consumerism—the popular ideology of late capitalism—is produced and disseminated in the form of commodified culture. Selves are made, class relations are masked or reproduced, and dominant values, norms, and definitions of reality are rendered unquestionably normal. None of this is done through "the dictator's call to die for the fatherland, but an internalized voice of the sponsor calling, 'Attention, K-Mart shoppers . . .'" (Langman n.d., 4). Thus the media are *productive* technologies of power in Foucault's sense, producing both signs and the users or consumers of these signs. Advertising thereby creates docile workers who are also desirous consumers dreaming of vacation travel, electronic gadgets, high-powered rifles, and other instruments of identity (Falk 1994, 55; Allen 1995).

All this points to a major change in the sources of selfhood. Formerly, people were more able to locate their "real self" in their institutional positions and family contexts. The social validation of identities depended on participation in communities of work, church, neighborhood, or kin that could grant personal recognition. For example, simple activities that formerly were infused with affect, conducted within the family, and served collective memories, such as preparing food or caring for children, are now available for purchase or hire. Processes of nurturing by which selves are formed are thus drawn into the calculus of the market (Langman 1992, 11). Similarly, in some segments of society where traces of Protestant-like callings still endure (such as the ministry, academy, or army), work may continue to provide affective gratifications and confirmations of self. Yet more people today are likely to locate the "real self" in their subjective states and personal feelings that are intertwined with various images and activities of consumption, each of which suggests a virtual membership or identity.

The aural and visual culture creates a world of commodified goods, images, and leisure activities that stands apart from shared stable networks, except those based on the often disconnected neo-worlds of consumption itself. This disconnection of selfhood from shared lived experience also encourages the proliferation of multiple identities for different locations, publics, and circumstances. As identity diffusion and turnover accelerate, contradictions and disjunctions increase between different expressions of the self that are specific to different times and places. In response, the self is either elevated into an increasingly remote and abstract transcendental essence, or is collapsed into its performances (Goffman 1959), only now the performance is more scripted by the representational practices of the corporate state.

Exemplars of this can be found in biographical essays posted on a retro Web site in 1998. Bryant Adkins, in "A Child of the Eighties," writes: "I am a child of the eighties. That is what I prefer to be called. The nineties can do without me. . . . 'Generation X' is a myth created by some over-40 writer trying to figure out why people wear flannel in the summer." More significant than the expectable resistance and intergenerational conflict of Bryant's essay is that these sentiments are expressed through an electronic media technology, the World Wide Web, which tends to depersonalize the life story because it is diffused to an unknown and potentially unlimited audience with whom the author has no direct contact or accountability. Moreover, the narrative is one "in which persons and experiences are subordinated to consumer objects and electronically stored and circulated images: 'I would sleep over at friends' houses on the weekends. We played army with G.I. Joe figures, and I set up galactic wars between Autobots and Decepticons. We stayed up half the night throwing . . . Velveeta at one another. We never beat the Rubik's Cube.' And again, 'Ronald Reagan was some old guy. Gorbachev was the guy who built a McDonald's in Moscow . . . I drank Dr. Pepper . . . Shasta was for losers. TAB was a laboratory accident. Capri Sun was a social statement'" (Murphy 1998, 10).

"Another essay, 'Children of the Eighties,' written by an anonymous twentysomething woman [and] posted on the same website, tells a similar story: 'We are the children of the Eighties. . . . We are the ones who played with Lego Building Blocks when they were just building blocks and gave Malibu Barbie crewcuts with safety scissors that never really cut . . .

We hold strong affection for the Muppets and The Gummy Bears . . . In the Eighties, *nothing was wrong.* Did you know the president was shot? . . . We *forgot* Vietnam and watched Tiananman's Square [*sic*] on CNN and bought pieces of the Berlin Wall at the store'" (Murphy 1998, 11).

These little biostatements suggest how electronic mass media present alternative choices of selfhood and style of life through different patterns of consumption, and how people define themselves through the TV shows they watch, the store toys they had, and the brand-name foods and beverages they consumed or tossed at each other. The realm of television, billboards, and other mass media begins to merge with that of the self. In both realms, images of the self differentiate, shift, and multiply until, finally, one's "essential" self is so diffused that it is easily absorbed into its various presentations. Indeed, the self largely *becomes* its presentations, leaving people with the anxious task of forever discovering, or at least seeking, "who I really am."

The secular quest to reconstruct both body and soul also is encouraged by new medical possibilities of cosmetic surgery, organ transplants, and transsexual surgery, in addition to diets, workouts, and spas. The project of self-definition also has become a major preoccupation of both modern TV shows and postmodern persons, as Eva Illouz and Timothy McGettigan suggest in this volume. Yet, because such reshaped bodies/selves are experienced as fluid and chosen, they perforce are somewhat arbitrary because disconnected from stable bonds and relationships. Indeed, such identities tend toward the hyperreal, in that their surface is their depth; they are, and are little more than, what they seem to be. The relation of television to viewer becomes similar to the relation of self to other, in that both are now more like hyped and hyperreal relations of seller to buyer. Alternate commoditized lifestyles, each with its fleeting relations of self and other, become models of what to buy, how to live, and what to be.

The multiplicity of clashing social standpoints and discourses has accelerated in the postmodern world as traditional templates of identity wither and new ones proliferate in such a blazing variety that none of them seems ultimately compelling, except for some persons through commitments to charisma or religious acts of will. In a context of dissolving families, evaporating communities, and work roles that disappear or change overnight, the "true self" tends to withdraw from social institutions into personal feelings and subjective states, which then are easily appropriated by mass-media imagery and linked to alternative forms of consumption. Recognition of selfhood is now granted by new and more fragile memberships, often spontaneously invented ones marked by body tattoos, Internet chat sites, magazine subscriptions, ecstasy and rave, or deep fandom. Every available surface, from the body to a banana, comes to display an advertisement, like the Harley-Davidson bicep tattoo, the Chiquita sticker, or the T-shirt with a logo. The consumer, indeed, has become a new global identity that expresses the ideology of transnational capitalism and is replacing or supplementing such older identities as Shi'ite, Sumatran, or citizen.

Media images and virtual communities offer magical transformations and new identities, associating changes in consumption, fashion, or appearance with metamorphosis into a new person, like the "makeovers" on talk TV. Individuals are taught to identify with values, role models, and social behaviors through advertising, which not only helps to manage consumer demand, but also socializes people into dominant ideologies of class(lessness), age categories, and gendered roles and behaviors, each with its own styles and obligations of consumption. As consumers, viewers are invited to identify with brand names and other symbolic constructs and therefore to use their associated products. The taste worlds that emerge from these processes are stratified vertically like classes, but also horizontally, as people in a wide range of social positions introject their preferred simulations. In this horizontal stratification, status is based on the tokens of imagined alter egos or media doubles that one possesses. For example, "gangs in New York wear athletic paraphernalia of professional football and basketball teams and some colleges. The wearing of the sign vehicle conveys something about who you are and associative status is conferred. . . . One can become a synecdochichal Michael Jordan by wearing his shoes. It is possible that people begin to 'think themselves' in terms of models or images of teams, that fantasy and reality merge and are indiscernible" (Manning 1995). Indeed, not only has consumption come to shape subjectivity, but also the mass-mediated signifiers of selfhood are experienced as authentic by the very persons whose identities they have constructed.

When cultural revolutionaries such as Rousseau, Schlegel, or Shelley were shifting the basis of selfhood from social conventions to inner feelings, little did they know that this inner realm also would be colonized by the conventions of commodification. The multitude of fragmented, floating signifiers of selfhood coincides with differentiated market sectors and lifestyle groupings that become new communities of identity, more important for many persons than such traditional categories as class, ethnicity, church, labor union, or political party. Thus, in advanced consumer societies, social differentiation is far more complex than in Marxian class theory (Brown

2002). Perhaps Weber's understandings of status based on honor, as refined by Bourdieu, anticipated the variety of consumption-based lifestyles—such as pools and patios, shotguns and pickups, or Brie and Chablis. Such categories are further nuanced by gender, ethnicity, and generation and are used by marketeers for target advertising by television, magazines, bus sides, direct mail, benchbacks, matchboxes, sponsored public-school programs, Web sites, and telephone to selected demographic groups, and the promos that one must listen to when corporate America keeps one on hold. It then becomes possible to talk about lifestyle enclaves and "imagined communities" of consumption that, like national identities, are largely invented in the interest of elites (Langman 1992,10–12; Anderson 1991).

The challenge of narrating a self and life seems more difficult as roles become more various and complex, as social change accelerates, and as economic and psychological turnover is ever more rapid. This often results in the experience of ambivalence. Even "basic" emotions such as love or hate become precarious, as do the rules for their proper expression. Should a woman love a man for what he is or for what he will become, or become after that? Should a man be angry at his spouse for her betrayal, or ashamed of himself for his patriarchal feelings? Image bombardment also accelerates the decay of older icons, encourages a faster intellectual turnover and a sense of the impermanence of all knowledge and values, and hence fosters greater instability of self, feelings, commitments, and relationships, as well as seemingly obsessive talk and negotiation of all of these.

Modern ambivalence is often resolved in the postmodern hybrid or mutant. This is expressed in the success of the artist Cindy Sherman, who "becomes" dozens of characters for her *Untitled Film Stills*, or in those public spectacles that celebrate difference, such as those of chameleon-like androgynes David Bowie or Bryan Ferry, who break gender conventions in celebration of their own malleability. Bowie's message was rupture, escape—from class, gender, persona, or any received commitment, into a fantasy past or a science-fiction future. In the provincial towns where he played, every Bowie concert spawned startling other Bowies, local look-alikes experimenting with their bodies, appearance, sexuality, and gender (Bukataman 1993, 17). Virtual bodies already are in use on TV, as in *Final Fantasy* and in medical research via computer through the National Library of Medicine. Indeed, your surgeon will soon be able to do a computer- and robot-assisted practice operation on a virtual body of you (Grice 2001).

In these and other realms of entertainment and leisure, people can inhabit new bodies/selves or travel from underwater marvels to outer space on starships. Pop stars such as Michael Jackson and Madonna, or groups like the Grateful Dead or the Rolling Stones, or events like Burning Man also provide new spaces for postmodern selves. Indeed, for increasing numbers of persons, celebrities are central in imagined communities that exist in the hyperspace of gossip magazines, spectacles, TV appearances, and celebrity Web sites (Langman 1992, 15). For example, we talk easily about TV stars or political celebrities such as Monica Lewinsky, commiserate with them on a first-name basis, or dislike them intensely, even though we have never had a conversation with them or even met them. In this sense, our imagined, media-generated connections to our social world are outstripping the actual contacts we have with it. Spectacles like the Super Bowl, for example, are not personal and participatory so much as unilateral and electronic. They operate as hegemonic ideology, not only by atomizing the population and creating pseudosolidarities of consumption, but also by displaying a surfeit of spectacular goods and lifestyles among which the viewer may electronically wander and experience simulations of satisfaction. Citizens, then, became consumers of illusions (Bukataman 1993, 36; Debord 1992).

Most of what people know about stars as images is from fan magazines, gossip columns, press releases, staged interviews, and prepared TV clips that are generated by entire organizations devoted to the production of personae. Within these image factories, dream invaders are crafted to enter people's psyches by stealth, without resistance or even awareness, to shape their patterns of consumption. The commodifiers of celebrity can even manufacture charisma to sell not only movie or rock stars and tickets to their films and concerts, but also soap, athletic shoes, cars, or politicians, as well as ideologies and identities. Corporations, governments, political and intellectual leaders also value an image appropriate to their presumed authority, power, and worth. The production and marketing of such images require considerable sophistication because stability of the image has to be retained even while stressing its adaptability, flexibility, and dynamism, and also because there is such intense competition for branding. Postmodern representation (Brown 1995) becomes, in effect, the means whereby an individualistic society of transients sets forth its nostalgia for stability and common values by identifying with brand names that seem more substantial than themselves.

In an earlier period in the West, the soul or spirit was conceived and experienced as distinct from the body, and as the nonmaterial essence of the person. For postmoderns, however, this relationship has become confused, even reversed. The search for a transcendental essence is abandoned and the body that can be immediately seen and felt now becomes the real and present manifestation of the self. The malleable self now resides in the malleable body, and the spirit is no longer trapped therein. The body comes to signify who the person "really is." To a great extent the body *is* the self, and to mold the self many feel that they must mold the body, through working out, diet, plastic surgery, or mood-enhancing drugs (Glassner 1990). As surface becomes indistinguishable from depth, we increasingly are what we appear to be.

A postmodern construction of the body/self also is evident in discourses that describe the "death" of the essential body and its technological replacements and extensions. In this discourse, the de-essentialized body loses its ontological depth and thereby becomes a surface to be worked upon. Indeed, death and eternal life may themselves become a lifestyle choice, as when Timothy Leary directed the production of his own death, or when people described Elvis's death as "a great career move," or when the film character of Dracula is portrayed as a cool seducer. "The postmodern Dracula is a lover, and when the heroine self-consciously chooses to go with him in one such genre film, it could only be said that she preferred his lifestyle. The hook of [today's] vampire film is that life among the undead is not that different, only more intense (Frank 1989, 7). Such views are matched by their opposite—a nostalgia for the spontaneity and emotional passions often associated with preindustrial, medieval, or Third World bodies, a desire for unmediated experiences and feelings, of the Nepalese monk or the Jamaican beach boy, for a body in which one can be at home (Mellor and Shilling 1997, 26).

Death, especially as experienced through participation in social rituals of death, is more clearly a narrative and, hence, an ethical affair, because it requires us to tell a story and find its meaning. People at a funeral tell stories, interpret character, and try to find a moral meaning for that life. "Unlike Durkheim's aborigines, modern mourners do not simply grieve. They have the occasion, albeit mediated by signs, to gather up from what is said and remembered of the deceased something which they can choose to take into their own lives. . . . But the immense problem remains, how do we 'get clear about who one wants to be'?" (Frank 1989, 15–17). One response to this condition is to merge with the entire universe. Indeed, this service is provided by a California firm that transports and releases ashes of dead persons in outer space, so that one's eternity can be lived among the stars.

The problematization of the body/self, of its definition and its boundaries, also is seen in postmodern art forms, which have been characterized as an antiaesthetics of the body. In the body art of Oppenheim, for example, a videotape titled *I'm Falling* shows the artist "trying to drown himself in a tank of water (a parody, perhaps, of Salvador Dali's earlier 'Inverted Submarine'). . . . Another video shows in slow motion rocks being dropped on Oppenheim's stomach. The videotape of his multimedia presentation, 'Disturbational Art' . . . shows Oppenheim eating 10 gingerbread men and then microscopic slides of the excreta of the gingerbread men, which are then projected in galleries (open to misreading as merely abstract painting), alongside a running loop videotape of the whole ingestion and excremental process" (Wall 1987). A second example is that of the Australian body artist Stelarc, who uses medical instruments to film the insides of his own body. The interiority of blood flows, muscles, heartbeats, and "acoustical landscape" shows the body as fascinating—that is, at once beautiful and repulsive" (Kroker and Kroker 1987, vi). Likewise, Cindy Sherman gets her anatomical/artistic materials from medical supply houses. She then breaks and tortures these prosthetic body parts and covers them in gore and vomit to create images of repulsive beauty that seduce in order to disgust (Tompkins 2000).

In a similar spirit, the French performance artist and professor Orlan used cosmetic surgery to shape her body/self to make a statement. Orlan devised a model of the classical Western ideal of feminine beauty and has had nine cosmetic surgeries to help her achieve it. She titled the entire project "The Ultimate Masterpiece: The Reincarnation of St. Orlan." As this is performance art as well as surgery, Orlan decorates the operating room and the surgical staff for her "theatrical production, and insists upon local anesthesia so that she can choreograph and interact throughout the entire surgical proceeding. [Another example is] Cindy Jackson, who founded the Cosmetic Surgery Network in order to consult with people contemplating cosmetic surgery. Ms. Jackson has undergone more than 20 procedures in 8 years, 'all by way of incrementally morphing herself in the general direction of her declared female paradigm, the Barbie doll. . . . Jackson believes that there is nearly limitless potential for changing the body, that your body doesn't have to be static through its entire life' (Siebert 1996:25)" (Med Mod & Pomo Self n.d., 20–22).

Modern thinkers from Robert Musil to Erving Goffman articulated a self that was defined by its social situation. But today subjectivity is located more in postmodern capitalism's dreamworlds of consumption. Persons' bodies/selves today can be sited anywhere from hyperreal worlds of desire such as glitz, fortune, and stardom to hyperreal places of consumption such as shopping malls, theme parks, rock concerts, fantasied restaurants, and enclave vacation resorts. In all these postmodern sites, the central feature is the production of hyperreal images, simulations to be consumed in hyperreal spaces that are themselves simulations. In the hands of artists such as Oppenheim, Stelarc, or Orlan, these processes are satirized through the inclusion of one's own intestines, heartbeats, and surgically stripped flesh.

Premodern social life was bifurcated into sacred and profane realms, where the sacred, though intensely experienced and demarcated from everyday routines, gave the group an identity and imbued the mundane with meaning and significance. Today, however, our tribal identities are affiliated not so much with alligators as reptiles but with alligators as little emblems on shirts. The sacred/profane is supplanted by the hyperreal/ banal. Identities once vested in tribal totems are now invested in ideal media images or brand-name identifications. Indeed, the consumption and performance of brand-name identities has become the postmodern form of narrative texts that today, like sacred myths of former times, give meaning to ordinary lives and profane experience (Langman 1992, 14; see Gottdiener 1997). Ads for Virginia Slims, as an instance, "seek to persuade women that it is liberating and progressive and perhaps even slimming to smoke that brand . . . The 'Virginia Slims woman' is exhibiting modernity, thinness, or female power when she lights up her Slim" (Kellner 1992, 164, 167). Similarly, the consumer who smokes and becomes the "Marlboro man" consumes stoic masculinity as much as a cigarette. Such ads point to new gender roles for women and reinforce old ones for men, both validated by the culture industry. The disenchantment promoted by industrialism is now reenchanted in a postindustrial world of signs.

The models of identity conveyed by the mass media are dreamlike images, but they do present an actual world; that is, dreams are not worlds that we merely observe from outside, but ones we also inhabit. As such, these dreamlike images acquire a lived personal significance. For example, when Melanie Griffith's character in Working Girl leaves the secretary pool to become a stockbroker and gets the man, all through her individual effort, we are induced to believe that class poses no barrier to success through personal initiative. TV also contributes to privatization simply by being usually watched in one's own home. In such ways, movies and television facilitate ideologies of individualized responses and private solutions to public problems. Although poor protagonists occasionally become prosperous heroines, patriarchal and capitalist domination endures, especially for the secretaries and sweepers who stay behind.

In sum, the electronic media shape our selves and sentiments. They play economic and cultural roles in society by fostering definitions of an esteemable body/self and quality of life in terms of commercial values.

The media have taken over the image banks and modes of expression of a vast number of viewers, generating the icons at which we gaze and the forms of homage that we pay them. Telepolitics reinforces civic privatism, the ideology of separated individuals for whom personal gratification or advancement, defined through consumption, are the major goals of life, all at the cost of civic engagement.

Postmodern Capitalism: A Fusion of Aesthetics and Consumption

We are now in a position to make some preliminary remarks on representations and relations of bodies and identities in global capitalism. One discourse in which these relations might be articulated is that of aesthetics or, more broadly, representation. The "aestheticization" of production and consumption refers to the rapid flow of signs and images that saturate and infuse products, consciousness, and consumption. The aestheticization of the body/self appears in its transformation from a social or natural given to a lifetime project of autocreation, a project that also is conducted largely through signs and images. In trying to theorize these processes, we can begin by extending Marx's fetishization of commodities to the commoditization of fetishes, including the fetishized body/self. Marx noted that exchange value obliterated and replaced the original use-value of things; but in doing so it allowed the commodity to freely float toward any secondary meaning, use-value, desire, or what Baudrillard (1975, 1981) called a "sign-value," a fetish that stands for itself. In this formulation, consumer capitalism does not merely extend the materialism of an earlier producer capitalism, but also confronts people with a new dreamworld of desires and aestheticized images that de-realize reality and realize appearances into a new hyperreal aesthetic/economic space (Featherstone 1992b, 270; Haug 1986, 52; 1987, 123).

With these changes, the Puritan ideology of early capitalism has collided with an increasingly hedonistic ethic of consumption now favored by capitalism itself. The need of today's entrepreneur to seduce, to compete with ever more complex pleasures, inscribes him in a consumerist ideology directly at odds with the "bourgeois" virtues of sobriety, thrift, and hard work that had assured the earlier development of production (Beneyto 1990, 8–9). In effect, the disciplined and inner-directed body/self of an earlier capitalism described, respectively, by Michel Foucault and David Reisman comes into contradiction with the hedonistic cyborg body/self of late capitalism as described by Brian Turner (1994) or Donna Haraway (1989). The moral liberation or even license necessary for consumption begins to erase the stricter morality necessary for production. Products, life, and capitalism itself become aestheticized as the manufacture of desire becomes indispensable in the making and selling of things.

As basic needs are satisfied or seen as essentialized constructions, the production of things further gives way to the production of wants. Here the principle of the classical economist Jean-Baptiste Say is pertinent—that supply precedes and creates demand. In this formulation there is no fixed, essential, or preexisting need that could be calculated or known in advance. Indeed, the great mistake of certain centrally directed economies has been to presume to calculate some natural demand or essential need that could be known in advance and to which production would respond. By contrast, market-oriented economies make no presumption about human desire as any metaphysical or given essence. Instead, capitalism must create such desire through the invention of the novel, the attractive, or, more often, the semblance or simulacra of the new and the attractive. Here late capitalism merges with the aesthetic avant-garde insofar as both supply their products in order to create desire, rather than merely to satisfy a desire that is already experienced by the consumer. Instead, before consuming the product, the consumer consumes the images (equivalent to the product) that create the desire which the product (equivalent to the images) seem to satisfy, at least until a new desire/product has been created.

Thus, it is precisely in the production of desire that aesthetics, body/ selves, and economics converge. Desire, the ultimate goddess of the aesthetic avant-garde, is the energizer of late capitalism and the "essence" of de-essentialized postmodern selfhood. The distinction is no longer between the necessary and the superfluous, between basic needs and luxuries, or between mere appearances and the real self, but between a multiplex of as yet unimagined possibilities. Capitalists and consumers both join artists as they become workers on and of the imagination. Far from becoming merely irrelevant or co-opted, aesthetic skills of representation are reintegrated into postmodern capitalism as even the body/self becomes a project of creative destruction and reconstruction. After expropriating desire, the system relegitimates itself in the now heroicized figure of the entrepreneur, the dream maker, the teaser and the pleaser, the economic artist who elicits and seems almost to fulfill human desires. Then the focus shifts from the older dynamics and mechanics of capitalist oppression to the production and manipulation of social reality and social subjects, and to how long the old ideology of economic rationality and the new theory of personal fulfillment can survive their next deconstructions.

Similar processes obtain in the postmodern crafting of bodies and identities. The symbolism of selves and the shaping of bodies through consumption is perhaps especially significant in complex societies with a high division of labor and high social and geographic mobility. As Helmut Staubmann noted (1993, 8), "high mobility requires an expressive symbolism demonstrating the status or features of the identity of a person in fluctuating interaction situations. The traditional ascriptive status and its stable expressive symbolism gets replaced by oscillating changes of fashions," including the appropriate body. A similar idea was suggested by Alexis de Tocqueville (1945) and Thorstein Veblen (1994) when they argued, respectively, that the differentiated and fluid American society generates expressive symbologies of fashion and money to display one's identity in interactions with new partners and unknown neighbors.

Such extensions of the "economic" into the "cultural" are matched by the reverse—the rise of a symbolic economy. This postmodern economy of signs has no precedent, and is barely recognizable in the works of Adam Smith or Karl Marx, neither of whom paid much attention to reproduction or consumption (Hickson 1992, 12–13). Marx, for example, largely took culture for granted and saw only relations of production as crucial, thereby fetishing the system of production and the market and neglecting processes and settings of labor formation, knowledge creation, and the constitution of the body/self and desire.

By contrast, it is much more obvious today how cultural production limits, shapes, and infuses economic reproduction, and not only the reverse. For example, in postmodern capitalism intellectual creativity is a major, perhaps *the* major, factor enabling changes in the means and relations of production. Innovations in cultural styles of consumption and identity similarly encourage new modes and outputs of production. Moreover, new modes of consumption such as shopping malls or credit cards have themselves elicited new production (Ritzer 1999). Thus, instead of taking bodies, identities, and forms of life for granted (and leaving them exterior to analysis), today a cultural economics needs to focus on the processes of cognitive innovation, identity formation, new definitions of lifestyles and modes of consumption, and, above all, the creation of desiring bodies.

Many authors have noted the extension of the market into the family and other areas of the life-world. But I am speaking here of a qualitative acceleration, and even reversal, of this process, in which the market itself is transformed into a sphere of ephemeral hyperrealities where "authentic feelings," "family values," and "economic calculation" all melt into each other. Such a transformation transforms the meaning of "economy." The market can no longer be plausibly understood as exterior to social settings and cultural values from which it emerges. Instead, postmodern capitalism requires, creates, and is reproduced by people who can engage in creative processes of consuming the new production.

As past and present or near and far are recycled and mixed into pleasing images, the artistic shaping of sentiments and desires finally everywhere infuses a reality that is inseparable from its aesthetic representation. "And so art is dead, not only because its critical transcendence is gone, but because reality itself . . . has been confused with its own image" (Baudrillard 1983b, 151). Mass tourism, films made in spectacular locations, and the micronarratives of advertisement set in exotic climes present an unlimited range of virtual experiences and simulated body/selves. What is experienced are processed images of beautiful flesh, persons, and places that are stylized and marketed like any other product in an age of electronic (re)production. Art ceases to be a distinct, closed-off sphere of experience, because the hyperreal blending of the actual and the virtual extends aesthetic fascination to things, bodies, and identities in a nonintentional surrealistic parody of the world.

To perform or even survive as a player in the volatile markets of style requires new skills in manipulating body, identity, taste, and opinion. One can project one's own image as a leader in personal style or one can saturate the market with images that ride the volatility to one's enrichment as an entrepreneur. In either case, this requires the creation of new logos, signs that are aimed at stimulating desires and associating them with products that otherwise have nothing to do with the original sign. Indeed, it could be said that capitalism now produces signs and sign systems more than commodities or, more precisely, that the commodity to be sold has become the image or icon of a sign system. Corporations seek to dominate markets and psyches by promoting fetish-like brand names that inspire and are re-created in ritual acts of consumption. Oligopolies like the big four in tobacco, or Nike and Reebok in sports gear, or Nestlé's in canned milk, achieve their global domination through sponsorship of spectacles and massive advertising campaigns around the world. Indeed, one feature of the new world economy is precisely the globalization and oligopolistic control of mass media that guide the taste preferences of customers, turn wants into needs, and alter patterns of selfhood to encourage consumption.

Advertising's primary cultural effect is a "democraticization" of desire for new and improved bodies, identities, and things. Although marketing does little to change the actual class or economic position of consumers (except perhaps to encourage indebtedness), it has yielded a homogenization and inflation of wants and aspirations. Yet such rising expectations generally have not led to revolution or even to significant protest. Why not? First, people who produce themselves through consumption have difficulty imagining alternatives to the consumer society in which they have become passive consumers, not active citizens. Second, for many people the capitalist system eventually does deliver. The democratization of desire stimulates innovation and larger production runs, so that goods that formerly were luxuries often become broadly available, aggressively marketed, and avidly consumed by more and more people as necessities. Even in China, the "three wants" of the 1970s—bicycle, radio, and sewing machine—became basic needs in the 1980s as the motorcycle, television, and refrigerator became the three new wants. Thus a democratization of goods arrives to satisfy a democratized desire even as other newer luxury goods emerge at the upper end of the market to restimulate desire and reinitiate the cycle. In the caste system of commodities, people may complain that the cargo of consumption is too meager, or that the rich receive an unfair measure, but not that the system itself is unjust, a system that, in any case, is constantly reinforced ideologically by the Capitalist Realism of commercial art and advertising, which in turn motivates the desire that fuels the dynamic of consumption, production, and creative destruction.

These remarks suggest that capitalism has won out over aesthetics, that it has absorbed the avant-garde and tamed the aesthetic and even the political critiques that have dogged it since the industrial revolution. But perhaps the reverse is true. Perhaps the aesthetics of irrationality, style, and desire have absorbed the disciplined and ascetic rationality of an earlier capitalism. Perhaps not capitalism but the cultural representation of desire has won by aestheticizing the political economy. Or perhaps it is impossible to tell the difference. As works of the cultural avant-garde often look like kitsch, and as entrepreneurship becomes a stylistic manipulation of images, it becomes more difficult to distinguish the impresario from the artist or the stockbroker from the swami.

Once they are recognized as symbolic action, however, economic activities cease to be an abstract or isolated facet of human experience. And once bodies and identities are understood as historical constructions they cease to be removed from political economy. Instead, one can talk of the political economy of corporal identities, even as the meanings of finance, production, and consumption are viewed as social-symbolic processes in which all the social categories are being continually redefined, including those of the body/self. This is true of local firms and markets as well as of national and international economic processes; it is true of individual body/selves as well as collective body politics and cultural identities, because ultimately producers and consumers alike remain embodied actors in the destructive creation of value.

Postmodern, Poststructuralist, and Narrative Ways of Knowing

If the body is not stable, what else possibly could be? Indeed, for Michel Foucault, some feminists, certain deconstructionists, Lacanian psycho-analysts, and poststructuralists generally, the body or the self sometimes disappears entirely. For example, most feminists considered sex to be bio-logical and gender to be a kind of cultural superstructure built up on that biological base. But now it appears that sexual differences too are ideo-logical constructions. Thus Julia Kristeva asks, "what can 'identity,' even sexual identity, mean in a new theoretical and scientific space where the very notion of identity is challenged?" As nature collapses into culture, all that was biological foundation melts into the air of social construction.

In this context, postmodernists and others have declared that inte-grated selfhood—and hence a master narrative of one's own identity—is impossible as a project and oppressive as an ideology. For example, the French structuralist psychoanalyst Jacques Lacan (1971, 190) argued that each person is divorced from himself or herself: "Life goes down the river, from time to time touching a bank, staying for a while here and there, without understanding anything—and it is the principle of analysis that nobody understands anything of what happens. The idea of the unifying of the human condition has always had on me the effect of a scandalous lie." Similarly, Jeffrey Mehlman (1974; see Staude 1990, 16) argues that "all autobiography is necessarily fictive; it creates a self whose very coher-ence is the sign of its falseness and alienation—just as the child's image in the mirror is false. The self as a fictive entity constituted in images or words . . . cannot refer back to the 'real' world because of the inherently non-referential nature of all signs." Michel Foucault, Jacques Derrida, and others deconstruct the subject even further, viewing it not as a personal entity but as a process of subjugation that is achieved through discourses of domination (Taylor 1989, 489). Such deconstruction undermines most of what was initially valued (except perhaps the power of critique or de-construction itself), and little is left to affirm except pure but uncommitted freedom, pure *because* it is uncommitted.

As the pace and complexity of societies accelerate, the body/self be-comes more porous and malleable. Indeed, postmodernists argue that the very notion of the autonomous subject is a myth or illusion, the product of a moment in modernity that is passing with the advent of postmodern culture and postindustrial capitalism. For example, Fredric Jameson (1991) argues that the subject has fragmented into a flux of hyperreal intensities, whereas Baudrillard (1983b) insists that we are absorbed into a world of signs without referents, and have become no more than a "term in the terminal," a mere effect of cybernetic systems of control. Likewise, Deleuze and Guattari (1983) celebrate schizoid, nomadic dispersions of desire and the decentering of subjectivity.

This postmodern or poststructural critique is radical. But it is not radical enough. Lacan, for example, believes that because we ultimately, or at least psychoanalytically, understand nothing, the idea of unity as a principle of understanding is a scandalous lie. But why should the psychoanalytic principle that nobody understands anything be any less scandalous than the hermeneutic or narrative principle that we can understand some things as unities? Lacan seems to feel that the artificial or constructed character of understanding particulars in terms of unities is inherently specious when placed against his fundamental conception of our *non*understanding. Here Lacan is a foundationalist. He absolutizes a principle of understanding/ nonunderstanding that is useful for Lacanian psychoanalysis as though it were useful for everything. By contrast, a more radically rhetorical and consistently (de)constructionist position would view different principles as generating, and appropriate to, distinct discourses, publics, and purposes. Instead of appreciating a pluralism of principles as relatively more (or less) valid for different purposes or domains, however, Lacan universalizes nonunderstanding as *the* human condition. Postmodernists thus join both positivists and existentialists in assuming that human life is meaningless, or that all versions of such meanings are invalid because artificial, illusionary, or laden with repressive power. But perhaps the standards of adequacy of all such thinkers are too high, insofar as they imagine that if life, or history, as a whole can have no total or unitary, no ultimate or objective meaning, then lives of particular persons or peoples cannot have even partial penultimate meanings, and that these cannot be more or less adequate for different forms of life.

Similarly, Mehlman (1974) insists that all autobiography is necessarily fictive insofar as it is a symbolic construction of coherence. But from a more radically relativist viewpoint, *all* human experience is symbolic construction of coherence. Indeed, this is what makes human experience *experience*, and not chaotic happenings or a buzzing, booming confusion of sensa. In Mehlman, also, one finds a lingering positivism or absolutism, an image of a reality that is outside of or prior to images, yet still accessible to our apprehension. But, as phenomenologists, language philosophers, and symbolic realists have argued, a view of human life as prior to social-symbolic construction or understanding conceives of human life as exterior to precisely that which makes it human (e.g., Merleau-Ponty 1962; Goodman 1978; Burke 1966; Brown 1989).

Moreover, to consider only the fictive, absent, or *différance* is to miss the claim of the theorists of the narrated self. For example, although Mehlman (1974) focuses on the inherent nonreferentiality of the autobiographical self, he nonetheless presumes that the false entity created in the text is a separate and distinct representation, much like Descartes's idea of the self as cogito. Likewise, by making a fetish of decentered fragmentation, some postmodern theorists deny what is part of their own text—the responsibility to realize the text of one's being that is implied in the radical freedom of deconstruction and in the metaphor of textuality itself (Brown 1989). What Heidegger called transcendental ego is eschewed in post-structuralist metaphors of aporia and *différance*, but it reappears again in the assumption of postmodern authors that their own texts are intelligible to readers, even readers constructed by that (authorless?) text. Discursivity, however self-referential, is no escape from the challenges of narration.

Thus these two views—the self as narrated and the self as absent, fictive, or subjection—are not so far apart. First, both positions accept that the self is a social-symbolic construction. Nor would the theorist of narrative disagree that the constitution or knowledge of selfhood involves power. But such theorists differ from Foucault and others in not reducing everything to power, in not seeing "discourse" as wholly dominating "speech." Foucault is nothing if not a social thinker. He does hope "to arrive at an analysis which can account for the constitution of the subject within an historical framework," but to do this, he says, "one has to dispense with the constituent subject, and to get rid of the subject itself" (Foucault 1980, 17). This can be a wholly legitimate method of approach and, in Foucault's hands, it is certainly fruitful. Yet the result is still a story, even a metanarrative, only now the protagonist is not persons or Progress, but agencies like discourse and the microphysics of power.

Although theorists of narration have much in common with deconstructionists, they differ from Derrida in not insisting on an opposition of "essence" and "absence." Indeed, Derrida is seen as sociologically naive in failing to recognize the shaping of varieties, degrees, and processes of essentialization, relativization, foundationalism, or fragmentation *through interaction*. By contrast, for narrative theorists the idea of the self as narration provides a needed moral and civic framework for the deconstructive critique. Indeed, the narrative theorist differs from most postmoderns (and many liberals) in the view that choice is not merely freedom from external constraints (such as metanarratives of patriarchy, reason, etc.) but, more, that to choose is to sacrifice one good for another—love or duty, family or nation—and it is of such ethically laden choices that chronologies become stories and lives become dramas. Politically, this implies that social constraint will always be with us, and that if such constraint is not that of legitimate public authority, it surely will resurge in other, likely more sinister, forms.

At the dawn of modern Western selfhood, persons were expected to exercise some authority over themselves. Indeed, from John Locke to Henry David Thoreau this was seen as a prerequisite for participation in public life (Fox-Genovese 1993, 12). Today this requirement of self-direction is waning. It is dismissed by many on the left as bourgeois or uptight, and on the right as a prideful resistance to the revealed authority of God or his spokesmen. Some postmodernists reconstruct postliberal individualism and a revised social contract in which persons can "take" from the polity, especially rights or equality, without having to give something in return, notably legitimacy. Yet the self, alone, cannot create equity, justice, or any other virtues or artifacts of political life.

Of course, none of this means that narratives are necessarily "liberating." Dominant ideologies also are stories of origin, nature, and destiny that foster identities to fit existing, often oppressive, roles. And they also provide frameworks of meaning and understanding, and even some degree of dignity and encapsulated power, despite their legitimation of what others, from different ideological or narrative perspectives, would call degradation. It is in the very contestation of such stories, however, that politics is enacted.

Indeed, we could say that the narrative perspective invites practical political critique beyond the usual postmodern deconstructive ideological or textual critique. For example, the theorists of narration see socialization into selfhood as shaped through cultural images and narratives of identity that are inherently laden with power. In this sense, culturally available scripts of selfhood are ideological constructions that define people or "subject positions" in ways to reproduce social arrangements. These identities can be seen as strategies that mediate the routines of everyday life and thereby reproduce or reshape the social order.

What we call the "self" of the person who tells her story becomes an artifact of her account of herself as it is defined in a social matrix of discourse. The identity of the narrator is itself inconstant, however, for it depends on listeners' conceptions of her role and intentions, which may change with each telling. On this account, the space for "deconstruction" and "genealogy" is located within the understanding that there is no ontological basis for fully harmonious unities, and hence that each such apparent unity can be deconstructed; that is, they can be shown not only to contain anomalous, irregular, or disparate elements upon which this unity has been imposed, but also silences and omissions that mask this process. Theorists of narration take all this seriously, but still affirm a place for public authorship, and, hence for civic authority. Thus a narrative theory of authority, or of ethics or politics, acknowledges the deeply ambiguous character of the achievements that it cherishes most.

And, in this perspective, the questions still remain: What discourses, what social formations, encourage what kinds of narratives, and what kinds of scripts for selfhood encourage a democratic civic life? In this more inclusive vision, it becomes clearer that paradigmatic narratives of contemporary selfhood have been largely captured by discourses such as therapy, expertise, advertising, and consumerism; that the personal autonomy and integrity of character that are cherished in modernist ideologies are deeply challenged; and that reflective self-direction of people and peoples remains not so much our condition as our quest and hope.

References

Adams, Henry. 1980. *The Education of Henry Adams*. Franklin Center: Franklin Library.
Allen, Henry. 1995. "A Billboard Lovely as a Tree." *New York Review of Books* (July 13): 34–35.
Anderson, Benedict. 1991. *Imagined Communities: Reflections on the Origins and Spread of Nationalism*. New York: Verso.
Anonymous. N.d. "Medical Modification and the Postmodern Self." Manuscript.
Arendt, Hannah. 1968. *Men in Dark Times*. New York: Harcourt, Brace and World.
Armstrong, Tim, ed. 1996. *American Bodies: Cultural History of the Physique*. New York: New York University Press.
Baudrillard, Jean. 1975. *The Mirror of Production*. Trans. Mark Poster. St. Louis: Telos Press.
———. 1981. *For a Critique of the Political Economy of the Signs*. Trans. Charles Levin. St. Louis: Telos Press.
———. 1983a. "The Ecstasy of Communication." In *The Anti-Aesthetic: Essays on Postmodern Culture*, ed. Hal Foster. Port Townsend, Wash.: Bay Press.
———. 1983b. *Simulations*. New York: Semiotext(e).
———. 1998. *The Consumer Society: Myths and Structures*. London: Sage.
Beneyto, José. 1990. "History Is Junk: Deconstructing Capitalism as Post-Histoire." Manuscript.
Bourdieu, Pierre. 1984. *Distinction: A Social Critique of the Judgment*. London: Routledge and Kegan Paul.
Brown, Richard Harvey. 1980. "The Position of the Narrative in Contemporary Society." *New Literary History* 11.3 (spring): 545–50.

———. 1983. "Dialectical Irony: Literary Form and Sociological Theory." *Poetics Today* 4.3: 543–64.

———. 1993. "Moral Mimesis and Political Power: Toward a Rhetorical Understanding of Deviance, Social Control, and Civic Discourse." In *Reconsidering Social Constructionism: Debates in Social Problems Theory*, ed. James A. Holstein and Gale Miller. New York: Aldine de Gruyter. 501–22.

———. 1997. *Society as Text: Essays on Rhetoric, Reason, and Reality.* Chicago: University of Chicago Press.

———. 1998. *Toward a Democratic Science: Scientific Narration and Civic Communication.* New Haven: Yale University Press.

———. 2003. *America in Transit: Culture, Capitalism, and Democracy in the United States.* New Haven: Yale University Press.

———. 1985. "Narrative, Literary Theory, and the Self in Comtemporary Society." *Poetics Today* 6.4: 573–90.

———. 1987. *Social Science as Civic Discourse: Essays on the Invention, Legitimation and Uses of Social Theory.* Chicago: University of Chicago Press.

———. 1989. *A Poetic for Sociology: Toward a Logic of Discovery for the Human Sciences.* Chicago: University of Chicago Press.

———, ed. 1995. *Postmodern Representations: Truth, Power, and Mimesis in the Human Sciences and Public Culture.* Urbana: University of Illinois Press.

Bruner, Jerome. 1987. "Life as Narrative." *Social Research* 54.1 (spring): 11–32.

Bukataman, Scott. 1993. *Terminal Identity: The Virtual Subject in Postmodern Science Fiction.* Durham, N.C.: Duke University Press.

Burke, Edmund. 1958. *Reflections on the Revolution in France.* London: Oxford University Press.

Burke, Kenneth. 1966. *Language as Symbolic Action.* Berkeley: University of California Press.

Calhoun, Craig. 1987. "Populist Politics, Communications Media and Large Scale Social Integration." *Working Paper 16*, Center for Psychosocial Studies, Chicago.

———. 1994. *Social Theory and the Politics of Identity.* London: Blackwell.

Cellini, Benvenuto. 1946 [1558]. *The Autobiography of Benvenuto Cellini.* Trans. John A. Symonds. Garden City, N.Y.: Doubleday.

Cmiel, Kenneth. 1991. *Democratic Eloquence: The Fight over Popular Speech in Nineteenth-Century America.* Berkeley: University of California Press.

Debord, Guy. 1992. *The Society of Spectacle.* Trans. Donald Nicholson-Smith. New York: Zone.

Deleuze, Gilles, and Félix Guttari. 1983. *Anti-Oedipus: Capitalism and Schizophrenia.* Trans. Robert Hurley, Mark Seem, and Helen R. Lane. Minneapolis: University of Minnesota Press.

Descartes, René. 1960 [1637]. *Discourse on Method, and Meditations.* Trans. Lawrence Lafleur. Indianapolis: Bobbs-Merrill.

Durkheim, Émile. 1960 [1893]. *La Division du travail social.* 7th ed. Paris: Presses Universitaires de France.

———. 1965. *The Elementary Forms of Religious Life.* New York: Free Press.

Durkeim, Émile, and Marcel Mauss. 1963. *Primitive Classification.* Chicago: University of Chicago Press.

Elias, Norbert. 1982. *The Civilizing Process.* Trans. Edmund Jephcott. New York: Pantheon Books.

————. 1987. *Involvement and Detachment: Contributions to the Sociology of Knowledge.* Cambridge: Blackwell.

————. 1991. *The Society of Individuals.* Cambridge, Mass.: Blackwell.

Ermarth, Elizabeth Deeds. 1984. *Realism and Consensus in the English Novel.* Princeton, N.J.: Princeton University Press.

Ewen, Stuart. 1988. *Captains of Consciousness.* New York: McGraw-Hill.

Falk, Pasi. 1994. *The Consuming Body.* London: Sage.

Featherstone, Mike. 1992a. " The Heroic Life and Everyday Life." *Theory, Culture and Society* 9 (February): 159–82.

————. 1992b. "Postmodernism and the Aesthetization of Everyday Life." In *Modernity and Identity,* ed. Scott Lash and Jonathan Friedman. Oxford: Blackwell. 265–90.

Foucault, Michel. 1973. *The Birth of the Clinic: An Archaeology of Medical Perception.* Trans. Alan Sheridan. London: Tavistock.

————. 1979a. *Discipline and Punish: The Birth of the Prison.* Trans. Alan Sheridan. New York: Random House.

————. 1979b. *The History of Sexuality,* vol. 1, *An Introduction.* Trans. Robert Hurley. London: Allen Lane.

————. 1980. *Power/Knowledge: Selected Interviews and Other Writings, 1972–1977.* Ed. and trans. Colin Gordon. New York: Pantheon Books.

————. 1988a. *The History of Sexuality,* vol. 3, *The Care of the Self.* Trans. Robert Hurley. London: Tavistock.

————. 1988b. *Madness and Civilization: A History of Insanity in the Age of Reason.* Trans. Richard Howard. New York: Random House.

————. 1987. *The History of Sexuality,* vol. 2, *The Use of Pleasure.* Trans. Robert Hurley. London: Allen Lane.

Fox-Genovese, Elizabeth. 1991. *Feminism without Illusions: A Critique of Individualism.* Chapel Hill: University of North Carolina Press.

————. 1993. "Beyond Individualism." Paper presented to the Meetings of the American Political Science Association.

Frank, Arthur. 1981. "Implications of the Self Experience of Biographical Discontinuity." *Reflections: Essays in Phenomenology* (winter): 46–53.

————. 1989. "The Self at the Funeral: An Ethnography of the Limits of Postmodernism." In *Studies in Symbolic Interaction,* ed. Norman Denzin. Greenwich, Conn.: JAI Press. 11.

————. 1990. "Bringing Bodies Back In: A Decade in Review." *Theory, Culture and Society* 7.1 (February): 131–162.

————. 1991. "For a Sociology of the Body, an Analytical Review." In *The Body, Social Process and Cultural Theory,* ed. Mike Featherstone, Mike Hepworth, and Bryan S. Turner. London: Sage. 36–102

Frentz, Thomas S. 1985. "Rhetorical Conversation, Time, and Moral Action." *Quarterly Journal of Speech* 71.1 (February): 1–18.

Friedman, Jonathan. 1994. *Cultural Identity and Global Processes.* Thousand Oaks, Calif.: Sage.

Glassner, Barry. 1990. "Fit for Postmodern Selfhood." In *Symbolic Interaction and Cultural Studies,* ed. Howard S. Becker and Michael M. McCall. Chicago: University of Chicago Press. 215–43.

Goffman, Erving. 1959. *The Presentation of Self in Everyday Life.* New York: Doubleday.

———. 1961. *Asylums: Essays on the Social Situation of Mental Patients and Other Inmates.* New York: Doubleday.

———. 1964. *Stigma: Notes on the Management of Spoiled Identity.* Englewood Cliffs, N.J.: Prentice Hall.

———. 1967. *Interaction Ritual, Essays in Face-to-Face Behavior.* Chicago: Aldine.

Goodman, Nelson. 1978. *Ways of Worldmaking.* Indianapolis: Hackett.

Gottdiener, Mark. 1997. *The Theming of America: Dreams, Visions, and Commercial Spaces.* Boulder, Colo.: Westview Press.

Grice, Gordon. 2001. "Slice of Life." *New Yorker* (July 30): 36–41.

Habermas, Jürgen. 1987. *The Theory of Communicative Action,* vol. 2, *Lifeworld and System: A Critique of Functionalist Reason.* Boston: Beacon Press.

———. 1989. *The Structural Transformation of the Public Sphere.* Cambridge: MIT Press.

Halberstam, Judith, and Ira Livingston, eds. 1995. *Posthuman Bodies.* Bloomington: Indiana University Press.

Haraway, Donna. 1989. "Manifesto for Cyborgs, Science, Technology, and Socialist Feminism in the 1980s." In *Feminism and Postmodernism,* ed. Linda Nicholson. London: Routledge. 190–234.

Harvey, David. 1989. *The Condition of Postmodernity: An Enquiry into the Origin of Cultural Change.* Oxford: Blackwell.

Haug, Wolfgang Fritz. 1986. *Critique of Commodity Aesthetics: Appearance, Sexuality, and Advertising in Capitalist Society.* Minneapolis: University of Minnesota Press.

———. 1987. *Commodity Aesthetics, Ideology and Culture.* New York: International General.

Hickson, John. 1992. "Postmodern Economy: Cultural Contradictions and Intellectual Practice." Manuscript.

Issacharoff, Michael. 1976. *L'Espace et la nouvelle.* Paris: Corti.

Jameson, Fredric. 1991. *Postmodernism, or, the Cultural Logic of Late Capitalism.* Durham, N.C.: Duke University Press.

Kellner, Douglas. 1989. *Critical Theory, Marxism, and Modernity.* Cambridge: Polity Press.

———. 1992. "Popular Culture and the Construction of Postmodern Identities." In *Modernity and Identity,* ed. Scott Lash and Jonathan Friedman. Oxford: Basil Blackwell. 141–77.

Kroker, Arthur, and Marilouise Kroker, eds. 1987. *Body Invaders: Panic Sex in America.* Montreal: New World Perspectives.

Kundera, Milan. 1984. "The Novel and Europe." *New York Review of Books* (July 19): 15–20.

Lacan, Jacques. 1971. *Écrits II.* Paris: Éditions du Seuil.

Lacqueur, Thomas. 1990. *Making Sex: Body and Gender from the Greeks to Freud.* Cambridge: Harvard University Press.

Langman, Lauren. 1992. "Citizen Madonna: The Politics of Modernity." Manuscript. Department of Sociology, Loyola University, Chicago.

———. N.d. "Identity and Hegemony: Toward a Critical Social Psychology." Manuscript. Department of Sociology, Loyola University, Chicago.

Langman, Lauren, and Valerie Scatamburla. N.d. "The Self Strikes Back: Identity Politics in the Postmodern Age." Manuscript. Department of Sociology, Loyola University, Chicago.

Langman, Lauren, and Wanda Harold. 1989. "The American Midas." Paper presented to the meetings of the American Sociological Association.

Lash, Scott, and Jonathan Friedman, eds. 1992. *Modernity and Identity*. Oxford: Basil Blackwell.

Lears, Jackson. 1994. *Fables of Abundance: A Cultural History of Advertising in America*. New York: Basic Books.

Locke, John. 1959. *Essay concerning Human Understanding*. New York: Dover.

Luban, David. 1983. "Explaining Dark Times: Hannah Arendt's Theory of Theory." *Social Research* 50.1 (spring): 215–47.

MacIntyre, Alasdair. 1989. *After Virtue: A Study in Moral Theory*. Notre Dame, Ind.: University of Notre Dame Press.

Manning, Peter. 1995. "The Copy." Manuscript. Department of Sociology. Michigan State University, East Lansing.

Marcuse, Herbert. 1969. *Eros and Civilization*. Boston: Beacon Press.

Mauss, Marcel. 1979 [1936]. *Sociology and Psychology: Essays*. London: Routledge and Kegan Paul.

Mehlman, Jeffrey. 1974. *A Structural Study of Autobiography: Proust, Leiris, Sartre, Lévi-Strauss*. Ithaca, N.Y.: Cornell University Press.

Mellor, Philip A., and Chris Shilling. 1997. *Re-forming the Body: Religion, Community, and Modernity*. London: Sage.

Merleau-Ponty, Maurice. 1962. *Phenomenology of Perception*. London: Routledge and Kegan Paul.

Murphy, Jim. 1998. "Excremental Capitalism." Manuscript. Department of Sociology, University of Maryland, College Park.

Musil, Robert. 1952. *Der Mann ohne Eigenshaften*. Hamburg: Rowohlt.

Nelson, Jenny L. 1986. "Television and Its Audiences as Dimensions of Being: Critical Theory and Phenomenology." *Human Studies* 9.1: 55–69.

Norton, Anne. 1988. *Reflections on Political Identity*. Baltimore: Johns Hopkins University Press.

O'Neill, John. 1985. *Five Bodies: The Human Shape of Modern Societies*. Ithaca, N.Y.: Cornell University Press.

Proust, Marcel. 1948. *Maxims of Marcel Proust*. Ed. and trans. Justin O'Brien. New York: Random House.

Ritzer, George. 1999. *Enchanting a Disenchanted World: Revolutionizing the Means of Consumption*. Thousand Oaks, Calif.: Pine Forge.

Sartre, Jean-Paul. 1966. *Being and Nothingness*. New York: Simon and Schuster.

Schochet, Gordon J. 1975. *Patriarchalism in Political Thought: The Authoritarian Family and Political Speculation and Attitudes in Seventeenth-Century England*. New York: Basic Books.

Schutz, Alfred. 1964. *Collected Papers*, vol. 2, *Studies in Social Theory*. Ed. Arvid Broderson. The Hague: Nijhoff.

Seligman, Adam B. 1992. *The Idea of Civil Society*. New York: Free Press.

Siebert, Charles. 1996. "The Cuts That Go Deeper." *New York Times Magazine* (July 7): 6, 20ff.

Simmel, Georg. 1971. *On Individuality and Social Forms: Selected Writing*. Ed. Donald N. Levine. Chicago: University of Chicago Press.

———. 1978. *The Philosophy of Money*. Trans. Tom Bottomore and David Frisby. London: Routledge and Kegan Paul.

Stanley, Manfred. 1978. *The Technocratic Conscience: Survival and Dignity in an Age of Expertise*. Chicago: University of Chicago Press.

Staubmann, Helmut. 1993. "The Aesthetics of Economics." Paper presented at the International Institute of Sociology, Sorbonne, Paris.

Staude, John-Raphael. 1990. "Autobiography, Identity and Modernity." Manuscript. Teeside Polytechnic, England.

Taylor, Charles. 1989. *Sources of the Self: Making of the Modern Identity.* Cambridge: Harvard University Press.

Thomas, William I. 1966. *On Social Organization and Social Personality: Selected Papers.* Chicago: University of Chicago Press.

Tocqueville, Alexis de. 1945. *Democracy in America.* New York: Alfred A. Knopf.

Tompkins, Calvin. 2000. "Her Secret Identities." *New Yorker* (May 15): 74–83.

Turner, Brian S. 1986. "Personhood and Citizenship." *Theory, Culture, and Society* 3.1: 1–16.

———. 1992. *Regulating Bodies: Essays in Medical Sociology.* London: Routledge.

———. 1994. *The Body and Society: Explorations in Social Theory.* London: Sage.

Turner, Ralph H. 1976. "The Real Self: From Institution to Impulse." *American Journal of Sociology* 81 (March): 989–1016.

———. 1994. "Race Riots Past and Present: A Cultural-Collective Behavior Approach." *Symbolic Interaction* 17.3 (fall): 309–24.

Veblen, Thorstein. 1994 [1899]. *The Theory of the Leisure Class: An Economic Study of the Evolution of Institutions.* New York: Penguin Books.

Weber, Max. 1991 [1904–5]. *The Protestant Ethic and the Spirit of Capitalism.* New York: HarperCollins.

Weigert, Andrew, and David Franks. N.d. "Ambivalence: A Touchstone of the Modern Temper." Manuscript. Department of Sociology, University of Calgary.

Contributors

RICHARD HARVEY BROWN has written broadly on the politics of knowledge, and, more recently, on relations of culture, identity, and globalization. His books include *Society as Text, A Poetic for Sociology, Social Science as Civic Discourse, Toward a Democratic Science,* and *America in Transit: Culture, Capitalism, and Democracy in the United States.* His first career was in international development, and he continues occasional policy research and consulting as president of the Washington Institute for Social Research. He is professor in sociology at the University of Maryland, College Park.

ANTONELLA FABRI is an anthropologist trained at the State University of New York, Albany. She conducted extensive fieldwork among internal refugees in Guatemala during the years of the civil war and also worked for MINUGUA, a United Nations peace process initiative, within which she investigated allegations of human rights violations. She has published on the politics of violence as it is manifested in the memories of Mayan women who survived the Guatemalan civil war. She has taught contemporary urban problems, with emphasis on Latin America, and is a research associate at John Jay College and at the New York Academy of Medicine, where she conducts studies on drugs in New York City.

EVA ILLOUZ teaches in the sociology and anthropology department at the Hebrew University of Jerusalem. She is the author of *Consuming the*

Romantic Utopia and is completing *An Essay on Cultural Interpretation: Oprah Winfrey and the Glamor of Misery.*

PHILIP W. JENKS, a political scientist, has written extensively on Hannah Arendt, Michel Foucault, and liberalism. In addition to pursuing political theory, he also writes poetry, including a recently published volume, *On the Cave You Live In.* He teaches in the university studies program at Portland State University and is currently engaged in a critical examination of birth- and population-control practices on Native American reservations.

LAUREN LANGMAN became involved in social protest as a graduate student because of the changing nature of civil rights and antiwar mobilization. As a result of his political activism, he moved from psychology to sociology and has remained politically active throughout his career, writing from the perspective of critical theory and organizing many conferences concerned with political critique and resistance. He is past chair of the Marxist section of the American Sociological Association and president of the Research Committee on Alienation of the International Sociological Association. He is on the editorial boards of *Sociological Theory, Current Perspectives in Social Theory,* and *Critical Sociology.*

TIMOTHY W. LUKE is University Distinguished Professor of Political Science at Virginia Polytechnic Institute and State University in Blacksburg, Virginia. He is the author most recently of *Museum Politics: Power Plays at the Exhibition* (Minnesota, 2002), and his other books include *Capitalism, Democracy, and Ecology: Departing from Marx, Shows of Force: Politics, Power, and Ideology in Art Exhibitions,* and *Ecocritique: Contesting the Politics of Nature, Economy, and Culture* (Minnesota, 1997).

TIMOTHY MCGETTIGAN has devoted his attention to broad questions relating to power, especially in the media and organizations. He is completing a study about how the categories of race, poverty, and addiction (and their relations) are shaped by the politics of representation.

MARGARET J. TALLY is a philosopher and sociologist trained at the New School for Social Research. She is assistant professor at the State University of New York, Empire State College, where she works in the area of social theory, structure, and change. She is the author of *Television Culture and Women's Lives: Thirtysomething and the Contradictions of Gender.*

Index

Arendt, Hannah, x, xi, 18, 19, 22, 26–31, 33, 36, 37, 120, 195

Aristotle, 33

art: hyperreality of, 215; performance, xix; postmodern, 209

assimilation, xi, xii; of indigenous cultures, 55; of Mayan culture, 50; rhetoric of, 51

Association for the Well-being of the Family (APROFAM), 46

Association of Voluntary Surgical Contraception, 46

athletics: amateur, 73

Australia, 64

authenticity: search for, 123, 202–3; of self, xix; service workers' lack of, 10

authority, xvii, 1, 51; alternative, 182; bourgeois claims to, 168, 177; civic, 221; claims to, 167; of companies, 6; decline of the father's, 169; and image, 208; legal-rational, 119; legitimate public, 220; narrative theory of, 221; of political leaders, 111; sovereign, 94; state, 79

autobiography: collective, 197; as fiction, 217–18; and talk shows, 124

autonomy: liberal claims to, 21; masculinist concept of, 22; personal, 221

Balzac, Honoré de, 190

Barthes, Roland, 81

Bartleby the Scrivener, 190

baseball, 72, 73

Bataille, Georges, 75

Baudelaire, vii, 153

Baudrillard, Jean, xvi, 35, 148, 153, 163, 212, 218

Beck, Ulrich, 123, 139

behaviorism, xviii, 30–31

Benhabib, Seyla, 28, 138, 142

Bentham, Jeremy, 181

Bible, 126, 198; wide-scale distribution of, 179

bioengineering, 89, 99, 101

biography, 125, 192; changes to, 193; commercialization of, 140; do-it-yourself, 124, 200; embattled, 141; of

presidential candidates, 190; public staging of, 114; responsibility for, 194; self-made, 120; standardized by state and market, 124

body, vii, viii, ix, x, xi, xvii, 19, 25, 32, 34, 88, 101, 104, 107, 191; abstractions of, 26, 34; athlete's, 71; built, 60; civilized, 178, 180, 186; as construction, xiv, 66, 216; control of, 64; and cosmetic surgery, 205; desiring, 214; development of, 99; disciplined, 24, 29, 65, 173, 174, 177–78, 180; disciplines of, xviii; docile, xii, 45, 50, 85; early modern, 197; erotic, 69, 77; essential, 209; ethnic, xii; female, ix, xii, 44, 62; fetishized, 199; fragmentation of, 100; gendered, xii; and global capitalism, 92, 212; and hegemony, 168; and ideological shifts, 168; image, 43, 102; impact of media on, 169, 183, 186; indigenous women's, xi, 17, 32; intelligence, 191; lived experience of, 35; malleability of, xix, 209; manipulation of, 209; markers, 65–66; and the market, 87, 95; Mayan, 42, 43, 56, 60; media influence on, xvii, 202; in motion, 93, 94, 95, 99; objectified, 45; perfect, 197; physical, 27; and pleasure, 199; politics of, ix, 106, 170, 216; postmodern, 213–14; power relations and, 18, 60; private, 17; public, 17; reproductive functions of, 48; as resistance, 5; rituals of, 64, 69; schooling of, xviii; secularization of, 198; and self, 201, 209; as sign, 49, 199; social, 60; socialization of, 171; and social life, 65; sovereign, 199; and state, 87; struggle over, 44; symbolism of, 46; and technics, 99; techno-, 100–102; transcendent, 57; of victims, 44; virtual, 207; visible, 201; welfare, ix, 24; women's 42, 43, 44, 46, 47, 52, 57; worker's, ix, 5

bodybuilding, xiii, 97, 105; and global capitalism, 87; as historical construction, 99; machinic, 99, 107; in marketplace, 88

body politic, xi, xiii, 42, 87, 89, 90, 94, 98, 100, 100–107, 170 body/self, vii, viii, x, xii, xix, 192, 211, 213, 216; aestheticization of, 212; American, xiii; constitution of, 214; in entertainment, 207; fetishized, 212; inner-directed, 212; lability of, 200; malleable, 217; Mayan, xi; narrativist view of, 192; postmodern, 192; of postmodern capitalism, 210; problematization of, 209; as project, 197; Protestant, 192; simulated, 215; Western transformation of, 199

body shop, xiii, 89–90, 94; of global capitalism, 107; in global markets, 99

Bordo, Susan, 36–37

Bourdieu, Pierre, vii, 5, 170, 186, 207

bourgeoisie: and Enlightenment, 168; Italian, 176; literate, 176

Bowie, David, 207

Brazil, xiii, 83; history of colonization, 69–70

Broadman, Howard, 22–23

Brown, Richard Harvey, vii–xxi, 189–26

bureaucracy, universalism of, 176

burnout, 4, 5

Bush, George W., 202

Butler, Judith, 19, 35–37

Calvin, John, 186

camera: being on, 155; effects on behavior, 155; gaze of, 147; generating excitement, 158; performance-making power of, 152–53; and self-reflection, 161; and spectacle, 163; structuring presence of, 160, 162; and surveillance, 200

Camp, Walter, 73, 74

Camus, Albert, 190

capacitacion, 52, 53, 57

capital, 88; accumulation of, 33; circulation of, 199; corporate, 102; cultural, 53; economic, 53; global, 19, 66, 103, 171; human, 95; systems of, viii

capitalism, 216; as commodity, 202; consumer, 34, 212; and desire, 213; global, vii, viii, ix, xiii, 31, 33, 85, 87, 90, 100, 212, 92, 99, 183; industrial, 168; late, xviii, 65, 214; liminal spaces of, 85; modern, 94; postindustrial, 218;

postmodern, xix, 214–15; print, 170, 178, 199; producer, 212; and production of signs, 215; Protestant, 199; rise and spread of, 179; spirit of, 65; transnational, 206

Capitalist Realism, 216

Caplan, Arthur, 22

Carbraugh, D. 117–18, 125

carnival, 67, 68, 85; popular aesthetic of, 115, and talk shows, 113–14

Carnival, xiii, 69–71, 74, 76–78, 83–85

Catholicism, xiii, 56, 70; confessional practices of, 197; hedonistic, 84; medieval, 192; Portugese, 69

celebrity, xix; charismatic, 119; commodified, 208

Céline, Louis-Ferdinand, 190

Cerezo, Vinicio, 42, 51

Cervantes, Miguel de, 190

character, vii, 169; integrity of, 221; social, 186

Charles II, 176

childhood: civilizing processes of, 181; as distinct stage in life cycle, 179; relaxed constraints of, 184

children, 22–25; bourgeois, 182; care of, 13; as community property, 48; distinction between parents and, 110; distressed, 132; Mayan, 51, 56; and the nation, 177; rebellious, 117; separation from adults, 179; socialization of, 180; on talk shows, 137; and television, 184; and traditional families, 51

Chile, 20

China, 33, 173; "three wants" of, 216

Christianity, 61; feudal, 84; muscular, 72, 73

church, 46, 48, 51, 196, 198; and divine right of rulers, 176; modernization and, 52

citizens, 43, 192; active, 216; hegemonic notions of, 44; as identity, 179; Mayas as, 42; national bodies of, 176; obedient, 43; self-disciplined, 182; of the state, 187; talk shows and, 111; transformation into consumer, 202

citizenship, 50, 72, 177, 183; the body
    and, 49; class rule and, 168
civil society. *See* society, civil
Civil War, American, 72
civilization, 185, 192; Freud's view of, 64
civilizing process, 180
class, xvii, 196; bodily expression as
    marker of, 5; disciplinary power and,
    24; privileges, 167; ruling, 167, 169,
    176; and social critique, 59; as unifying
    discourse, 53
classification: as negotiable, 122
classism, 23
Clinton, Bill, 185, 202
cognitive science, vii
colonialism, 58
colonization: legacy of, 58; of the New
    World, 84
Commission on Human Rights of the
    Organization of American States, 45
commitment, 113
commodity: fetishization of, 212
communication: electronic, xvii, 182, 183;
    linguistic, 131; mass, viii, ix; means of,
    182; media of, 170; modes of, xvii; oral,
    xvii; print, xvii; public, 134; scribal, xxii;
    and social bonds, 130; with strangers,
    202; talk shows as, xvi; written, 172
community, 52, 68; abstract, 176, 178,
    186; benevolent, 133; church, 203;
    crisis of, 177; declining significance
    of, 198; disintegration of, 55, 130, 205;
    imagined, 208; inclusion into, 172; iso-
    lated, 174; local, 52; and narrative, 194;
    national, 105, 178; new forms of, 133;
    of pride, 82; rural, 59; spontaneous, 77;
    of work, 203
companies: transnational, ix; workers'
    loyalty to, 1
Company of Critics, The, 142
computers, 105; games, xviii
confession: public, 128; staged, 131
conflict: interpersonal, 136; staged, 127,
    135; on talk shows, 130, 140; therapeu-
    tic approach to, 134
consciousness, xvii, 34, 192, 212; acquisi-
    tion of, 44; camera, 147; collective,

106; colonization of, 185; hegemonic
    control of, 167; impact of media on,
    170; individual, 198; machinationalized,
    104; of Mayan women, 42, 43; modes
    of, 171; political, 114; raising, 42, 43,
    52, 57; willing assent of, 169; women's,
    54, 59
consumer, 187; choice, xiii; desirous, 203;
    experience of the, 213; as global iden-
    tity, 206; of Norplant, 21; passive, 216
consumerism, 85, 168, 186, 221; culture
    of, 182; and erosion of the nation, 182;
    global, xiii; and global economy, 187; as
    hegemony, 183, 187; as ideology of late
    capitalism, 203; mass-mediated, xiii
consumption, ix, xii, xviii, 34, 182, 184,
    202, 212, 216; aestheticization of, 212;
    alternative forms of, 205; and body,
    214; and body/self, 197; cultural, 84;
    encouragement of, 199; globalized, 74;
    hedonistic, 183, 212; imagined com-
    munities of, 207; of intoxicants, 82;
    life-worlds of, 183; ludic, 65; modes of,
    214; patterns of, 205, 208; and pleasure,
    85; rituals of, 85, 215; and self, 204; of
    signs, 183; and subjectivity, xix, 206;
    unlimited, 203
contraception, 20–23, 30, 33; forced, 23;
    invasive, 22; natural, 47; prohibitions
    against, 61
control: bodily, 54, 179, 181; of culture,
    167, 185; of desire, 181; of depiction of
    self, 152; discourse of, 50; of fertility,
    45–46; of the id, 182; internalized, 180;
    labor process and, 3; of mass media,
    215; of means of communication, 169;
    of means of production, 169; normative,
    2–4; physical, 174; of population, 48;
    resistance to, 90; of self, 115–16; social,
    67, 171–73, 185; by the state, 43, 177;
    techniques of, 44
conversation, xv, 136; mediation of ide-
    ology through, 169; as natural speech,
    116, 130; and oral culture, 172; tele-
    vision as, 116
Corea, Gena, 24
corporations: transnational, 183

Norplant, 18; paternalistic, 58; political, xi, 142; positivist, 19; postcolonial, xii; postmodern, 19, 205; procedures of, 135; public, 148; purification of, 92; scientific, 25; of sexuality, 43; technical, xi; therapeutic, 118; on women's bodies, 48
dispute, 110, 129–31
diversity, 37, 98
divestiture, ix, 8, 9
documentary film, 149, 152, 164; crew, 149–50, 152, 155, 158, 159, 163, 164
domestic sphere, 114, 120, 179
domination, ix, x, xii, xiii, xviii, 58, 60, 79, 83, 167; assent to, 186; and the body, 106; capitalist, 211; class, xii; compliance with, xvii; discourses of, 217; gender, 76; genealogy of, 18; government, 57; and hegemony, 172; hierarchies of, 171; and integration, 50; of the Other, 75; patriarchal, 211; structures of, 28; theological justifications for, 173; theories of, 19; and violence, 76; visual, 81
Donahue, Phil, 118, 140
Don Quixote, 190
Dostoyevsky, Fyodor, vii, 190
Douglas, Mary, viii, 43
downsizing, ix, 1, 2; impact of, 4, 8; and work environment, 11
Dumm, Thomas, 32
Durkheim, Émile, vii, 64–65, 66, 68, 128, 172, 185–86, 209

Easton, Nina, J., 23
ecology: deep, 98
economics: image-based, 141; market-oriented, 213; modern, 106
economy, 98; agricultural, 56; as bodily discipline, 170; flexible, 17; globalization of, 1; industrial, 1; merchant, 178; postindustrial, 1, 17; postmodern, 214; premodern, 112; and Protestant ethic, 199; rationalization of, 175; symbolic, 214; world, 193; world political, 17, 38
Education of Henry Adams, The, 196
Elias, Norbert, vii, 65, 180, 182

elites, vii, 74, 168; and authority, 171; bourgeoisie, 178; Brazilian, 70; celebration of power by, 67; control of culture, xvii; economic, 85; feudal, 180; and identity 207; imposition of ideas by, 186; ladino, 50, 51; national, 72; parodies of, 68; political, 175; proto-nationalism of, 178; as representatives of the people, 167; scribal, 173; and talk shows, xv, 109; transnational, 183; white, 50
emancipation, 134; patronizing discourse of, 139–40
emotion, xv, 67, 112, 120, 136, 171, 207; dramatization of, 113, 130; exhibition of, 128; female, 72; and identity, 129; and intuition, 91; liberation of, 131; and morality, 128; on Oprah, 129; in oral cultures, 172; and pleasure, 199; and self, 126; socialization of, 171; talk, 127; on talk shows, 115, 125, 127; warehousing of, 79
emotivism, 129, 130
empiricism, 32; feminist, 59
empowerment, xii, xiii
Enlightenment, 32, 91, 100, 168, 178, 186; philosophies of, 176; spread of, 178
environment, 96, 97; artificial, xiv; machine, 103; natural, xiv; social, 111; work, 1–3, 6, 7, 10, 11
equality, 125
Equal Opportunity Employment Commission, 9
eroticism, 79
essentialism, 47, 58, 59
ethics: of care, 132; narrative theory of, 221
ethnicity, 42, 196, 207
ethnocide, 48, 49
eugenics, 45
everyday life, xiv, xv, 122, 169, 171, 186; contentious character of, 109; dramatization of, 113; as embattled, 129; management of, 118; metaphors for, 143; micropolitics of, 138; psychology in, 110; routines of, 220

exchange value, 212
exhibitionism, 80; and electronic media, 185
experience, 26, 195, 201, 216, 218; alternative, 70; of ambivalence, 207; bodily, 200; corporeal, 32; of dominated groups, 141; embodied, 38, 193; emotional, 68; of Green Tortoise trips, 152, 158; immediate, 184; limits on, viii; lived, 32, 35; and narrative, 194; phenomenological, viii; psychological, vii; simulated, 164; transgressive, 75; unmediated, 209; virtual, 215; of women, 25, 33, 57, 215; of workers, 3, 4
experts, 144; gaze of, 133; intervention of, 131; opinion of, 178; on talk shows, 113; uncertain knowledge of, 135
exploitation, 168; of Mayan women, 61

Fabri, Antonella, 42–63
family, xiv, 46, 51, 120, 136, 179, 220; as corporate metaphor, 3, 5, 7–10, 14–15; displaced, 62; dissolving, 205; and the home, 50; as institution, 50; Mayan, 45; middle-class, 49, 51; nuclear, 49; planning, ix, 44, 45; recent transformations in, xv, 110; single-parent, 122; sociology of the, 122; unity of the, 52
Family Medical Leave Act (FMLA), 11
fashion, xviii, 214
fast-food outlets, 89
favelas, 70, 78
Featherstone, Mike, 65
feelings, xiv, 67, 171; personal, 204, 205; unmediated, 209; of workers, 3. See also emotion
feminism, xi, 20; Anglo, 59; Mayan, 59; poststructural, 35; racial and ethnic exclusions in, 37; and the Super Bowl, 83
feminists, 77, 217; ladino, 47, 49
feminist theory, vii, viii
Ferry, Bryan, 207
fetish: commoditization of, 212
fetishism, 140
Fichte, Johann Gottlieb, 168, 177
film, xviii, xix; 215. See also documentary film

Final Fantasy, 207
Fiske, John, 115
flexible specialization, 103
folktales, 111, 112
football, 85; history of, in America, 72–75
Foucault, Michel, vii, x, 5, 19, 22, 24, 27, 32–37, 65, 87, 135, 170, 174, 203, 212, 217, 219; analytics of power, 18; on modernity, 18; on power and discipline, 29; on resistance 18, 25, 26, 28, 29; and social change, 28
Frankfurt School, xvii, 167, 169
Fraser, Nancy, 37
freedom, 177, 178
Freud, Sigmund, 64, 65, 134, 169, 171
Fromm, Erich, 186
Frye, Northrop, 116
Fukuyama, Francis, 30

Galileo, 29–30, 93
García, Romeo Lucas, General, 44
gaze: of camera, 149, 154–56, 158, 162, 163; documentary, 147, 156; inward, 156; male, 81; medical, 30; scientific, 30, 148, 151, 156; of talk shows, 115; voyeuristic, 115, 164
Geertz, Clifford, 111
gender, xix, 53, 57, 66, 196, 207; classification of, 65; construction of, 19, 35; as cultural artifact, 217; discourse of, 200; essentialism, 58; experimentation with, 207; hierarchy of, 80; ontologies, 36; as performance, 35–36; and power, 22; privileges of males, 76; restraints of, 71; skepticism, 36; stereotypes, 82; and work, 3, 6
genetic engineering, 101
genocide, xi, 23; against Indian people, 42
genre, xviii; of talk shows, 116, 130
Giddens, Anthony, 119, 123, 139
Girard, René, 75
Goffman, Erving, 143, 170, 210
Goody, Jack, 170
governance, 175
Gramsci, Antonio, xvii, 88, 167, 169, 184, 186

Green Tortoise, xvi, 148–64; television news cameras and, 162–63
Greider, William, 88, 89
Griffith, Melanie, 211
Grosz, Elizabeth, 18
Guatemala, xi, xii, 43, 45, 50, 61, 62; Congress of, 47; U.S. intervention in, 45
Guattari, Félix, 218

Habermas, Jürgen, xv, 134, 143, 192
habitus: invisible, 185; reproduction of, 169
Haiti, 20
Haraway, Donna, 19, 37, 92, 95–98, 212
Hardon, Anita, 20
health, xi, xii, 42, 73; community, 45; and development agencies, 50; discourse on, 54; of Mayan women, 49, 54; and nation-states, 43; organizations, 48, 50–52; politics of, 55; professionals, 44; in Russia, 107; women's, 47, 57
Health Association of Community Services (ASECSA), 45, 52, 53
health care, xii; problems, 13; programs, 45, 50–51, 60
Heckscher, Charles, 2
hedonism: visual media and, 185
Hegel, Georg Wilhelm Friedrich, 120
hegemony, xvi, xvii, 19, 20, 33, 167–68, 171, 186; and culture, 187; and desire, 172; of global capital, 168; Gramscian equation for, 19; social, 26
Heidegger, Martin, 219
Herder, Johann Gottfried von, 168
hierarchy: organizational, 6; residues of, 79; reversal of, 78
history, 98, 190; of groups, 172; invented, 177; and schooling, 177; social, vii; Western, 178
History of Sexuality, 24
Hitler, Adolf, 186
Hobbes, Thomas, 87, 89, 92–94, 98–99, 103
Hochschild, Arlie, 2–3
home, 51; in Brazilian culture, 70; talk shows and the, 117; as women's space, 50, 52; work and, 110

homelessness, xiv, 130
Homer, vii
Horatio Alger, 190
Hugo, Victor, 190
Huizinga, Johan 65
Human Condition, The, 30
humanism, 191; and emergence of modernity, 90; spread of, 180
human rights, 59, 168
humanware, 22
Hume, David, 189
hybridization, 105–6
hybrids, 91, 95, 97, 98
hygiene, xii; family, 45; of Mayan women, 49, 54, 57; programs of, 60
hyperreality, 214

ideal speech situation, xv, 109
identity, vii, viii, ix, 46, 65–66, 110, 120, 148, 162, 164, 192–94, 196, 203–5, 220; aggressive, 75; American, 69, 72, 85; assimilationist, 49; and the body, 83, 200; brand-name, 211; Brazilian, 69, 74; and citizenship, 168, 178; collective, 64, 66–67, 76; as commodity, 208; communities of, 171, 177, 206; construction of, 35, 74, 125, 156, 171, 216; consumer-based, 183; crisis of, 177; cultural, xviii, 47, 66, 74, 84, 216; deconstructed, 125; economic change and, 5; essential, vii, 58; and everyday life, 118–19; fantasied, 77; formation of, 110, 214; fragmentation of, x, 17; gender, 73; and global capitalism, 212; hypermasculine, 81, 85; hyperreal, 205; individual, vii, 177, 179; interrogations of, 65; media's impact on, xv, 187; liminal, 76; manipulation of, 215; markers of, 50; media and, 184, 202; national, xi, 72, 85, 196, 207; and oppression, 220; partial, 95; performance of, 74, 81, 83; personal, 191; politics of, viii, ix; postmodern, 22, 31, 35, 153; reflexive exploration of, xvi; religious, 196; as resistance, 4; rituals of, 69, 84; shared, 67; socialization and, 170; submerged, 85; tribal, 211; value of, 192; Western,

memory: collective, 177, 203; repressed, ix; of violence, 62
metaphor, 93, 110, 201
Mexico, 50
micropolitics, 139
migration: forced, 44; and violence, 55
Mill, John Stuart, 89
mind: and body, 191, 201; Protestant emphasis on, 197
Miss America, 74
modernity, 71, 153, 217; burden of, 199; consequences of, 124; late, xv, 110, 122, 130–31, 143; as moral shift, 119; power of, 91; project of, 191; reflexive, 112, secularism of, 66
modernization, 42, 44, 56, 60, 62, 91, 106; as cyborganization, 106; in Guatemala, 53; reflexive, 124, 139
Montel Williams, 113, 114, 115
Montesquieu, 26
Montt, Efraín Ríos, General, 44, 62
morality, 191; boundaries of, 114; competing definitions of, 125; early codes of, 174; middle-class, 122; plays, 110; on talk shows, 138
morals: destabilized, 121; foundation of, xv
motherhood: deconstruction of, 122; meaning of, 121; redefinition of, 124
movements: guerilla, 45; indigenous, 57; ladino feminist, 47; machinational, 90, 105–6; popular, 62; resistance, 57, 61; pro-choice, ix; pro-life, ix; women's health, 33; workers' divisions within, 6
Mumford, Lewis, 98, 99
Musil, Robert, 210
myth, 111; of autonomous subject, 217; invented, 177; of origin, 66, 70, 196; of return to nature, 97

Naess, Arne, 98
Napoleon Bonaparte, 177
narration: challenges of, 219; emotional, 172
narrative, xviii, 131, 191, 218; of Henry Adams, 196; approach to identity, 197, 220; of the body, xviii, 169; corporal,

200; cultural, 66; death as, 209; deconstruction of, xix; of the good life, 113; of inclusivity, 37; of legitimation, 88; and media, xix; as metaphor, 192; of oppression, 142; as organizing device, 195; popular, 190; postmodern, 211; of selfhood, xix, 221; subjects of, 194; of talk shows, 130
natality, xi, 18, 27–29, 31
nation, vii, viii, 71, 220; capitalist, 182; Guatemalan, 60; as imaginary community, 177, 183; loyalty to, 176; Russian, 106. *See also* nation-state
National Committee of Guatemalan Widows (CONAVIGUA), 46, 47, 58, 62
National Council for Population and Development, 47
nationalism, xviii, 71, 175, 178; as anachronism, 183; as dominant political trope, 182; eroding, 187; popular, 168; print-based, 184
nation-state, xiv, 42, 43, 48, 50, 51, 58; and the body, 49; capitalist, 179, 187; Guatemalan, 44, 51, 52, 56; modern, 66, 168, 171, 174; repressive, 45; rise of the, 178; and universal rights, 177
Native Americans, 158
nature, 31, 90–91, 96, 97, 107
Newton, Isaac, 93
Nietzsche, Friedrich, vii, xii, 64, 66, 68, 96
nihilism, x, 18, 25
Nordic Track, 89, 102–4, 107
norms, xiv, xviii, 2, 121, 129, 143, 150; of cleanliness, 66; competing, 125; of conflict resolution, 113; of emotional control, 115; inversions of, 67, 71; of justice, 139; loyalty, 128; as negotiable, 122; of physical contact, 137; and private life, 123–24; reproductive, 20; and socialization, 170; stated vs. tacit, 3; talk shows and, 123; validity of, 138
Norplant, x, 17–26, 28, 32–33; cultural logic of, 20; as disciplinary apparatus, 28; discourses of, 23; side effects of, 20–21
Notes from the Underground, 190

private sphere, x, xv, 29, 109, 136, 185;
  staging of, 114; and subjectivity, 184
production: aestheticization of, 212
productivity: ideology of, 116
progress, 31–32, 219
property: control of, 167
Protestantism, 64, 72, 84, 179, 197, 180
Protestant Reformation, 84, 178, 197–98
psyche, 87, 97, 105, 134, 191
psychiatry, vii
psychoanalysis, vii, xvii, 110, 118;
  and self-knowledge, 134, and self-
  revelation, 197
public and private: distinction between,
  x, xv, 17, 29, 97, 110, 114, 120–21, 134,
  137, 185
punishment: as public ceremony, 174; as
  reform of the spirit, 198
Public Service Commission, 9
public sphere, xv, 22, 29, 32, 109, 115,
  138; agonistic, 120; debate within, 136;
  emergence of, 176, 198; growth of, 176,
  178; liberal view of, 137; modern, 142;
  and talk shows, 111
purification, 91, 115
Puritanism, xiii, 72

race: restraints of, 71
racism, 23; in Arendt's philosophy, 18
rational choice theory, xviii
rationality, 64, 115, 134; economic, 213;
  postmodern, 141
rationalization, 24, 80
reading, xvii, xviii, 198–99; as bodily discipline, 181; feminist, 19; revolutionary
  consequences of, 180
reality: dominant definitions of, 203;
  simulation and, 163; virtual, 184; and
  voyeuristic, 156
reason, vii, 36, 64, 197; public sphere
  and, 120
Red and the Black, The, 193
reeducation, 52. See also capacitacion
reflexivity, 171, 179
Reformation. See Protestant Reformation
Regnier, Sebsian, 155

Reich, Robert, 1
Reisman, David, 212
relations: class, 169; of domination,
  19; force, 18, 25; gender, 18, 75, 84;
  human, 18, 31; incestuous, 117; interpersonal, viii; intimate, xiv, xv, 129, 130;
  mass, viii; with others, 118; personal, xv;
  124; political, x, 18; of power, 22, 25,
  113, 203; private, x, 18; of production,
  20; of reproduction, 20; sexual, 65; social, viii, x, 18, 110, 129; sociopolitical,
  26; and talk shows, 122
relationships. See relations
religion, 75; nationalism and, 178; public
  world of, 184
Renaissance, 180
Renan, Joseph, 168
representation, viii; political, x; postmodern, 208; of the self, xii
representatives. See representation
repression: and cannibalization, 50; cultural, xi; and extermination, 50; military,
  44
resistance, xii, 19, 25, 47, 167, 183;
  agents of, ix; to assimilation, 58; to
  authority of God, 220; democratic, 31,
  33; discourse of, 57, 58; in Foucault's
  work, 18, 25, 26, 28, 29; and identity,
  56; liminal, 68; passive, x; places of, 67;
  politics of, 26; postmodern, 34; and self,
  202; technified, 102; of workers, 2, 4,
  14–15
revolution, 216; threat of, 44
ritual, 64, 66, 83; Carnival as, 70; collective, 66, 111; of consumption, 85;
  cultural, 81; of death, 209; ludic, 66;
  of manners, 65; and meaning, 111;
  patriotic, 178, 196; performance of, 66,
  68; religious, 172; of violence, 83; and
  social life, 77; of solidarity, 82; of voyeurism, 200
Robinson Crusoe, 190
Rocky, 190
Rolonda, 113, 121
Roosevelt, Teddy, 73
Rorty, Richard, xv

Rousseau, Jean-Jacques, 96, 177, 206
Rowland, Robyn, 24
Russian federation, 107

Sartre, Jean-Paul, 96, 194
Say, Jean-Baptiste, 213
Scheper-Hughes, Nancy, 43
Schlegel, Freidrich von, 206
school: as bureaucracy, 13; identity and, 196; and national government, 177; and socialization, 169
science, 88, 90, 91; applied, 93; discourse of, 133; postmodernist critique of, 147; procedures of, 99
Scott, James, C., 19, 141
Second National Encounter of Indigenous People and People in Resistance, 57
self, vii, viii, ix, 32, 73, 124, 131, 132, 148, 163, 201, 210, 220; affirmation of, 79; as authentic, xix; as autonomous, xix; and the body, 199; and camera's gaze, 152, 164; Carnival as repair of, 79; celebrity culture and, xix; as cogito, 219; and consciousness, 189; construction of, xvi, 59, 69, 196; consumer, 183; control of, 118; corporeal, 31, 35; creation of, xviii; definition of, viii, 205; denial of, xviii; documentary, 156; embattled, 113, 118, 120, 129; embodied, viii, 72; emotional, 123; employee's, 2; entrepreneurial, 118; as essence, 204, 205; -esteem, 79; expressions of, 184; as fiction, 217, 219; gendered sense of, 10; -help, 117; image of, 156, 200, 205; -improvement, 51; love of, 101; malleable, 209; mastery of, 189; media and, xvi, 211; narcissistic, 115; as narrated, 191, 193–94, 219; normalization of, 56; and other, 129, 201, 205; as performance, 204; postmodern, 1, 35, 37; presentation of, 83 152, 155–56, 170, 201; "real," 162, 203–5, 214; realization of, xviii, 98, 123, 194, 201; -restraint, 115; simulated, 152; speech, 133; and society, 171, 191; sovereign, 189; symbolism of, 214; virtual, 193; wounded, 132

selfhood: autonomous, 182; changes in, 119, 203, 206; consumer-based, xiii; contemporary, 203; expressions of, 83; integrated, 217; late-modern, 112; and lived experience, 204; mass-mediated, 182, 205, 206; modern Western, 220; patterns of, 215; postmodern, 213; question of, 113; recognition of, 205; reflexive, 171, 193; scripts for, 221; social context of, 191
self-identity. *See* identity
self-representation: subaltern, 59
sensationalism, xiv, 109, 118
senses, xvii; media assaults on, xviii; privatization of, xix; shift in priority among, 198
sensuality, viii; of Middle Ages, 198; repression of, 179
Serrano, Jorge, 46, 61–62
service sector, 83
sex, viii; as historical construct, 90; as ideological construction, 217; privatization of, 198; as regulatory fiction, 35–36; safe, ix
sexism, 23; in Arendt's philosophy, 18
sexuality: coerced, 71; control of, 180, 181; discourse of, 200; egalitarian, 80; experimentation with, xix, 207; female, 77; relaxed, 80; restrictions on, 174; standards of, 66; and television, 185; women's, 50, 57
shame, 46; erosion of, 185; public, 128
Sheets-Johnstone, Maxine, 18, 26–27, 37
Shelley, Percy Bysshe, 206
Sherman, Cindy, 207, 210
shock, xiv, 109
sickness. *See* illness
signification, 19
signified: as normative grounding, 122
signs: as commodity, 168
sign value, 212
silence, xii
Simmel, Georg, 199
simulation, xvi, xix, 35, 154, 160, 163–64, 210; cameras and, 154; of combat, 69; documentary, 160; identity and, 156; of

the new and attractive, 213; power of, 148; preferred, 206; visual, 164

Sirianni, Carmen, 13

slavery: African, 69; in Brazil, 70

Smith, Adam, 87, 89, 92–95, 99, 101, 214

Smith, Lynn, 23

social bonds, xvi

social engineering, xii, 23

socialization, xvii, xviii, 170; childhood, 179; into dominant ideologies, 206; as historically specific, 169; into selfhood, 201, 220

social movements, vii; Mayan, 55; theory, 80

social science: vii, 142, 189, 191

social theory, viii, 5; modern, xviii

social workers: on talk shows, 135

society: advanced, viii, xiv, 185, 202; American, 133, 214; amusement, 184; bourgeois, 76; capitalist, ix, 31; civil, 44, 176, 190; communal, 65; consumer, 183–84, 206, 216; courtly, 71; in crises, ix; feudal, 171; hopes of, 191; horticultural, 167; individualistic, 208; industrial, 182; information, 182; late-capitalist, 85, 184; liberal, 136; market, 168, 176; and media, 202; modern, 1, 106, 177, 197; moral fabric of, 141–42; patriarchal, 54; postindustrial, 2; post-modern, ix, 31, 147–48, 197; seculariza-tion of, 90; traditional, 177; wealthy, 196; Western, 2

sociobiography, 132, 133

sociology: of the body, vii, xvii; and historians, 111–12; neo-urban, viii; and talk shows, 128

solidarity, 129, 186; group, xii; local, 174; personal, viii; in scribal cultures, 174; social, 128, 130

Songs of the Open Road, xvi, 148, 156

sovereignty: popular, 168, 178

space: aesthetic/economic, 212; biased, 173; and cyborgs, 92; disciplinary, 24; feminist, 28; of Green Tortoise bus, 148; as historical construct, 90; hyper-real, 211; individual, 103; for the ludic,

67; ontological, 18; partitioning of, 24; physical, 190; and postmodern self, 208; psychological, 190; public, xi, 18, 28, 38, 70; of resistance, 60; social, 110; of speech and action, 28; subversive, 44; for women, 57, 59

spectacle, xiii, xvi, xviii, 67, 70, 208; and cinema, 153; commodified, 85; and dif-ference, 207; and documentary, 159; of emotions, 120; of globalized capital, 187; sponsorship of, 215; of suffering, 125; talk shows as, 115; televised, 202; visual, 161

Specters of Marx, 19

speech: and action, 28; as emancipatory, 131; talk show as, 116, 133

spirit, viii, 208

Spivak, Gayatri Chakravorty, 59

sport: in consumer capitalist societies, 81; discussion of, 82; as global spectacle, ix; and media, 74; as myth, 67

Sri Lanka, 20

state, xiv, 48, 89, 96; agents of, 44; au-thoritarian, 174; capitalist, 55; and citizenship, 168; and contracts, 175; economic-legal structure of, 22; forma-tion of, 60; Guatemalan, x, 42, 46, 52; as historical construct, 90; and individu-als, 129; institutions of, 139; liberal, 26; machinic force of, 87; neoliberal corpo-rate, ix; regulation of reproduction, 21, 29, 37; and self, 123; welfare, x. *See also* nation-state

status, 1; and horizontal stratification, 206; middle-class, 85

Staubmann, Helmut, 214

Stedman, Graham, 119

Stelarc, 210, 211

Stendahl, 190, 193

step policy of sick leave, 11–13

stereotypes, 114; in talk shows, 117

sterilization, 20, 23–25, 48, 49; and Gua-temalan government, 56; involuntary, 45; mass, 46; of Mayan women, 45

stress, ix, 5; off-the-job, 13; stress-leave, 4; work-related, 4, 13, 15 structuralism, xviii, xix; of Durkheim, 68

subaltern, xii, 59–60; indignities experienced by, 79; as other, 83

subject: analyzing, 18; autonomous, 92, 129; confessing, 119; cyborg, 105; decentering of, x, 18; deconstruction of, 217; of documentary, 152, 158; free, 200; formation of, 105; human, 91; manipulation of, 18, 213; passive, 174; production of, xi, 18, 22, 32; reconstitution of, 44; of the state, 25; of the throne, 176, 187; of voyeur's gaze, 156; women as, 57

subjectivity, 87, 101; body shops and, 99; and consumption, xii, 210; corporeal, 65; cyborg, 104; decentering of, 218; disciplined, 186; inscribed, 170; and media, 184, 187; migration of, 184; modes of, 171; narcissistic, 127; and talk shows, 115; transformations of, 179

subpolitics, 139

superacion, 52

Super Bowl, xiii, 69, 72, 74–76, 80, 82–84, 202, 208

surrogacy, 20

surveillance, xii, xvi; direct, 172; internalized, 24; pervasiveness of, 200; of workers, 6

Swiss Family Robinson, The, 190

symbolic rewards, 2

symbols: dominant bourgeois, 114

systems, viii; machinic, 99; medical, xii; technological, 191

taboos: incest, 121; on talk shows, 138

talk shows, xiv, xv, xvi, 109, 112, 123, 125, 134, 185, 197; attacks against, 113–14; audience responses to, 109; as carnival, 113–16; and conflict resolution, 135; conventions of, 110; as courtrooms, 137–38; cultural codes of, 110; demography of, 113; and discourse, 116, 142; as hybrids, 113, 136; as infrapolitics, 141; language of, 130, 143; and modernization, 124; and morality, 128, 140; participants,

110; psychoanalysis and, 134, 135; as rituals, 111; role of the host, 132; structure of, 116–17, 121, 130, 143; and support groups, 132–33; surface meaning of, 112; taboos, 138; therapeutic character of, 117; and victimization, 126, 127, 141; as voyeuristic, 125

Tally, Margaret J., 1–16

taste: boundaries structuring, 114; manipulation of, 215

Taylor, Charles, 119

Taylor, Frederick Winslow, 73

Taylorism, 7

technics, 88, 98, 100

Technics and Civilization, 99

techniques: filming, 164; observational, 147, 151

technology, 1, 91, 105; and armies, 176; co-evolving, 98; communication, 173; of control, 51; cutting-edge, 105; deep, 90, 106; fusion with workers, 22; genetic, 25; reproductive, xi, 17–26, 28, 29, 31, 33; rereading of, 87; telecommunications, 9; visual media, 153

telecommunications: technology of, 9; workers in, 14

telegraph, 90

telephone, 89, 106, 170

television, 106, 182, 184, 211, 216; carnival spirit of, 115; children and, xviii; and football, 74; as parasocial medium, 116; productions, 201; and self, 205; viewers, 205. *See also* talk shows

Thailand, 20

therapy, 118, 134, 195, 196, 221

Thirty Something, 116

Thoreau, Henry David, 220

Tierney, Thomas F., 87

time: and cyborgs, 92; as historical construct, 90; leisure, 72; organization of, 24

time-space compression, 184

Tocqueville, Alexis de, 214

tradition, 45, 172; fading of, 130; Greco-Roman and Christian, 69; and the

home, 50; invented, 177; oral, 178; and schooling, 177
truth, 30, 31, 36–37; and camera's gaze, 156, 164; divine, 189; modernist view of, 134; prior, 135; will to, 191
Turner, Brian, 65, 212
Tuyuc, Rosalina, 47, 58, 59
typography: changes in, 74

Unbearable Weight, 36
United Nations Mission for the Verification of Human Rights in Guatemala (MINUGUA), 55
Untitled Film Stills, 207
urbanization, 72, 73, 199
use-value, 212

Vallas, Stephen, 6, 7
values, xiv, 44, 123; civic, 191; collective, 111; commercial, 211; cultural, xv, 48, 66, 109; dominant, 203; and economy, 171; of ethnicity, 44; family, 214; foundational, 136; of gender, 44; of the good life, 113; hegemonic control of, xvii; impermanence of, 207; imposition of, 58; national, 99; patriarchal, 80; of scribal culture, 173; shared, 67; and socialization, 170; talk shows and, 117; traditional, 49; of women, 57; in workplace, 2
Veblen, Thorstein, 214
violence, 60; campaigns of, 43; epistemic, 59; erotic male, 83; in Guatemala, xi, xii, 46, 48, 54, 61; in-group, 75; justifications of, 44; moral effect of, 54; against natality, 30; will to, 76; against women, 46, 48, 59
voyeurism, xvi, 80–81, 149; and electronic media, 185, 200; feminist critiques of, 147

Wall Street, 10
Walzer, Michael, 142
Warner, Lloyd, 72
wealth, xvi; as deserved, 167; national, 175

Weber, Max, 64, 65, 75, 76, 119, 138, 167, 186, 197, 207
welfare, x, 13, 17; ties between Norplant and, 17, 24, 32
willing assent, xvii, 169, 176, 184
Willis, Paul, 110, 143
Winfrey, Oprah, 113, 119–20, 122, 124, 127, 132–33, 135, 138, 143, 202
women, ix, 110; as agents, 53; bodies of, 59–60; Brazilian, 77; castrated, 81; desiring, 77; emancipated, 59, 128; empowerment of, 52; experience of, 33; image of, 47; indigenous, xi, xii, 43, 59–60; middle-class, 47; and Norplant, 20–28; and poststructural critique, 36; productivity of, 24; and reproduction, 48; roles of, 48, 73; single mothers, 13; and slavery, 78; sterilized, 45; as subjects, 53; and tradition, 50; violence against, 46; welfare mothers, 32; workers, 4–15
work, 1, 2, 73, 90, 203, 205; agricultural, 55; alienating, 4; environment, 11, 14, 18; ethic, 14, 15, 178–79; feminization of occupations, 6; and the home, 179; knowledge, 1, 2; managerial, 73; and masculinity, 75; mechanization of, 8; as motion, 94–95; public world of, 184; rationalized, 4, 7, 15; and selfhood, 203; service, 1, 2, 7, 13–14; scripted nature of, 7; in sweatshops, 55; Taylorized, 4, 7, 10, 11, 15
workers, ix, 1, 2, 182; absenteeism of, 4, 15; adaptation to new organizational cultures, 2; African-American women, 12; airline stewardesses, 3; autonomy of, 7; bodily control over, 6; emotional control over, 6; food-service, 3; fusion with technology, 22; identification with company, 8, 11; and identity, 179; immigrant, 7; insurance industry, 3; knowledge industry, 1; loyalty of, 1, 7; and the nation, 177; new hires, 8; service industry, 2–4; surveillance of, 6; unhappiness of, 2; use of sick leave, 5, 6, 11–15